MEDITERRAN

CLASSIC RECIPES FRO

ITALY, FRANCE, SPAIN, NORTH AFRICA, THE MIDDLE EAST, GREECE, TURKEY AND THE BALKANS

MEDITERRANEAN

CLASSIC RECIPES FROM

ITALY, FRANCE, SPAIN, NORTH AFRICA, THE MIDDLE EAST, GREECE, TURKEY AND THE BALKANS

CHRISTINA BLASI   GABRIELLA MARI   MARTA BUSQUETS NET   ROSALBA GIOFFRÈ   CARLA BARDI

APPLE

First published in the UK in 2004 by Apple Press
Sheridan House
112-116a Western Road
Hove
East Sussex
BN3 1DD
UK
www.apple-press.com

ISBN 1-84092-461-6

This book was conceived, edited and designed by McRae Books Srl
Borgo Santa Croce, 8 - 50122 Florence, Italy
info@mcraebooks.com

Project Director: Anne McRae
Design Director: Marco Nardi, Sara Mathews
Text: Carla Bardi, Rosalba Gioffrè, Scuola di Arte Culinaria Cordon Bleu, Florence
(Gabriella Mari, Cristina Blasi), Marta Busquets Net
Home Economists: Scuola di Arte Culinaria Cordon Bleu, Florence
Photography: Marco Lanza, Walter Mericchi
Cover Design: Rod Teasdale, White Rabbit UK
Layouts: Yotto Furuya, Paola Baldanzi, Adina Stefania Dragomir
Editing: Helen Farrell, Anne McRae
Color separations: Fotolito Toscana, Florence – Litocolor, Florence

Printed in China by C&C Offset Printing Co.
10 9 8 7 6 5 4 3 2 1

TABLE OF CONTENTS

Mediterranean food, and the so-called "Mediterranean diet," are hailed the world over as both delicious and healthy. With over 400 recipes drawn from the eight major regions of the Mediterranean basin, this book is one of the most comprehensive single-volume overviews available today. The recipes, compiled by a team of Italian and Spanish food writers, were chosen to reflect the special character of each region. Here you will find many of the classic pasta and rice dishes (ravioli, risotto, paella), alongside cereals such as bulgur wheat (tabbouleh), couscous, and polenta. But for those looking for low-carb, high protein alternatives, there is a wonderful array of grilled and baked fish and meat dishes (kofta, kebabs), and nourishing soups (bouillabaisse). The sheer variety of Mediterranean food means that it will never go out of fashion. *Mediterranean* will be a cornerstone addition to any food lover's library.

ITALY

Italian cooking, in all its brilliant regional diversity, is probably the best known of the Mediterranean cuisines. In the 19th and early 20th centuries, Italian migrants spread their love of cooking wherever they went, while in recent years tourism and celebrity cooks have done the rest. But Italian cooking deserves its fame—it is a simple cuisine (or a host of simple cuisines), firmly based in rural traditions that rely on the finest quality ingredients.

Rice and potato fritters
(see page 14)

SIMPLE STUFFED BELL PEPPERS

Peperoni ripieni semplice

- 4 medium yellow bell peppers/capsicums, halved lengthwise and seeds removed
- 2 tablespoons salted capers, rinsed and chopped
- 2 cloves garlic, finely chopped
- $^1/_4$ cup/30 g fine dry bread crumbs
- 2 tablespoons finely chopped fresh parsley
- 2 tablespoons raisins, soaked in warm water for 1 hour, then drained
- 2 tablespoons pine nuts
- $^1/_2$ cup/125 ml extra-virgin olive oil
- salt and freshly ground black pepper

This is just one of many variations on the stuffed bell peppers theme. Many fillings call for ground beef, pork, or chicken, often flavored with Parmesan or Pecorino cheese, garlic, parsley, and other Mediterranean herbs. This recipe is especially easy and flavorful.

Preheat the oven to 400°F/200°C/gas 6. • Place the bell peppers in a roasting pan, skin-side down. Bake for 5 minutes. • Meanwhile, mix the capers, garlic, bread crumbs, parsley, raisins, pine nuts, oil, salt, and pepper in a medium bowl. • Spread the mixture on the partly cooked bell peppers. • Bake for 10–15 minutes more, or until the filling begins to brown. • Serve warm.

Serves 4 • Prep: 10 min • Cooking: 15–20 min • Level: 1

PROSCIUTTO WITH MELON

Prosciutto con melone

Slice the melon in half lengthwise. Scoop out the seeds and cut into wedges about 1 inch (2.5 cm) wide. Remove the rind from each slice, but place the wedge of melon back into its rind to serve. • Place the melon on a large serving platter and cover with the slices of prosciutto.

Serves 6 • Prep: 10 min • Level: 1

- 1 melon (cantaloupe or honeydew)
- 12 paper-thin slices prosciutto (preferably top-quality Parma ham)

STUFFED BAKED TOMATOES

Pomodori gratinati

- 8 medium tomatoes
- salt and freshly ground black pepper
- 2 medium onions, finely chopped
- 2 cloves garlic, finely chopped
- 2 tablespoons extra-virgin olive oil
- $^1/_4$ cup/45 g fresh bread crumbs
- 8 black olives, pitted/stoned and chopped
- 1 tablespoon pine nuts
- 1 tablespoon raisins
- 1 tablespoon salted capers, rinsed

Preheat the oven to 350°F/180°C/gas 4. • Cut the top off each tomato and use a teaspoon to scoop out the flesh. Place the flesh in a bowl. Season the hollow tomatoes with salt and pepper. • Sauté the onions and garlic in the oil until translucent. Add the tomato flesh and cook for a few minutes until it reduces a little. • Remove from the heat and stir in the bread crumbs, olives, pine nuts, raisins, and capers. • Spoon the mixture into the tomatoes and place in an oiled ovenproof dish. • Bake for 25–30 minutes, or until lightly browned. • Serve hot or at room temperature.

Serves 4 • Prep: 10 min • Cooking: 30–35 min • Level: 1

RICE AND POTATO FRITTERS

Polpette di riso e patate

These fritters are generally served as finger food to accompany an early evening drink. If served with a mixed salad, however, they make an excellent vegetarian main course.

Boil the potatoes in 1 quart (1 liter) cold water in a large deep saucepan until tender. • Add the rice and simmer until the rice is cooked, 15–18 minutes. • Drain well, place in a bowl, and let cool. • Add the parsley, garlic, Parmesan, eggs, salt, and pepper. Shape into oblong fritters. • Roll the fritters in the flour. • Heat the oil in a large frying pan and fry the fritters, a few at a time, for 5–7 minutes, or until golden brown all over. • Remove with a slotted spoon and drain on paper towels. • Serve hot.

Serves 6 • Prep: 15 min • Cooking: 45 min • Level: 2

- 1 lb/500 g potatoes, peeled and cut into cubes
- 1 cup/200 g short-grain rice
- 1 tablespoon finely chopped fresh parsley
- 1 clove garlic, finely chopped
- $^1/_4$ cup/30 g freshly grated Parmesan cheese
- 2 large eggs, lightly beaten
- salt and freshly ground black pepper
- 2 cups/300 g all-purpose/plain flour
- 1 cup/250 ml olive oil, for frying

Appetizers

SICILIAN-STYLE EGGPLANT FRITTERS

Polpette di melanzane alla Siciliana

- 2 eggplants/aubergines
- 1 tablespoon finely chopped parsley
- 10 leaves fresh basil, torn
- 1 clove garlic, finely chopped
- ¹⁄₄ cup/30 g freshly grated Parmesan cheese
- 2 large eggs, lightly beaten
- salt and freshly ground black pepper
- 1 cup/100 g fine dry bread crumbs
- 1 cup/250 ml olive oil, for frying

In a variation on this recipe, the freshly fried fritters are served in a hot tomato sauce. Try them with the sauce on page 28.

Preheat the oven to 400°F/200°C/gas 6. • Cut the eggplants in half lengthwise and place them on a baking sheet. • Bake for 15–20 minutes, or until tender and golden brown. Let cool and scoop out the flesh with a spoon, mashing it coarsely with a fork. • Stir together the eggplant, parsley, basil, garlic, cheese, eggs, salt, pepper, and enough bread crumbs to obtain a firm mixture. Shape into balls the size of walnuts. Roll in the remaining bread crumbs. • Heat the oil in a medium cast-iron frying pan. Fry the fritters in batches for 5–7 minutes, or until golden brown all over. • Drain on paper towels and serve immediately.

Serves 4 • Prep: 15 min • Cooking: 40 min • Level: 2

Preparing eggplants

Some varieties of globe eggplants can be bitter. To eliminate the bitterness, cut the eggplants lengthwise and sprinkle them with coarse salt. Let stand for 1 hour in a colander, then rinse under cold running water and pat dry with paper towels.

Sicilian-style eggplant fritters

Bell pepper crostini

MUSHROOM TOASTS

Crostini con funghi

- 1¼ lb/625 g fresh porcini mushrooms
- 2 tablespoons butter
- ¼ cup/60 ml extra-virgin olive oil
- 1 small white onion, finely chopped
- 2 cloves garlic, finely chopped
- 1 tablespoon finely chopped fresh mint, parsley, or thyme
- salt and freshly ground black pepper
- ½ cup/125 ml vegetable stock or broth
- firm-textured bread for the crostini (a French baguette or Italian ciabatta are ideal), sliced and toasted

This mushroom mixture is also very good when spread on squares of cold polenta and baked in a preheated oven at 400°F/200°C/gas 6 for 10 minutes.

Remove any grit or dirt from the mushrooms, rinse carefully under cold running water, and pat dry with paper towels. • Separate the stems from the caps and dice only the firm, unblemished parts of the stems. Chop the caps coarsely. • Heat the butter and oil in a frying pan over medium heat and sauté the onion, garlic, and mint for 5 minutes. • Add the mushrooms and season with salt and pepper. Cook for 5 minutes, stirring constantly. • Gradually stir in enough stock to keep the mixture moist and cook for 8–10 minutes more. • Spread each toast with a generous helping of the mushroom mixture and serve.

Serves 4 • Prep: 20 min • Cooking: 20 min • Level: 1

BELL PEPPER CROSTINI

Crostini di peperoni

Crostini are a favorite antipasto (appetizer) throughout Italy and are served all year-round. Toppings, and the type of bread used, change from region to region and also according to the season. These bell pepper crostini are best served during the summer when bell peppers are at their tastiest.

Broil (grill) or roast the bell peppers whole in the oven until the skins are blackened, turning as needed. • Wrap them in a paper bag for 5 minutes, then remove the skins and seeds. • Slice the bell peppers into small, thin strips and place in a large bowl. Add the garlic, basil, olives, oil, salt, and pepper and marinate in the refrigerator for 4 hours. • Spread the bell pepper mixture on the freshly toasted bread and serve.

Serves 4 • Prep: 20 min + 4 hr to marinate • Cooking: 10–15 min • Level: 1

- 1 red bell pepper/ capsicum
- 1 yellow bell pepper/ capsicum
- 1 clove garlic, finely chopped
- 4 leaves basil, torn
- 2 tablespoons pitted/ stoned black olives, coarsely chopped
- ¼ cup/60 ml extra-virgin olive oil
- salt and freshly ground black pepper
- firm-textured bread for the crostini (a French baguette or Italian ciabatta are ideal), sliced and toasted

Appetizers

TOASTED BREAD WITH GARLIC AND OIL

Fettunta

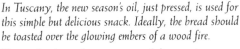

- 8 thick slices firm-textured white bread
- 2 large cloves garlic, peeled and left whole
- salt and freshly ground black pepper
- $^1/_4$ cup/60 ml best quality extra-virgin olive oil

In Tuscany, the new season's oil, just pressed, is used for this simple but delicious snack. Ideally, the bread should be toasted over the glowing embers of a wood fire.

Toast the bread over a wood fire or in a preheated oven at 400°F/200°C/gas 6 until crisp. It is important that the bread dries out while toasting, which it won't if browned in a toaster. • Rub each slice all over with the garlic. • Arrange the toasted bread on a serving plate. Season with salt and pepper and drizzle with the oil.

Serves 4 • Prep: 10 min • Cooking: 5–10 min • Level: 1

TOASTED BREAD WITH BLACK TUSCAN KALE

Fettunta col cavolo

These crostini are made with cavolo nero, or black Tuscan kale. This very dark green member of the cabbage family has a strong, almost bitter flavor. Replace with regular green kale if you can't find cavolo nero.

Boil the kale in salted water in a large deep saucepan for 15–20 minutes, or until tender. • Toast the bread and rub it with the garlic. Arrange the kale on the toasted bread. Season with salt, pepper, and a generous drizzle of oil.

Serves 4 • Prep: 5 min • Cooking: 15–20 min • Level: 1

- 1 head black Tuscan kale (lacinato kale, dinosaur kale), stems removed, leaves coarsely chopped
- 4 large slices firm-textured bread, such as ciabatta
- 1–2 cloves garlic, peeled and left whole
- salt and freshly ground black pepper
- 6 tablespoons extra-virgin olive oil

TOASTED BREAD WITH FRESH TOMATOES

Bruschette

This dish can be prepared ahead of time, but keep the tomato topping and toast separate until just before serving so the toasts don't become soggy.

Preheat the oven to 400°F/200°C/gas 6. Toast the bread until lightly browned. • Cut the tomatoes into small cubes. Transfer to a medium bowl and stir in the oil, basil, and oregano. Season with salt and pepper. • Top the toast with the tomato mixture.

Serves 4 • Prep: 10 min • Cooking: 5 min • Level: 1

- 8 slices firm-textured white bread
- 2–3 large ripe tomatoes
- $^1/_4$ cup/60 ml extra-virgin olive oil
- 8 leaves fresh basil, torn
- 1 teaspoon dried oregano (optional)
- salt and freshly ground black pepper

Breads

Every region of Italy has its own special selection of breads. In Tuscany, for example, the traditional loaves are unsalted and have been so at least since the time of Dante. But Tuscany also has the salty schiacciata, which is better known in other regions as focaccia. Some regional breads have become famous all over Italy and can be found in almost every bakery. Pane pugliese and altamura are two very popular breads from Apulia in the south, while ferrarese has become a favorite in many regions outside its native Ferrara, in central Italy. Grissini, or bread sticks, originally come from Turin, the capital of Piedmont, but have spread all over the world.

Pizza with artichoke topping

PIZZA WITH ARTICHOKE TOPPING

Pizza ai carciofi

- Pizza Dough for one 12-inch/30-cm pizza (see recipe, below)
- salt and freshly ground black pepper
- 5 tablespoons extra-virgin olive oil
- 2–3 tender, young artichokes, trimmed and thinly sliced
- 1 cup/250 g coarsely crumbled or grated Ricotta salata cheese
- 4–6 anchovy fillets, coarsely chopped

Only the tenderest young artichoke hearts, without any choke, are used in this recipe. If you can't get them, use 6–8 thinly sliced defrosted frozen baby artichoke hearts.

Preheat the oven to 425°F/220°C/gas 7. • Roll out the dough to fit into an oiled 12-inch (30-cm) pizza pan. • Press the surface of the dough with your fingertips to make little dimples in it. • Season with salt and pepper. Drizzle with half the oil, then spread the artichoke slices out in a single layer. • Distribute the cheese and anchovy fillets on top. • Bake for 25–30 minutes. • Drizzle with the remaining oil and serve.
Serves 2–4 • Prep: 25 min + 1 hr to rise • Cooking: 25–30 min • Level: 2

Cleaning artichokes

Only the tender inner cores of artichokes are edible. To clean an artichoke, cut off the top third of the leaves, then remove the tough outer leaves by pulling them down and snapping them off at the base. Cut the artichoke in half lengthwise using a sharp knife and remove any fuzzy choke. Drizzle the artichokes with fresh lemon juice to stop them from turning black.

Preparing yeast

In Italy, fresh compressed yeast is used to make pizza, but active dry yeast works just as well. To prepare fresh yeast, crumble the cake of yeast into a small bowl of warm water. If you are using active dry yeast, sprinkle the yeast over a small bowl of warm water. Let stand for 10 minutes, or until the mixture looks creamy.

MAKING PIZZA DOUGH

- 1 oz/25 g fresh yeast or 2 (¼-oz/7-g) packages active dry yeast
- about ⅔ cup/150 ml warm water
- 2½ cups/375 g all-purpose/plain flour
- 1 teaspoon salt

1. Prepare the yeast as explained above. Sift the flour and salt into a large bowl. Make a well in the center and pour in the yeast mixture and water. Use a wooden spoon to stir the mixture until the flour has been absorbed.

2. The dough will be a rough ball in the bottom of the bowl. Sprinkle a clean work surface, preferably made of wood, with a little flour. Note that the flour used to prepare the work surface is not included in the quantities given in the recipe. You will need about ½ cup (75 g) extra for this. Use a spatula to transfer the dough to the work surface. Curl your fingers around the dough and shape into a ball.

3. Press down on the dough with your knuckles to spread it a little. Take the far end of the dough, fold it a short distance toward you, then push it away again with the heel of your palm. Flexing your wrist, fold it toward you again, give it a quarter turn, then push it away. Repeat these motions, gently and with the lightest possible touch, for 8–10 minutes. When the dough is firm and no longer sticky, lift it up and bang it down hard against the surface a couple of times.

4. Place the kneaded dough in a large bowl greased with oil and cover with a cloth. The dough should double in volume during rising. This will take about 1 hour. To test whether it has risen sufficiently, poke your finger gently into the dough; if the impression remains, then the dough is ready.

Focaccia & Bread

FLATBREAD

Piadina

- 3 1/3 cups/500 g all-purpose/plain flour
- 1 teaspoon baking soda
- 1/4 teaspoon salt
- 1/4 cup/60 g lard, melted
- 1/4–1/2 cup/80–125 ml warm water

Sift the flour, baking soda, and salt into a large bowl. Shape into a mound and make a well in the center. Add the lard and 1 tablespoon of water. Gradually mix in the flour, adding enough water to make a firm dough. • Knead the dough on a clean, lightly floured work surface until smooth. Return to the bowl greased with oil and cover with a cloth. Set aside for 30 minutes. • Roll the dough out into a very thin sheet (less than 1/8 inch (3 mm) thick). • Cut out disks 6–8 inches (15–20 cm) in diameter. • Cook on a griddle or dry-fry in a very hot cast iron frying pan, turning once, until lightly browned. • Serve very hot.

Serves 6–8 • Prep: 25 min + 30 min to rest • Cooking: 15 min • Level: 2

CHEESE-FILLED FOCACCIA

Focaccia di Recco

This unleavened focaccia comes from Recco, near Genoa. Try other fillings, but always use ingredients that cook quickly, such as sliced mushrooms or ham.

Preheat the oven to 400°F/200°C/gas 6. • Oil a 9 x 13-inch (23 x 33-cm) baking pan. • Sift the flour and salt into a large bowl and make a well in the center. Stir in 1/4 cup (60 ml) of oil and enough water to form a fairly soft dough. Divide in half and shape into two balls, cover with a clean cloth, and set aside for 15 minutes. • Roll both pieces of dough out to fit the pan. Place one in the pan. Cover with the cheese, leaving a 1/2-inch (1-cm) border. Cover with the other piece of dough, pressing down to seal the edges. • Brush with the remaining 2 tablespoons oil and sprinkle with salt. • Bake for 15–20 minutes, or until lightly browned. If the dough puffs up while baking, prick with a fork.

Serves 6 • Prep: 30 min • Cooking: 15–20 min • Level: 2

- 3 1/2 cups/500 g all-purpose/plain flour
- 1 teaspoon salt, + more for sprinkling
- 6 tablespoons extra-virgin olive oil
- 3/4–1 cup/180–250 ml water
- 1 1/4 cups/300 g Gorgonzola or Taleggio cheese, melted with 1 tablespoon milk

Cheese-filled focaccia

Ciabatta

CIABATTA

- 1 oz/25 g fresh yeast or 2 (¹/₄-oz/7-g) packages active dry yeast
- 1¹/₂ cups/375 ml + 1 tablespoon lukewarm water, + more as needed
- 3¹/₃ cups/500 g + 2 tablespoons all-purpose/plain flour
- ¹/₂ teaspoon natural or organic honey
- 1 teaspoon salt
- ¹/₄ cup/60 ml extra-virgin olive oil
- durum wheat flour, to dust

This is one of the most versatile and beloved of Italian breads. Although it takes some time to rise (about 20 hours in all), it can be made at home.

Dissolve the yeast in 1 tablespoon of warm water. Let stand 10 minutes, or until foamy. • Sift the 3¹/₃ cups (500 g) of flour onto a work surface and make a well in the center. Add the yeast mixture and enough water (about 1 cup/250 ml) to make a smooth dough. • Knead the dough until smooth and elastic, about 5 minutes. Place in a well floured bowl and cover with plastic wrap. Set aside for 18 hours. • Turn the dough out onto a lightly floured work surface. Make an indentation in the center. • Dissolve the honey in the remaining ¹/₂ cup (125 ml) water. Mix in the remaining flour and

salt. Knead in the honey mixture until well blended. Transfer the dough to a bowl greased with the oil. Cover with plastic wrap and let rise for 30 minutes. • Turn out onto a lightly floured surface. Shape into a ciabatta (a rounded loaf). Sprinkle the top and sides of the dough with the remaining 2 tablespoons flour. • Cover with a cloth and set aside for 1 hour. • Preheat the oven to 425°F/220°C/gas 7. • Dust the dough with durum wheat flour. Place the dough on a baking sheet. • Bake for 10 minutes. Lower the oven temperature to 350°F/180°C/gas 4 and bake for 40 minutes more.

Makes one 2-lb/1 kg loaf • Prep: 40 min + 19¹/₂ hr to rise • Cooking: 50 min • Level: 3

Savory Pies

AGRIGENTO-STYLE COUNTRY PIE

Torta di Agrigento

- Pizza Dough for 1¹/₂ 12-inch/30-cm pizzas (see page 20), made with ¹/₄ cup/60 ml oil instead of water
- 2 lb/1 kg spinach, trimmed and cooked
- 1 medium cauliflower, trimmed, cut into small florets, and cooked
- ¹/₄ cup/60 ml extra-virgin olive oil
- 8 oz/200 g Provolone cheese, diced
- 6 oz/180 g tuna canned (tinned) in oil, drained and flaked
- 12 black olives, pitted/stoned and coarsely chopped

Prepare the dough and let rise for 1 hour. • Drain the cooked spinach well, squeezing out excess moisture. • Sauté the spinach and cauliflower in 2 tablespoons of oil. • Preheat the oven to 400°F/200°C/gas 6. • Grease a deep 9-inch (23-cm) in diameter springform pan. • When the dough has risen, divide it into two unequal parts (about two-thirds/one-third) and roll out the larger piece into a disk ¹/₈-inch (3-mm) thick. Use it to line the bottom and sides of the pan, slightly overlapping the edge. • Spread with the spinach and cover with the cauliflower, cheese, tuna, and olives. • Roll out the smaller piece of dough to the same thickness and slightly larger than the diameter of the pan. • Place on top of the filling. Pinch the edges together, then fold them over toward the center and tuck under to make a neat rolled edge. • Brush the surface with the remaining 2 tablespoons oil and prick with a fork. • Bake for 30–35 minutes or until the crust is golden brown. • Serve hot.

Serves 4–6 • Prep: 1 hr + 1 hr to rise • Cooking: 30–35 min • Level: 2

APULIAN POTATO PIE

Torta di patate alla pugliese

This is just one of the many vegetable pies that are traditional in Italy, especially in the south. The filling is reminiscent of the gattò di patate, a Neapolitan mold made with potatoes, Mozzarella, prosciutto, and Parmesan cheese.

Boil the potatoes in 1 quart (1 liter) cold water in a large saucepan until tender. • Drain and mash until smooth. • Sauté the pancetta in the oil in a frying pan until crispy. Drain well and pat dry on paper towels. • Preheat the oven to 325°F/170°C/gas 3. • Butter a 9-inch (23-cm) round cake pan. Line with waxed (greaseproof) paper. Butter the paper. • Unfold the dough and cut into a disk large enough to cover the bottom of the baking pan. Place in the prepared pan. Cut the remaining dough into strips long and wide enough to cover the pan sides with a sufficient overlap to enclose the filling. • Mix the mashed potatoes, sautéed pancetta, butter, milk, egg, egg yolk, Parmesan, salt, and pepper in a large bowl. Spoon the filling mixture into the prepared pan. Fold the overlapping edges of the dough over the filling. • Bake for 40–45 minutes, or until golden brown. • Serve hot or at room temperature.

Serves 6–8 • Prep: 15 min • Cooking: 40–45 min • Level: 2

- 2 lb/1 kg potatoes
- 3 oz/90 g pancetta (or bacon)
- 2 tablespoons extra-virgin olive oil
- 1 package (17-oz) puff pastry (such as Pepperidge Farm)
- ¹/₂ cup/125 g butter, melted
- 1 cup/250 ml milk
- 1 large egg + 1 large egg yolk
- ¹/₂ cup/50 g freshly grated Parmesan cheese
- salt and freshly ground black pepper

Pancetta

Pancetta is a pork product cut from the belly of the pig. It ranges in color from pinky white to dark red in the leaner versions. Either flat or rolled, it is usually chopped and used to flavor pasta sauces, risottos, and many other dishes. Substitute bacon if you can't get pancetta; bacon is similar in flavor although (unlike pancetta) cured by smoking.

RIBBON PASTA WITH LEMON

Tagliolini al limone di Amalfi

- 1 lb/500 g tagliolini or other fresh ribbon pasta
- 1 tablespoon butter
- ¹/₂ cup/125 ml white wine
- ¹/₂ cup/125 ml light cream
- ¹/₈ teaspoon paprika
- ¹/₄ cup/30 g freshly grated Parmesan cheese
- grated zest of 1 lemon
- 1 tablespoon fresh lemon juice

This extremely simple sauce is perfect for fresh pasta, whether homemade or purchased from a specialty store or supermarket. Always use fresh lemons.

Cook the pasta in a large pot of salted boiling water until al dente. • Melt half the butter in a frying pan over low heat. Pour in the wine and cook until evaporated. Add the cream and paprika. • Drain the pasta and add to the sauce. • Stir in the remaining butter, Parmesan, and lemon zest and juice. Toss carefully over high heat to reduce the sauce, if necessary, and serve.

Serves 4 • Prep: 10 min • Cooking: 10 min • Level: 1

PASTA WITH BLACK OLIVES

Pasta con olive nere

Simmer the tomatoes and garlic in a medium saucepan over medium-low heat for 15 minutes. • Add the oil, olives, oregano, and red pepper flakes and cook for 2 minutes more. Season with salt. • Meanwhile, cook the spaghetti in a large pot of salted boiling water until al dente. • Drain and add to the tomato sauce. Toss briefly and serve.

Serves 4 • Prep: 10 min • Cooking: 20 min • Level: 1

- 1 lb/500 g fresh or canned/tinned tomatoes, coarsely chopped
- 2 cloves garlic, finely chopped
- 6 tablespoons extra-virgin olive oil
- 1²/₃ cups/160 g black olives, pitted/stoned and coarsely chopped
- 2 teaspoons dried oregano
- ¹/₂ teaspoon red pepper flakes
- salt
- 1 lb/500 g spaghetti or bucatini

Ribbon pasta with lemon

Bucatini with pancetta, cheese, and parsley

BUCATINI WITH PANCETTA, CHEESE, AND PARSLEY

Bucatini all'amatriciana bianca

- 1 lb/500 g bucatini or spaghetti
- ¹/₄ cup/60 ml extra-virgin olive oil
- 1 fresh chile pepper, left whole
- 5 oz/150 g pancetta or bacon, finely chopped
- 1 white onion, finely chopped
- 1 cup/100 g finely chopped fresh parsley
- 2 cups/250 g freshly grated Pecorino cheese

This dish takes its Italian name from the hill town of Amatrice, in central Italy. There is also a "red" version made in the same way, but with the addition of about 1¹/₄ lb (625 g) peeled and chopped tomatoes after the onion has been sautéed.

Cook the pasta in a large pot of salted boiling water until al dente. • Meanwhile, heat the oil in a medium saucepan over high heat. • Sauté the chile pepper and pancetta until browned. Remove the pancetta, pat dry on paper towels, and set aside. Discard the chile. • In the same saucepan, sauté the onion for 8–10 minutes over medium heat. Return the pancetta to the saucepan and let it flavor the onion. • Drain the pasta and add to the sauce. • Season with parsley and Pecorino. Toss well and serve.

Serves 4 • Prep: 5 min • Cooking: 20 min • Level: 1

PASTA WITH RICOTTA SALATA AND EGGPLANT

Pasta alla Norma

Slice the eggplants quite thinly lengthwise. Place in a colander and sprinkle with the salt. Let stand for 1 hour. Rinse well and pat dry on paper towels. • Use a fork to break the Ricotta salata into fairly small, crumbly pieces (or chop the Pecorino into small pieces with a knife). • Simmer the tomatoes in a large saucepan with the garlic and oil for 30 minutes, stirring occasionally. • Strain the tomato sauce (or process in a blender) and return to the pan to keep hot over very low heat. • Fry the eggplant slices in hot oil until browned on both sides and drain on paper towels. • Meanwhile, cook the spaghetti in a large pot of salted boiling water until al dente. Drain well and transfer to a serving bowl. Add the tomato sauce and mix in just over half the cheese and the basil. • Serve immediately, topping each portion with eggplant slices and the remaining Ricotta salata or Pecorino.

Serves 4 • Prep: 20 min + 1 hr to drain • Cooking: 40 min • Level: 2

- 3 medium eggplants/aubergines
- 1–2 tablespoons coarse sea salt
- 5 oz/150 g Ricotta salata cheese or semi-hard Pecorino cheese
- 1¹/₄ lb/625 g fresh or canned/tinned tomatoes, peeled and chopped
- 1 clove garlic, finely chopped
- 6 tablespoons extra-virgin olive oil
- 1 lb/500 g spaghetti
- 1 cup/250 ml olive oil, for frying
- 8 leaves basil, torn

Pasta

Ravioli Sardinian-style

Ravioli Sardi

Pasta Dough
- 3 cups/450 g all-purpose/plain flour
- 2 large eggs, lightly beaten
- ¹/₄–¹/₂ cup/60–125 ml water

Filling
- 1²/₃ cups/400 g Ricotta cheese
- 2 large eggs, lightly beaten
- ¹/₃ cup/70 g granulated sugar
- 1 tablespoon finely chopped fresh parsley
- grated zest of ¹/₂ lemon
- ¹/₂ cup/60 g fine dry bread crumbs
- ¹/₈ teaspoon ground nutmeg
- ¹/₈ teaspoon ground cinnamon
- salt and freshly ground white pepper

Sauce
- 3 tablespoons extra-virgin olive oil
- 2 lb/1 kg tomatoes, peeled and chopped
- 1 clove garlic, peeled and left whole
- salt and freshly ground white pepper
- 1 tablespoon finely chopped fresh parsley
- 2 tablespoons butter
- ¹/₄ cup/30 g freshly grated Parmesan cheese
- 4 leaves basil, torn

These ravioli come from the beautiful island of Sardinia. The slightly sweet flavor of the ricotta filling is offset by the fresh tang of the tomato sauce. Delicious!

Pasta Dough: Sift the flour onto a work surface and make a well in the center. Add the eggs and enough water to make a smooth dough. Add more water if needed. Roll out the dough using a pasta machine or by hand. Cut into long sheets about 4 inches (10 cm) wide. • Filling: Mix the Ricotta, eggs, sugar, parsley, lemon zest, bread crumbs, nutmeg, cinnamon, salt, and pepper until well blended. • Place heaped teaspoons of the filling down the center of the sheets of pasta at intervals of about 2 inches (5 cm). Moisten the edges of the dough and fold over to seal, pressing down gently between the mounds of filling. Use a sharp knife or a wheel cutter (for fluted edges) to cut between the mounds. • Sauce: Heat the oil in a large frying pan over medium heat. Stir in the tomatoes and garlic. Season with salt and pepper. Cook for 8–10 minutes, or until the sauce has reduced. Remove the garlic and add the parsley and butter. • Cook the ravioli in 2–3 batches in a large pot of salted boiling water for 5–7 minutes, or until the edges of the pasta are cooked al dente. • Scoop the cooked ravioli out of the pot with a slotted spoon and place on a heated serving plate. Spoon the sauce over the top and sprinkle with the Parmesan and basil. • Serve hot.
Serves 6 • Prep: 1 hr • Cooking: 30 min • Level: 3

Stuffed pasta roll

Rotolo ripieno

Prepare the pasta dough. Shape the dough into a ball, wrap in plastic wrap, and let rest for 1 hour. • Roll the dough out into a thin, rectangular sheet measuring 12 x 16 inches (30 x 40 cm) and cover with a clean cloth or plastic wrap to prevent it from drying out. • Filling: Wash the spinach leaves thoroughly. Place in a saucepan and cook until tender with just the water left clinging to the leaves. • Squeeze out excess moisture, then chop coarsely. • Sauté the spinach in 2 tablespoons of butter and add 1 tablespoon of Parmesan. • Sauté the mushrooms in 2 tablespoons of butter for 4–5 minutes. • Poach the chicken livers in a little water until tender. Drain and chop finely. • Melt 4 tablespoons of butter in a frying pan and sauté the sausage meat, chicken livers, and beef over low heat until browned. Season with salt and cook for 10 minutes, moistening with a little water if the sauce begins to dry. • Spread this mixture over the sheet of pasta dough, stopping about ³/₄ inch (2 cm) short of the edges. Cover with the spinach in an even layer. • Fold over the edge of one of the longer sides and roll up, forming a long sausage. • Wrap firmly in a large piece of cheesecloth (muslin). Tie the gathered ends of the cloth with string. • Place the roll in boiling water in an oval Dutch oven. Simmer gently for 50 minutes. • Remove from the water carefully and set aside to cool a little. Untie and remove the cloth. • Preheat the oven to 450°F/220°C/ gas 8. • Cut the roll into ¹/₂-inch (1-cm) thick slices and place in an overlapping layer in a lightly buttered ovenproof dish. Melt the remaining 6 tablespoons butter and pour over the slices, then sprinkle with the remaining 11 tablespoons Parmesan. • Bake for 5–10 minutes, or until the cheese is lightly browned.
Serves 4 • Prep: 1 hr + 1 hr to rest • Cooking: 90 min • Level: 3

- 1 Pasta Dough made with 3 cups/450 g all-purpose flour (see opposite recipe)

Filling
- 2 lb/1 kg spinach leaves
- ³/₄ cup/180 g butter
- ³/₄ cup/90 g freshly grated Parmesan cheese
- 8 oz/200 g fresh mushrooms, thinly sliced, or 1 oz/30 g dried Italian porcini mushrooms, soaked in warm water and drained
- 8 oz/200 g chicken livers, trimmed
- 4 oz/125 g fresh Italian sausage meat
- 8 oz/200 g finely ground/minced lean beef
- salt

STUFFED PASTA WITH PUMPKIN FILLING

Cappellacci di zucca

Filling

- 2³/₄ lb/1.3 kg pie pumpkin or winter squash
- 1³/₄ cups/200 g freshly grated Parmesan cheese
- 1 large egg
- pinch of freshly grated nutmeg
- ½ cup/50 g fine dry bread crumbs
- salt
- Pasta Dough made with 3 cups/450 g all-purpose flour (see page 28)
- 7 tablespoons butter, melted

Preheat the oven to 400°F/200°C/gas 6. • Cut the pumpkin in half lengthwise, scrape away the seeds and fibers, and cut it into slices 1½ inches (4 cm) thick. • Bake for 25–30 minutes, or until tender. • Remove the flesh from the skin. Strain the flesh into a large bowl while still hot. • Mix well with 1¼ cups (150 g) of the Parmesan, egg, nutmeg, bread crumbs, and salt. • Cover the bowl with plastic wrap and let stand for 2 hours. Prepare the pasta dough. Shape the dough into a ball, wrap in plastic wrap, and let rest for 1 hour. • Roll the dough out into a very thin sheet. Use a fluted pastry wheel to cut it into 3-inch (7.5-cm) squares. Place ½ tablespoon of the filling in a mound in the center of each square. Fold into triangles and seal well with a little water. • Cook the pasta in batches in a large pot of salted boiling water until the edges of the pasta are cooked al dente. Scoop out with a slotted spoon, drain well, and place in a heated serving dish while you cook the rest. • Serve hot, drizzled with the butter and sprinkled with the remaining ½ cup (60 g) Parmesan.

Serves 4–6 • Prep: 1 hr + 3 hr to rest the pasta dough and filling • Cooking: 30 min • Level: 3

Pasta

BAKED SPINACH LASAGNA

Lasagne verde al ragù

- 3 cups/750 ml Meat Sauce (see page 39)
- generous 1 cup/250 g cooked, drained spinach
- 1 quantity Pasta Dough (see page 28)

Béchamel Sauce
- 1/4 cup/60 g butter
- 5 tablespoons all-purpose/plain flour
- 2 cups/500 ml hot milk
- salt and freshly ground white pepper

- salt
- 2 cups/300 g freshly grated Parmesan cheese
- 2 tablespoons butter

This recipe is especially good when made with fresh pasta, if you have the time to make it. If not, use store-bought dried lasagna sheets and cook as indicated on the package.

Prepare the meat sauce. • Squeeze as much moisture out of the cooked spinach as possible and chop very finely. • Prepare the pasta dough as explained on page 28, incorporating the spinach into the dough with the eggs. Shape the dough into a ball, wrap in plastic wrap, and let rest for about 1 hour. • Roll the pasta dough out into a slightly thicker sheet than usual, about 1/8 inch thick. Cut into rectangles measuring 6 x 4 inches (15 x 10 cm). • Béchamel Sauce: Melt the butter in a small saucepan. Stir in the flour and cook and stir over medium heat for 2–3 minutes. • Add the milk, a little at a time, stirring constantly, and continue cooking for 5 minutes, or until thick and smooth. • Remove from the heat. Season with salt and pepper. • Bring a very large saucepan of water to a boil with the salt. Add the lasagna in batches and cook for 2–3 minutes, or until al dente. • Scoop the cooked sheets of lasagna out with a slotted spoon and spread them out on clean cloths to dry off for a few minutes. • Preheat the oven to 375°F/190°C/gas 5. • Spoon a thin layer of the meat sauce over the bottom of a fairly deep, rectangular ovenproof dish and cover with a layer of lasagna sheets. Spread with a layer of Béchamel and sprinkle with Parmesan. Repeat this process until all the ingredients are used up. The top layer should be lasagna, covered with Béchamel sauce and sprinkled with the remaining Parmesan. • Dot with the butter and bake for 25–30 minutes, or until golden brown. • Let stand for 5 minutes before serving.
Serves 4 • Prep: 45 min + 4 hr for the meat sauce • Cooking: 45 min • Level: 3

BAKED STUFFED CRÊPES

Cannelloni alla Barbaroux

This recipe comes from Piedmont, in the northeast. Cooking in this region shows a strong French influence.

Butter a shallow ovenproof dish. • Preheat the oven to 400°F/200°C/gas 6. • Crêpes: Beat the egg, flour, milk, 1/2 tablespoon olive oil, and salt in a large bowl with an electric mixer at medium speed until smooth. • Heat 1 teaspoon oil in a medium frying pan. Pour in 2 tablespoons of batter and quickly tip and rotate the pan to distribute the batter evenly. The crêpe should be very thin. Use a spatula to turn it after 40–50 seconds and cook for about 30 seconds, or until golden brown. Slide the crêpe onto a plate. • Add another teaspoon of oil to the pan and repeat the operation until all the batter has been used. The batter should yield 12 crêpes. • Filling: Chop the veal and prosciutto finely in a food processor. Transfer to a medium bowl and and add the egg and Parmesan. • Spread some of the filling onto each crêpe and roll up loosely. • Place the filled crêpes in the prepared dish. • Béchamel Sauce: Melt the butter in a small saucepan. Stir in the flour and cook, stirring constantly, over medium heat for 2–3 minutes. • Add the milk, a little at a time, stirring constantly, and continue cooking for 5 minutes, or until thick and smooth. • Remove from the heat. Stir in the Parmesan. Season with salt and pepper. • Pour the Béchamel over the stuffed crêpes. • Bake for 25–30 minutes, or until lightly browned. • Serve piping hot.
Serves 4 • Prep: 1 hr 20 min • Cooking: 25–30 min • Level: 3

Crêpes
- 1 large egg
- 2/3 cup/100 g all-purpose/plain flour
- 2/3 cup/150 ml milk
- 3 tablespoons extra-virgin olive oil
- salt

Filling
- 8 oz/250 g lean roasted veal or beef
- 3 oz/90 g prosciutto
- 1 large egg
- 1 tablespoon freshly grated Parmesan cheese

Béchamel Sauce
- 2 tablespoons butter
- 3 tablespoons all-purpose/plain flour
- 1 cup/250 ml hot milk
- 1 tablespoon freshly grated Parmesan cheese
- salt and freshly ground white pepper

Pasta

SPAGHETTI WITH ORANGE

Spaghetti all'arancia

- 1 lb/500 g spaghetti
- ¹/₃ cup/80 ml extra-virgin olive oil
- 2 cloves garlic, finely chopped
- 8 anchovy fillets
- 2 tablespoons fine dry bread crumbs
- ¹/₄ cup/60 ml white wine
- 4 oranges, peeled and cut into segments, blood oranges if available
- salt
- 1 tablespoon finely chopped fresh parsley

Cook the pasta in a large pot of salted boiling water until al dente. • Heat the oil in a large frying pan over medium heat. Add the garlic and anchovies. Let the anchovies dissolve gently, taking care not to burn them. Add the bread crumbs and cook 2–3 minutes. Pour in the wine and cook until evaporated. • Add the oranges and their juice. Cook for 2 minutes over high heat. Season with the salt. • Drain the pasta and place in a heated serving dish. Spoon the sauce over the top. Toss gently, sprinkle with the parsley, and serve.

Serves 4 • Prep: 15 min • Cooking: 15 min • Level: 1

PASTA WITH CAULIFLOWER

Pasta con cavolfiori

- 1 small cauliflower, trimmed
- salt
- 1 lb/500 g pasta, such as bucatini or spaghetti
- 1 medium onion, finely chopped
- ¹/₃ cup/80 ml extra-virgin olive oil
- 2 salted anchovies, rinsed and boned, or 4 anchovy fillets
- 3 tablespoons golden raisins/sultanas
- 3 tablespoons pine nuts
- ¹/₄ teaspoon saffron threads, dissolved in 3 tablespoons hot water
- freshly ground black pepper
- ¹/₄ cup/30 g freshly grated Pecorino cheese (optional)

Preheat the oven to 425°F/220°C/gas 7. • Boil the cauliflower in plenty of salted water until just tender. Lift the cauliflower out of the water. Divide the cauliflower into small florets. • Return the water to a boil and add the pasta. • Meanwhile, sauté the onion for 1–2 minutes in the oil in a large saucepan. Add the anchovies, raisins, pine nuts, and saffron. Stir for 2–3 minutes, then add the cauliflower and continue cooking over low heat, stirring occasionally. • When the pasta is cooked al dente, drain and add to the cauliflower mixture. • Combine carefully, then transfer to a heated serving dish and sprinkle generously with pepper. • Serve hot. • For a hearty winter dish, transfer the pasta and cauliflower mixture to a heated ovenproof dish and sprinkle with the Pecorino. • Bake in the oven for 10–15 minutes, or until the cheese is golden brown. • Serve hot.

Serves 4 • Prep: 15 min • Cooking: 40 min • Level: 1

HOMEMADE PASTA WITH SPICY TOMATO SAUCE

Maccheroni al ferretto

This dish is one of the many possible variations prepared throughout southern Italy. The Italian word maccheroni is a generic and age-old term that describes many different shapes of pasta, throughout the Italian peninsula and islands. This Calabrian version is marked by its generous use of chile pepper.

Tomato Sauce: Heat the oil in a large saucepan over medium heat. Sauté the chile pepper, onion, and beef until browned. Stir in the garlic and wine and cook until the wine has evaporated. Add the tomatoes, basil, salt, and pepper. Bring to a boil. Lower the heat, and simmer gently, partially covered, for at least 2 hours. Add hot water if the sauce begins to dry. • Serve the meat separately as a main course. • Pasta: Mix the flour and enough warm water (110–115°F) to form a soft dough. Knead on a lightly floured surface for 10 minutes, or until smooth and elastic. Wrap in plastic wrap and let rest for about 30 minutes. • Roll the dough into long strips and cut into 4-inch (10-cm) long pieces. With a *ferretto* (or knitting needle), shape them into hollow cylinders, like bucatini, about 8 inches (20 cm) long. Place them on a clean kitchen towel and sprinkle with cornmeal. • Cook the pasta in a large pot of salted boiling water for 7–10 minutes, or until cooked al dente. Drain well and transfer to a heated serving dish. • Spoon the tomato sauce over the top and sprinkle with the Pecorino.• Serve hot.

Serves 6 • Prep: 1 hr 40 min + 30 min to rest • Cooking: 2 hr 10 min • Level: 3

Tomato Sauce
- ¹/₄ cup/60 ml extra-virgin olive oil
- 1 dried chile pepper, crumbled
- 1 large red onion, finely chopped
- 1 lb/500 g chuck steak, in a single cut
- 2 cloves garlic, finely chopped
- ¹/₂ cup/125 ml dry red wine
- 3 lb/1.5 kg ripe tomatoes, peeled and chopped
- 1 tablespoon coarsely chopped fresh basil
- salt and freshly ground black pepper
- ¹/₄ cup/60 ml water

Pasta
- 2²/₃ cups/400 g durum-wheat flour
- 2 tablespoons fine ground cornmeal
- ¹/₂ cup/60 g freshly grated Pecorino cheese

Rice

CHICKEN RISOTTO

Risotto alla sbirraglia

- 4 tablespoons butter
- 2 tablespoons extra-virgin olive oil
- 1 stalk celery, finely chopped
- 1 onion, finely chopped
- 1 carrot, finely chopped
- 1 chicken (about 1¹/₂ lb/750 g), cut into 8 pieces
- salt and freshly ground white pepper
- 1 cup/250 ml dry white wine
- 2 cups/400 g short-grain rice (preferably Italian arborio)
- 2 chicken livers, trimmed and finely chopped
- 1¹/₂ quarts/1.5 liters chicken stock or broth
- 6 tablespoons freshly grated Parmesan cheese

Melt 3 tablespoons of butter with the oil in a saucepan and sauté the celery, onion, and carrot for 2 minutes. • Sprinkle the chicken with salt and pepper and add to the pan. Increase the heat and cook until brown all over, after 8–10 minutes. Sprinkle with a little wine. Cover and cook, gradually adding the wine until tender, 25–30 minutes. Remove and set aside in a warm oven. • Put the rice and chicken livers in the pan with the cooking juices and cook over high heat for 2 minutes. • Begin stirring in the stock, ¹/₂ cup (125 ml) at a time. Cook, stirring, until each addition has been absorbed, until the rice is tender, 15–18 minutes. • Stir in the remaining 1 tablespoon butter and Parmesan. Transfer the risotto to a heated serving dish. Arrange the chicken on top and serve.

Serves 6 • Prep: 20 min • Cooking: 1 hr • Level: 2

PUMPKIN RISOTTO

Risotto di zucca

- 2 lb/1 kg orange-fleshed pie pumpkin or winter squash
- ¹/₃ cup/80 g butter
- ¹/₄ cup/60 ml extra-virgin olive oil
- 2 cups/400 g short-grain rice (preferably Italian arborio)
- ¹/₂ cup/125 ml dry white wine
- salt and freshly ground black pepper
- 2 cups/500 ml stock or broth
- 1 cup/150 g freshly grated Parmesan cheese

Peel the pumpkin, cut in half lengthwise, and remove the seeds and fibers. Slice thinly. • Heat half the butter and oil gently in a saucepan. Add the pumpkin, cover tightly, and cook over low heat until almost tender, 12–15 minutes. • Add the rice, stirring well to flavor the grains. Pour in the wine and stir until the wine has evaporated. Season with salt and pepper. • Begin stirring in the stock, ¹/₂ cup (125 ml) at a time. Cook, stirring, until each addition has been absorbed, until the rice is tender, 15–18 minutes. • The risotto should be moist but not sloppy. • Remove from the heat and stir in the remaining butter and the Parmesan.

Serves 6 • Prep: 10 min • Cooking: 40 min • Level: 1

RICE WITH SEAFOOD

Riso alla pescatora

The dish is sometimes called a risotto, although that is technically incorrect. A true risotto is stirred during cooking to release some of the starch from the kernels of rice and to give the finished dish its typically creamy consistency. This rice dish is low-maintenance and does not require constant stirring. This same recipe can be made without the tomatoes.

Soak the mussels in cold water for 1 hour to purge them of sand. • Drain well and cook with the water until they open up, 10 minutes. Discard any that haven't opened. • Bring the stock to a boil. • Cut the shrimp into pieces if they are very large. • Heat 2 tablespoons of oil in a large saucepan over medium heat. Sauté the onion for 8–10 minutes, or until browned. Add the garlic and chile pepper. • Add the squid and cook for 5–7 minutes over medium heat. Add the tomatoes, season with salt and pepper, and continue cooking over low heat. • Heat the remaining oil in a medium frying pan, add the rice, and stir over high heat for 1 minute. • Add the rice to the squid mixture. Pour in the wine and cook until it has evaporated. • Pour in enough stock to generously cover the rice. Lower the heat, cover, and cook for 10–15 minutes, or until the rice is tender. Add the shrimp and the mussels and clams and cook until heated through. When the rice is done, add the butter and garnish with the parsley.

Serves 6 • Prep: 20 min • Cooking: 30–35 min • Level: 2

- about 1¹/₂ quarts/1.5 liters fish stock (made with fish bones, the shrimp shells, 1 onion, parsley, white peppercorns, and other herbs as desired)
- 1³/₄ lb/800 g shrimp, shelled (reserve the shells for the stock)
- ¹/₄ cup/60 ml extra-virgin olive oil
- 1 onion, finely chopped
- 2 cloves garlic, finely chopped
- 1 dried chile pepper, crumbled
- 14 oz/400 g small squid, cleaned and cut into rings
- 6 tomatoes, peeled and cut into cubes
- salt and freshly ground white pepper
- 2 cups/400 g short-grain rice (preferably Italian arborio)
- ¹/₄ cup/60 ml white wine
- 3 lb/1.5 kg mussels and clams
- ¹/₄ cup/60 ml water
- 2 tablespoons butter
- 2 tablespoons finely chopped parsley

Gnocchi

PRUNE GNOCCHI

Gnocchi de susini

- 8 oz/250 g prunes
- 7 tablespoons granulated sugar
- salt
- 2 lb/1 kg potatoes
- 1²/₃ cups/250 g all-purpose/plain flour
- 1 large egg, lightly beaten
- 2 tablespoons butter
- fine dry bread crumbs
- ¹/₂ teaspoon ground cinnamon

This recipe from Trentino, in northwestern Italy, is a close relative of the Austrian knödel. It is an excellent first course to serve before game. You can replace the prunes with fresh plums. Use half a plum for each dumpling and add a little more sugar to counteract the acidity of the fresh fruit.

Soak the prunes in warm water for 30 minutes, then drain. Pit (stone) them and fill each cavity with ¹/₂ teaspoon sugar. • Peel the potatoes, boil until tender, and mash them. Spread out on a chopping board and season with salt. Let cool. • Add the flour, egg, and 1 tablespoon butter to the potatoes. Use your hands to mix the potato mixture until well blended. • Shape the dough into dumplings about the size of a golf ball. Insert a prune into the center of each. • Cook the gnocchi in batches in a large pan of salted boiling water until they bob up to the surface, 4–5 minutes. • Scoop out with a slotted spoon, drain well, and transfer to a heated serving dish. • Brown the bread crumbs in the remaining 1 tablespoon butter and remaining sugar. Dust with the cinnamon. Sprinkle over the gnocchi and serve hot.

Serves 6 • Prep: 20 min + 30 min to soak • Cooking: 30–40 min • Level: 3

POTATO GNOCCHI

Gnocchi del giovedì

Wash the potatoes thoroughly, but do not peel. Cook in lightly salted boiling water until tender. • Slip the skins off the cooked potatoes and mash them. Stir in the flour and salt. • Beat the egg yolks with a fork. Add to the mixture and stir well. • Take a handful of the mixture and, on a lightly floured work surface, roll it out into a long sausage, about ¹/₂ inch (1 cm) in diameter. Use a sharp knife to cut into ³/₄-inch (2-cm) lengths. Repeat until all the mixture is used up. Place the little dumplings on a clean cloth to dry. Let stand for 1 hour before cooking. • Bring a large pot of salted water to a boil and add the dumplings in batches. When the dumplings have risen to the top, let them bob around for about 2 minutes, then scoop out with a slotted spoon and place in a heated serving dish. Continue until all the dumplings are cooked. • Drizzle with the butter and sprinkle with the Parmesan.

Serves 4–6 • Prep: 20 min + 1 hr to rest • Cooking: 40 min • Level: 2

- 3 lb/1.5 kg potatoes
- ³/₄ cup/125 g all-purpose/plain flour
- salt
- 2 large egg yolks
- ¹/₂ cup/125 g butter, melted
- 1 cup/150 g freshly grated Parmesan cheese + more to serve

BAKED SEMOLINA GNOCCHI

Gnocchi alla Romana

- 1 quart/1 liter milk
- 1²/₃ cups/250 g semolina
- salt
- ¹/₂ cup/125 g butter
- 2 large egg yolks
- 1 cup/125 g freshly grated Parmesan cheese + more to serve
- 1 tablespoon grated Gruyère cheese
- freshly ground white pepper

Bring the milk to a boil in a large saucepan. • Sprinkle the semolina in little by little, stirring all the time so that no lumps form. Stir for 25–30 minutes, or until the mixture is dense. • Remove from the heat and season with salt. Stir in ¹/₄ cup (60 g) butter, the egg yolks, ¹/₂ cup (60 g) Parmesan, and the Gruyère. • Spread the mixture out on a lightly floured surface to about ¹/₂-inch (1 cm) thick. Let cool. • Preheat the oven to 350°F/180°C/gas 4. • Use a glass to cut out disks of the mixture. Butter an ovenproof dish and use the pieces

leftover after cutting out the disks to form a first layer in the dish. Sprinkle with a little of the remaining Parmesan. Lay the disks over the top, one overlapping the next. • Melt the remaining ¹/₄ cup (60 g) butter and drizzle over the top. Sprinkle with the remaining Parmesan and dust with pepper. • Bake for 25–30 minutes, until a lovely golden color. • Serve hot.

Serves 4 • Prep: 20 min • Cooking: 1 hr • Level: 2

Polenta

POLENTA

- 4 quarts/4 liters cold water
- 2 tablespoons coarse sea salt
- 3¹/₂ cups/450 g coarsely-grain yellow cornmeal

Bring the water and salt to a boil in a saucepan large enough to hold at least 4 quarts (4 liters) of liquid. • Add the cornmeal gradually, stirring constantly so that no lumps form. Polenta should always be perfectly smooth. • Stir the polenta over high heat by moving a long, wooden spoon in a circular motion. At a certain point the polenta will begin to draw away from the sides of the pot on which a thin crust will form. The polenta should be stirred constantly for the 40–45 minutes it takes to cook. • Pour the cooked polenta onto a serving board or platter. Serve hot with sauce or let cool to make fried or baked polenta crostini.

Serves: 4 • Prep: 5 min • Cooking: 40–45 min • Level: 2

Polenta

Polenta

Polenta is made with coarsely ground cornmeal, salt, water, and lots of hard work! There are some good precooked polenta mixes available now that reduce the cooking time considerably, although many claim that the resulting polenta lacks authenticity. Originally from northern Italy, polenta is served with vegetable, meat, and cheese sauces. Leftover polenta can be grilled or fried and topped with sautéed mushrooms, chopped tomatoes, or a variety of other toppings.

POLENTA WITH MEAT SAUCE

Matuffi con il ragù

Meat Sauce

- 2 tablespoons extra-virgin olive oil
- 2 red onions, finely chopped
- 2 carrots, finely chopped
- 2 stalks celery, finely chopped
- 2 cloves garlic, finely chopped
- 8 oz/250 g sausage
- 8 oz/250 g ground/minced beef
- 1 tablespoon all-purpose/plain flour
- 1/2 cup/125 ml red wine
- 1 lb/500 g tomatoes, peeled and chopped
- 1 tablespoon finely chopped parsley
- 1/4 teaspoon freshly grated nutmeg
- sprig rosemary
- sprig sage
- 1 bay leaf
- 1 small piece lemon zest
- salt and freshly ground black pepper
- meat stock or broth, or water, if needed

Polenta

- 3 quarts/3 liters water
- 2 teaspoons coarse salt
- 2²/₃ cups/400 g coarsely ground yellow cornmeal
- 1/4 cup/30 g freshly grated Parmesan cheese

Meat Sauce: Heat the oil in a medium saucepan over low heat. Add the onions, carrots, and celery. Cook, covered, for 25–30 minutes. Add the garlic and sausage, turn up the heat to high, and add the beef. Brown until cooked. • Stir in the flour. Pour in the wine and cook until it has evaporated. • Add the tomatoes, parsley, nutmeg, rosemary, sage, bay leaf, lemon zest, salt, and pepper. • Cook for at least 4 hours over low heat, adding a little stock or water to keep it moist. • Polenta: Bring the water almost to a boil in a large deep saucepan. Add the salt and sprinkle in the cornmeal. Bring to a boil and let simmer for 40–45 minutes, stirring constantly. If it becomes too thick, add a little boiling water or milk. • When cooked, pour onto a warm serving plate. Top with the meat sauce and sprinkle with Parmesan.

Serves 6 • Prep: 30–35 min • Cooking: 4 hr • Level: 2

POLENTA WITH BEANS AND PANCETTA

Polenta fasiolada

Sauté the pancetta and onion in the oil in a large saucepan until the pancetta is crispy. • Add the beans, sage, and enough cold water to cover the beans. Bring to a boil, then cover, and simmer gently for 1 hour. • When the beans are nearly done, add salt to taste and, stirring constantly, gradually sprinkle in the cornmeal. • Cook slowly for 45 minutes, stirring often, and adding warm water if necessary. The polenta should be fairly soft. • Turn out onto a board or platter and serve.

Serves 6 • Prep: 20 min + overnight to soak • Cooking: 2 hr • Level: 1

- 1¹/₃ cups/250 g dried cranberry, borlotti, or pinto beans, soaked overnight and drained
- 1/2 cup/100 g diced pancetta or bacon
- 3 tablespoons extra-virgin olive oil
- 1 small onion, finely chopped
- 6 leaves fresh sage
- water
- salt
- 2¹/₄ cups/350 g coarsely ground yellow cornmeal

Polenta with meat sauce

Soups

TUSCAN CABBAGE AND RICE SOUP

Minestra di cavolo e riso

- 2 carrots, finely sliced
- 2 stalks celery, sliced
- ½ small Savoy cabbage, coarsely chopped
- 1 quart/1 liter meat or vegetable stock or broth
- 1 cup/200 g short-grain rice
- freshly ground black pepper
- 2 tablespoons extra-virgin olive oil
- 2 tablespoons freshly grated Parmesan cheese

Traditionally this Florentine soup was made with the juices produced when cooking tripe. Tripe is still popular in Tuscany; and tripe sandwiches are a classic street food in Florence.

Bring the stock to a boil in a large saucepan with the carrots, celery, and cabbage. Lower the heat and simmer for 25–30 minutes, or until the vegetables are tender. • Add the rice and cook for 15–18 minutes, or until the rice is cooked. Season with the pepper, oil, and Parmesan.

Serves 4 • Prep: 5 min • Cooking: 40–50 min • Level: 1

SPINACH AND RICE SOUP

Minestra di riso e spinaci

Wash the spinach leaves thoroughly and place in a saucepan. Cover tightly and cook over medium heat for 2–3 minutes with just the water left clinging to the leaves. • Remove from the heat and, when cool enough to handle, squeeze out as much moisture as possible. Chop coarsely. • Melt the butter in the same saucepan, and add the spinach and salt. Stir over medium heat for 3 minutes. Set aside. • Bring the stock to a boil in a large saucepan. Add the rice and cook for 15–18 minutes, or until the rice is cooked. • Add the spinach. • Beat the egg lightly in a bowl with salt, pepper, and Parmesan. Pour this mixture into the hot soup while beating with a whisk. Remove from the heat. • Let stand for 30 seconds before serving.

Serves 4 • Prep: 10 min • Cooking: 20–25 min • Level: 1

- 12 oz/350 g fresh spinach leaves
- 2 tablespoons butter
- salt
- 1¼ quarts/1.25 liters meat stock or broth
- 1 cup/200 g short-grain rice
- 1 large egg
- freshly ground white pepper
- 3 tablespoons freshly grated Parmesan cheese

Tuscan cabbage and rice soup

Neapolitan Christmas soup

SICILIAN EASTER SOUP

Sciusceddu pasquali

- 8 oz/250 g ground/ minced lean beef or pork
- 3 large eggs
- 3 tablespoons freshly grated Pecorino cheese
- 1 clove garlic, finely chopped
- 1 tablespoon finely chopped fresh parsley
- freshly grated nutmeg
- salt
- 1 quart/1 liter meat stock or broth
- 8 oz/250 g Ricotta cheese
- 3 tablespoons fine dry bread crumbs
- 1 tablespoon golden raisins/sultanas (optional)

Place the meat in a large bowl and add 1 egg, the Pecorino, garlic, parsley, nutmeg, and salt. • Mix well and shape heaped teaspoons into small meatballs. • Bring the stock to a boil in a large saucepan. Drop in the meatballs and cook for 4–5 minutes, or until cooked through. • Beat the remaining 2 eggs and combine with the Ricotta, bread crumbs, and raisins (if using), adding salt to taste, to make a creamy mixture. • Pour the egg mixture into the hot stock and stir with a fork for about 1 minute, or until the egg sets into tiny shreds. • Serve immediately.

Serves 4 • Prep: 10 min • Cooking: 10 min • Level: 1

NEAPOLITAN CHRISTMAS SOUP

Minestra maritata

This hearty soup is a classic Neapolitan Christmas dish.

Bring 3 quarts (3 liters) of water to a boil with the pancetta, sausage, spareribs, and parsley. Boil for 80–90 minutes, or until the meat is tender. Remove the meat from the stock, discarding the bone. Cut the meat into small pieces. Cool the stock and skim off the fat. Return to a boil and add the chopped meat. • Boil the turnip greens, chicory, lettuce, broccoli, cabbage, and spinach in 1 quart (1 liter) salted water until the vegetables are tender. • Drain the vegetables and add to the meat stock with the garlic, chile pepper, Parmesan, and Caciocavallo cheese. Cook for 30 minutes more, or until piping hot.

Serves 6 • Prep: 30 min • Cooking: 2 hr 30 min • Level: 2

- 4 quarts/4 liters water
- 6 oz/180 g pancetta, or bacon, chopped
- 3 oz/90 g sausage (such as luganega), chopped
- 1 lb/400 g pork spareribs
- bunch parsley
- 1 lb/500 g turnip greens, coarsely chopped
- 2 bunches chicory, coarsely chopped
- 2 bunches prickly lettuce or curly kale, coarsely chopped
- 2 heads broccoli, coarsely chopped
- 1/2 Savoy cabbage, coarsely chopped
- 1 bunch spinach
- 2 cloves garlic, finely chopped
- dried red chile pepper
- crusts of Parmesan cheese
- 1 oz/30 g Caciocavallo cheese or Ricotta salata, crumbled

Soups

MEAT STOCK WITH EGG

Stracciatella alla Romana

- 1¹/₂ quarts/1.5 liters meat stock or broth
- 5 large eggs
- salt
- pinch of freshly grated nutmeg
- ¹/₄ cup/30 g freshly grated Parmesan cheese + more to serve

Bring the stock to a boil in a medium saucepan. • Beat the eggs with a pinch each of salt and nutmeg. Add the ¹/₄ cup (30 g) Parmesan and beat until smooth. • When the stock is boiling, pour in the egg mixture. Beat with a fork for 3–4 minutes over medium heat until the egg begins to cook and has solidified in tiny lumps or shreds. • Serve at once, sprinkled with extra Parmesan.

Serves 4 • Prep: 5 min • Cooking: 15 min • Level: 1

ITALIAN FAVA BEAN SOUP

Maccu di favi

- 1¹/₄ quarts/1.25 liters water
- 1¹/₂ cups/300 g dried fava/broad beans, soaked overnight and drained
- small bunch of common or wild fennel, coarsely chopped
- ¹/₂ dried chile pepper, seeded, whole or crumbled
- salt
- 4 slices of 2–3-day-old firm-textured white bread, toasted
- ¹/₄ cup/60 ml extra-virgin olive oil

Bring the water to a boil in a saucepan and add the beans. Partially cover and simmer for 1¹/₂ hours over low heat, stirring occasionally. Add the fennel and chile pepper and cook for another 1¹/₂ hours, stirring more frequently, crushing the beans as much as possible with a large wooden spoon. They should gradually turn into a coarse puree. Add a little boiling water if the soup becomes too thick. • Season with salt only when the beans are cooked, after about 3 hours total cooking time. • Place the toasted bread in heated soup bowls and drizzle with a little oil. Ladle the soup over the bread, drizzle with the remaining oil, and serve piping hot.

Serves 4 • Prep: 5 min + 8–10 hr to soak • Cooking: 3 hr • Level: 1

MEAT AND VEGETABLE SOUP

Garmugia

This soup comes from the beautiful town of Lucca, in northern Tuscany, where it is served in springtime.

Heat the oil in a large saucepan over medium heat. Sauté the scallions until translucent. • Add the beef, stirring constantly, for 2–3 minutes, until browned. Stir in the pancetta and cook for 5 minutes more. • Add the fava beans, peas, artichokes, and asparagus. Season with salt and pepper. • Cook for 10–15 minutes, or until the meat is cooked. • Pour in the stock and cook for 20 minutes more. • Serve in individual soup bowls with the cubes of fried bread.

Serves 4 • Prep: 15 min • Cooking: 45 min • Level: 2

- ¹/₄ cup/60 ml extra-virgin olive oil
- 4 scallions/spring onions, thinly sliced
- 4 oz/90 g ground/minced beef
- 2 oz/60 g pancetta or cubed lard
- ³/₄ cup/90 g fresh fava/broad beans
- ³/₄ cup/90 g fresh peas
- 2 artichokes, cleaned and sliced
- ³/₄ cup/90 g asparagus tips
- salt and freshly ground black pepper
- 2 cups/500 ml beef stock or broth
- firm-textured bread, cut into cubes and sautéed in olive oil (see page 69)

Fava beans

Cultivation of the fava bean (also known as the broad or horse bean) dates so far back in time that no one knows quite where it comes from. The beans are a common ingredient in Italian regional cuisines. In Tuscany, they are served raw with Pecorino cheese as an appetizer. In southern Italy, there are many fava beans soups and purees.

Seafood

TURBOT WITH MUSHROOMS

Rombo ai funghi

- 2 tablespoons extra-virgin olive oil
- 6 tablespoons butter, cut up
- 1 turbot or brill, weighing about 4 lb/2 kg, cleaned
- $1/2$ cup/75 g all-purpose/plain flour
- salt and freshly ground white pepper
- 1 cup/250 ml Italian Tocai wine or Pinot Grigio
- 10 oz/300 g mushrooms, cleaned, trimmed, and sliced

Preheat the oven to 400°F/200°C/gas 6. • Pour the oil and 2 tablespoons of butter into the bottom of an oval ovenproof dish. • Rinse and dry the fish. • Coat the fish lightly all over with flour and place in the dish. Season with salt and pepper. Dot the fish with 2 tablespoons of butter. • Bake for 10 minutes. • Remove from the oven. Sprinkle the wine over the fish and return to the oven for 15 minutes more. • Sauté the mushrooms over medium heat in the remaining 2 tablespoons butter for 15 minutes. Season with salt and pepper and remove from the heat. • Remove the fish from the oven and transfer to a heated serving plate. Add the cooking liquid to the mushrooms and reduce over medium heat for 5 minutes. • Spoon the mushrooms and liquid over the fish and serve.

Serves 4–6 • Prep: 20 min • Cooking: 35 min • Level: 1

CLAMS SAUTÉED WITH WINE

Caparossoli in cassopipa

Heat the oil in a large frying pan over medium-high heat and sauté the onion until pale golden brown. • Add the clams, followed by the wine and water. Cover tightly and simmer over low heat for 15 minutes until the clams should have opened. Discard any that have not opened. • Sprinkle with parsley and serve.

Serves 6 • Prep: 15 min • Cooking: 20–25 min • Level: 1

- $1/4$ cup/60 ml extra-virgin olive oil
- 1 onion, finely chopped
- $2^1/3$ lb/1.3 kg clams in shell
- 1 cup/250 ml Italian Tocai wine or Pinot Grigio
- 3–4 tablespoons hot water
- 2 tablespoons finely chopped fresh parsley

Turbot with mushrooms

Swordfish in Sicilian tomato sauce

BAKED SALT COD WITH POTATO

Baccalà al forno con patate

- 1¹/₂ lb/750 g salt cod, cut into small pieces
- ¹/₄ cup/60 ml extra-virgin olive oil
- 1¹/₂ lb/750 g potatoes, peeled and cut into fairly large cubes
- 1 tablespoon finely chopped fresh parsley
- 1 medium onion, finely chopped
- 2 cloves garlic, finely chopped
- 1 teaspoon dried oregano
- salt and freshly ground black pepper
- ¹/₂ cup/60 g fine dry bread crumbs

Soak the salt cod in a large bowl of cold water for 2–3 days, changing the water every few hours. This will remove the excess salt. • Drain well and set aside. • Preheat the oven to 350°F/180°C/gas 4. • Brush 2 tablespoons of the oil over the bottom and sides of a wide, shallow ovenproof dish. • Arrange the pieces of cod in a single layer and cover with the potatoes. • Sprinkle with the parsley, onion, garlic, oregano, salt, and a generous sprinkling of pepper. Sprinkle with the bread crumbs and drizzle with the remaining 2 tablespoons oil. • Bake for 40–45 minutes, or until the potatoes and fish are tender.

Serves 4 • Prep: 15 min + 2–3 days to soak the cod • Cooking: 40–45 min • Level: 1

SWORDFISH IN SICILIAN TOMATO SAUCE

Pesce spada a ghiotta

This Sicilian dish, enriched with raisins, pine nuts, and olives, is called "a ghiotta" after the thick sauce in which it is served. The tomato sauce can be store-bought or made using the recipe on page 32.

Sprinkle the swordfish with flour. • Heat 2 tablespoons of oil in a large frying pan over high heat. Add the garlic and sear the fish on both sides. Season with salt and pepper. Pour in the wine and cook until it has evaporated. Remove the fish from the pan and transfer to a heated serving platter. • Heat the remaining 2 tablespoons oil in a large saucepan over medium heat. Stir in the pine nuts, raisins, olives, tomato sauce, sugar, and vinegar. Cook for 5 minutes, or until the sauce has reduced. Season with the salt and pepper. • Serve the swordfish with the sauce.

Serves 4 • Prep: 15 min • Cooking: 15 min • Level: 1

- 4 thick slices swordfish
- ¹/₄ cup/30 g all-purpose/plain flour
- ¹/₄ cup/60 ml extra-virgin olive oil
- 2 cloves garlic, finely chopped
- salt and freshly ground white pepper
- ¹/₄ cup/60 ml white wine
- 2 tablespoons pine nuts
- 2 tablespoons raisins
- 1 cup/100 g green olives, pitted/stoned and coarsely chopped
- 1 cup/250 ml tomato sauce
- 1 tablespoon granulated sugar
- 1 tablespoon white wine vinegar

CHICKEN WITH FENNEL SEEDS

Pollo ai semi di finocchio

- 1 young, oven-ready roasting chicken, about 3 lb/1.5 kg
- 4 oz/125 g pancetta, finely chopped
- 2 cloves garlic, finely chopped
- 1 teaspoon finely chopped sage
- 1 teaspoon finely chopped rosemary leaves
- 1 tablespoon finely chopped fresh parsley
- 1 teaspoon fennel seeds
- salt and freshly ground black pepper
- 6 tablespoons extra-virgin olive oil

Preheat the oven to 400°F/200°C/gas 6. • Wash the chicken inside and out and dry with paper towels. • Mix the pancetta, garlic, sage, rosemary, parsley, and fennel seeds with a good pinch each of salt and pepper and place in the cavity. Use a trussing needle and thread to sew up the opening. • Pour 3 tablespoons oil into a roasting pan, place the chicken in it and drizzle with the remaining 3 tablespoons oil. Season generously with salt and pepper. • Roast for 55–60 minutes, or until the juices run clear when a knife is inserted deep into the thigh. • Serve hot or at room temperature.

Serves 4 • Prep: 20 min • Cooking: 1 hr • Level: 1

CHICKEN WITH BELL PEPPERS

Pollo ai peperoni

Melt 2 tablespoons butter with 1 tablespoon of oil in a large frying pan over medium heat. Add the rosemary and, after 30 seconds, the chicken and bay leaf. • Increase the heat slightly and fry the chicken pieces for 6–8 minutes, turning to brown evenly. • Add half the stock and cover. Cook for 20–25 minutes or until tender, adding more hot stock if needed. • Melt the remaining 2 tablespoons butter in a saucepan. Add the anchovies, crushing them so that they dissolve in the butter. • Add the bell peppers and garlic. Season with salt and pepper. • Simmer over medium heat for 15 minutes, then drizzle with the vinegar. • Remove the garlic and bay leaf and discard. • Add the bell pepper mixture to the chicken and simmer for 10 minutes more. • Serve hot.

Serves 4 • Prep: 1 hr • Cooking: 45 min • Level: 1

- ¹/₄ cup/60 g butter
- 6 tablespoons extra-virgin olive oil
- 1 tablespoon finely chopped fresh rosemary leaves
- 1 roasting chicken, cut into 8 pieces
- 1 bay leaf
- 1³/₄ cups/400 ml hot chicken stock or broth
- 6–7 anchovy fillets
- 4 green or yellow bell peppers/capsicums, cut into ³/₄-inch/2-cm strips
- 2 cloves garlic, lightly crushed
- salt and freshly ground black pepper
- ¹/₄ cup/60 ml white wine vinegar

Chicken with bell peppers

Ligurian-style chicken

LIGURIAN-STYLE CHICKEN
Pollo alla ligure

- ¹/₄ cup/60 ml extra-virgin olive oil
- 1 large onion, finely chopped
- 2 cloves garlic, finely chopped
- 1 teaspoon fennel seeds
- 1 roasting chicken, cut into 4 or 8 pieces
- ¹/₂ cup/125 ml dry white wine
- 2 tablespoons finely chopped fresh herbs, such as rosemary, sage, thyme, or marjoram
- grated zest and juice of ¹/₂ lemon
- ¹/₂ cup/60 g black olives
- salt and freshly ground black pepper

Traditionally, this dish was made with rabbit instead of chicken. Rabbit is still widely available in many butcher shops and supermarkets. You may also replace the rabbit in the next recipe with chicken if preferred.

Heat the oil in a saucepan over medium heat. Sauté the onion for 8–10 minutes, or until translucent. • Stir in the garlic and fennel seeds. • Add the chicken and sear it all over. • Pour in the wine and cook until it evaporates. • Add the herbs, lemon zest, olives, salt, and pepper. Cover and cook over low heat for 35–40 minutes. When the chicken is done, add the lemon juice and serve immediately.

Serves 4 • Prep: 15 min • Cooking: 50 min • Level: 2

RABBIT IN SWEET AND SOUR SAUCE
Coniglio in agrodolce

Bring the wine, parsley, sliced onion, bay leaf, and peppercorns to a boil in a small saucepan. Boil for 1 minute, remove from the heat, and set aside to cool. • Place the rabbit pieces in a large bowl. Pour the wine marinade over and let marinate for 6–8 hours. • Remove the rabbit from the marinade and dry with paper towels. Strain the marinade and reserve 1 cup (250 ml). Season the rabbit with salt and pepper and coat with flour, shaking off the excess. • Heat the oil in a large frying pan until very hot. Add the rabbit and cook for about 10 minutes, until well browned all over. Season with salt and pepper. • Remove the rabbit from the pan and set aside. • In the same oil, sauté the finely chopped onion, celery, carrot, capers, raisins, and olives for 5 minutes over medium heat, stirring often. • Add the rabbit and sprinkle with the sugar. Pour in the vinegar. • Simmer for 2 minutes, then add the reserved marinade, cover, and simmer over low heat, until the rabbit is very tender, about 1 hour. • Serve hot.

Serves 4–6 • Prep: 30 min + 6–8 hr to marinate • Cooking: 75 min • Level: 2

- 1¹/₄ cups/310 ml dry red wine
- 3–4 sprigs parsley
- 2 medium onions, one sliced + one finely chopped
- 1 bay leaf
- 1 teaspoon black peppercorns
- 1 young, tender rabbit or chicken, cut into 6–8 pieces
- salt and freshly ground black pepper
- 3 tablespoons all-purpose/plain flour
- ¹/₃ cup/80 ml extra-virgin olive oil
- 2 stalks celery, chopped
- 1 small carrot, finely sliced
- 1 tablespoon capers
- 3 tablespoons golden raisins/sultanas, briefly soaked in hot water, then drained
- 15 large green olives, pitted/stoned and chopped
- 2 tablespoons sugar
- ¹/₄ cup/60 ml red wine vinegar

Pork & Lamb

BREADED COTECHINO SAUSAGE WITH ZABAIONE

Cotechino in galera con lo zabaione

- 1 1-lb/500-g fresh cotechino sausage (or precooked with skin removed)
- Pizza Dough for one 12-inch/30-cm pizza (see page 20)
- 2 tablespoons fennel seeds
- 1 large egg yolk

Zabaione
- 4 large eggs, separated
- $^1/_4$ cup/50 g granulated sugar
- $^1/_4$ cup/60 ml Marsala wine
- 2 tablespoons brandy

Cotechino sausage, originally from Emilia-Romagna, is served at or around Christmastime throughout Italy. Precooked cotechino sausages are now widely available. If you buy one of these, remove the skin just before wrapping in the pizza dough.

Soak the cotechino in water for at least 4 hours. Pat dry with paper towels. • Use a fork to prick the cotechino all over. Wrap in cheesecloth (muslin) and tie securely with cooking string. • Cook in a large pan of boiling water for at least 2 hours. • Remove from the pan and cool to warm. Remove the muslin and let cool completely. • Roll the pizza dough out on a lightly floured work surface. Sprinkle with the fennel seeds and roll it to a thickness of about $^1/_8$ inch (3 mm), making sure that the fennel seeds are pressed deep into the dough. It should be about $^1/_2$ inch (1 cm) thick. • Carefully remove the skin and wrap the cotechino in the dough. Brush with the egg yolk and let rise for 45 minutes. • Preheat the oven to 400°F/200°C/gas 6. • Butter a baking sheet. • Place the cotechino on the prepared sheet. • Bake for 40–45 minutes, or until golden brown. • <u>Zabaione</u>: Beat the egg yolks and sugar in a double boiler with an electric mixer at high speed until pale and thick. Stir in the Marsala and brandy. • Place over barely simmering water and continue cooking, stirring with a wooden spoon until very pale and thick, about 15–20 minutes. Remove from the heat and pour onto individual serving plates. • Slice the wrapped cotechino $^1/_2$ inch (1 cm) thick, place on the zabaglione, and serve.

Serves 6 • Prep: 1 hr + 4 hr to soak + 45 min to rise • Cooking: 3 hr • Level: 3

LAMB STEW

Scottiglia di agnello

- $^1/_4$ cup/60 ml extra-virgin olive oil
- $^1/_4$ teaspoon finely chopped fresh rosemary
- 4 cloves garlic, finely chopped
- 1 dried chile pepper, crumbled
- 1 lb/500 g boneless lamb, cut into cubes
- $^1/_2$ cup/125 ml white wine
- $^1/_2$ lb/750 g tomatoes, peeled and chopped
- salt
- $^1/_4$ cup/60 ml water, + more as needed (optional)
- 4 slices firm-textured bread, toasted and rubbed with garlic
- 1 tablespoon finely chopped fresh parsley

Lamb is a common ingredient in Italy, and this recipe, and its many variations, was developed long ago to create something tasty and filling from a few inexpensive ingredients.

Heat the oil in a cast-iron frying pan over medium heat. Add the rosemary, garlic, and chile pepper. Add the meat and brown well. Pour in the wine and cook until it evaporates. • Stir in the tomatoes. Season with the salt and cook, partially covered, over low heat for 25–30 minutes, or until the tomatoes have broken down. Add water if the stew dries out. • Place the bread in individual plates and spoon the meat and its fairly liquid sauce over the top. Garnish with the parsley and serve hot.

Serves 4 • Prep: 15 min • Cooking: 55–65 min • Level: 1

Lamb stew

PORK, VEGETABLE, AND POLENTA CASSEROLE

Puccia

- 1 lb/500 g pork tenderloin, cut in bite-sized cubes
- 1¼ lb/625 g Savoy cabbage, cut into thin strips
- 1 small onion, coarsely chopped
- 1 small carrot, sliced
- 1 stalk celery, sliced
- salt
- ½ cup/125 ml hot water + 1½ quarts/1.5 liters salted water
- 1½ cups/200 g coarsely ground yellow cornmeal
- 5 tablespoons butter, cut into small pieces
- ¼ cup/30 g freshly grated Parmesan cheese

Place the pork in a Dutch oven (casserole) with the cabbage, onion, carrot, and celery. Add a pinch of salt and the hot water. Cover and bring to a boil. • Reduce the heat to medium and simmer for 30 minutes. • Bring the salted water to a boil in a large saucepan. Sprinkle in the cornmeal while stirring constantly to prevent lumps from forming. Continue cooking over medium heat, stirring constantly for 20–25 minutes, or until the mixture begins to pull away from the pan sides. • Add the meat, vegetables, and their cooking liquid to the polenta and stir well. • Simmer for 20–25 minutes more, stirring often, and adding a little boiling water if needed to keep the polenta very moist and soft. • Stir in the butter and Parmesan. Serve immediately.

Serves 4 • Prep: 15 min • Cooking: 70–80 min • Level: 1

LAMB AND POTATO CASSEROLE

Agnello con patate

- 2 lb/1 kg boneless lamb, cut into bite-sized pieces
- 1½ lb/750 g yellow, waxy potatoes, thickly sliced or in wedges
- 3 large fresh tomatoes, quartered or cut into 6 wedges
- 1 medium onion, sliced
- ¼ cup/60 ml extra-virgin olive oil
- salt and freshly ground black pepper
- leaves from a small sprig of fresh rosemary
- 1 teaspoon dried oregano
- hot water

Preheat the oven to 400°F/200°C/gas 6. • Place the lamb, potatoes, tomatoes, and onion in a Dutch oven (casserole). • Drizzle with the oil and season with salt and pepper. Sprinkle with rosemary and oregano. • Cover and bake for about 1 hour, or until very tender, basting at frequent intervals with a little hot water. • Serve hot.

Serves 4 • Prep: 15 min • Cooking: 1 hr • Level: 1

Veal & Beef

GENOESE STUFFED VEAL

Cima alla genovese

- 2 lb/1 kg boneless tenderloin veal or beef, in 1 piece
- 8 oz/200 g ground/ minced veal or beef
- 8 oz/200 g ground/ minced pork
- 4 oz/125 g lard or pancetta, very finely chopped
- 8 slices day-old bread, without crust, soaked in milk, and squeezed
- 3 tablespoons freshly grated Parmesan cheese
- 7 oz/200 g cooked Swiss chard, squeezed and finely chopped
- 2 tablespoons finely chopped fresh marjoram
- 1/4 cup/25 g pistachios, blanched and peeled
- 4 large eggs, lightly beaten
- 1/8 teaspoon freshly grated nutmeg
- salt and freshly ground white pepper
- 3 quarts/3 liters vegetable stock or broth

This recipe is typical of the cuisine of the region of Liguria—intricate yet aromatic. Serve with pickled vegetables and mayonnaise.

Cut a pocket into the piece of veal or beef. • Mix the ground veal, pork, lard, bread, Parmesan, Swiss chard, marjoram, pistachios, eggs, nutmeg, salt, and pepper in a large bowl. Stuff the meat with the mixture. Use a trussing needle and thread to stitch up the pocket. • Place in a large saucepan and cover with hot stock. Place over high heat and bring the stock to a boil. • Lower the heat and simmer gently for about 2 hours, or until the meat is very tender. • Cool the veal completely in the stock. Slice thinly and transfer to a serving plate.

Serves 6 • Prep: 25 min • Cooking: 2 hr • Level: 2

SICILIAN STUFFED BEEF ROLL

Farsumaru

Mix the ground beef and sausage meat in a large bowl. • Add the raw egg, Pecorino, parsley, onion, garlic, salt, and pepper, and combine well. • Place the slice of beef flat between 2 sheets of parchment paper and beat gently until it is about 1/4 inch (5 mm) thick. • Lay the meat flat and cover with the prosciutto and pancetta. Spread the ground meat mixture over the top, leaving a border around the edge. • Slice the pointed ends off the eggs and place them "nose to tail" down the center of the beef. • Lay the Provolone on either side of the eggs. • Carefully roll up. Tie with string at regular intervals. • Heat the oil over high heat in a large Dutch oven (casserole), and brown the meat roll all over. • Pour in the wine and cook, uncovered, until it has reduced. • Add the tomato paste. • Cover and simmer over very low heat for about 1 hour, turning several times, until the meat is tender and the juices run clear. • Just before serving, remove the string and transfer to a heated serving plate. • Carve into thick slices and spoon the cooking liquid over the top. Serve hot.

Serves 6 • Prep: 30 min • Cooking: 75 min • Level: 2

- 4 oz/125 g lean ground/ minced beef or veal
- 8 oz/200 g Italian sausage meat
- 1 large egg
- 1/4 cup/60 g freshly grated Pecorino cheese
- 1 tablespoon finely chopped fresh parsley
- 2 tablespoons finely chopped onion
- 2 cloves garlic, finely chopped
- salt and freshly ground black pepper
- a single, thick slice of lean beef from top round, rib, or chuck/ topside, sirloin, or chuck, weighing about 1 1/2 lb/750 g
- 8 oz/200 g prosciutto or ham, sliced
- 4 slices pancetta, chopped
- 3 hard-cooked eggs
- 4 oz/125 g Provolone cheese, cut into narrow strips
- 1/4 cup/60 ml extra-virgin olive oil
- 1/2 cup/125 ml dry red wine
- 1 tablespoon tomato paste, diluted in 1 cup/ 250 ml hot water

Vegetables

FAVA BEAN PUREE WITH VEGETABLES

Fave e foglie

- 3 cups/300 g dried fava/broad beans, soaked for 3 hours, drained and well rinsed
- 3 mealy/floury potatoes, peeled and sliced
- 2 medium eggplants/ aubergines
- $^1/_3$ cup/80 ml extra-virgin olive oil
- 2 teaspoons red wine vinegar
- salt
- 1 lb/500 g zucchini/ courgettes, cut into thin wheels
- 1 clove garlic, lightly crushed
- 1 tablespoon finely chopped fresh mint
- 2 teaspoons white wine vinegar
- 4 lb/2 kg greens (wild chicory or Swiss chard), cooked and chopped

Place the beans and potatoes in a large saucepan. Pour in enough water to cover them completely. Bring to a boil over low heat. Simmer, covered, for 3 hours, or until tender. • Preheat the oven to 400°F/200°C/gas 6. • Cut the eggplants in half lengthwise and place them on a baking sheet. • Bake for 15–20 minutes, or until tender. • Slice them thinly and drizzle with 2 tablespoons oil, the red wine vinegar, and season with salt. • Sauté the zucchini and garlic in 2 tablespoons oil in a frying pan until golden. Drain the zucchini on paper towels. Add the mint and white wine vinegar. • Mash the fava beans and potatoes until smooth. Reheat and mix in the remaining oil and salt. • Serve hot, with the vegetables.

Serves 6 • Prep: 15 min + 3 hr to soak • Cooking: 3 hr • Level: 2

Fava bean puree with vegetables

MIXED BRAISED BELL PEPPERS

Peperonata

Place the bell peppers, onions, and tomatoes in a large saucepan. Add the oil and garlic and season with salt and pepper. Cover and cook over medium heat for about 15 minutes. • Turn the heat up to high and partially uncover to let some of the liquid evaporate. Cook until the bell peppers are tender, about 15 minutes. • Garnish with basil leaves and serve hot or at room temperature.

Serves 4–6 • Prep: 10 min • Cooking: 30 min • Level: 1

- 4–6 mixed red, green, and yellow bell peppers/capsicums, cut into thin strips
- 2 large onions, thinly sliced
- 1 lb/500 g peeled and chopped fresh or canned/tinned tomatoes
- $^1/_4$ cup/60 ml extra-virgin olive oil
- 3 cloves garlic, finely chopped
- salt and freshly ground black pepper
- 6 leaves basil, torn

Roman-style spinach

SWEET-SOUR ARTICHOKES

Capunata di caciuocculi

- 8 fresh artichokes
- 3 tablespoons all-purpose/plain flour
- 6 tablespoons extra-virgin olive oil
- 3 tablespoons finely chopped onion
- 1 tablespoon capers
- 12 green olives, pitted/stoned and chopped
- 1 small carrot, diced
- 2 stalks celery, sliced
- salt and freshly ground black pepper
- ¹/₂ cup/125 ml hot water
- 4 tomatoes, chopped
- 2 salted anchovies
- 2 teaspoons sugar
- 6 tablespoons red wine vinegar

Clean the artichokes as explained on page 20. Cut each artichoke lengthwise into six pieces. • Coat the artichokes lightly with flour and sauté in a saucepan over high heat for 2–3 minutes, turning once or twice. • Remove the artichokes, letting the excess oil drain back into the casserole. • Add the onion, capers, olives, carrot, celery, salt, pepper, and hot water and simmer over medium heat for about 10 minutes. • Stir in the tomatoes and then add the artichokes and anchovies. Cover and simmer over low heat for 20–25 minutes, or until the artichokes are tender and the tomatoes have broken down. • Mix the sugar with the vinegar and stir into the vegetables. Cook for 4–5 minutes more. • Serve warm.

Serves 4 • Prep: 15 min • Cooking: 35–40 min • Level: 1

ROMAN-STYLE SPINACH

Spinaci alla romana

This dish can be made with boiled or fresh spinach. If using fresh spinach, remember to rinse and drain it at least 5 times. Add the fresh spinach to the frying pan a handful at a time.

Plump the raisins in cold water for 30 minutes. Drain well. • Heat the oil in a large frying pan over high heat. Add the garlic and pine nuts. Cook for 1 minute. Stir in the spinach and raisins. Cook for 5 minutes, stirring often. Season with salt and pepper. • Serve hot.

Serves 4 • Prep: 20 min + 30 min to soak • Cooking: 6 min • Level: 1

- 1 teaspoon raisins
- 3 tablespoons extra-virgin olive oil
- 2 cloves garlic, finely chopped
- 1 teaspoon pine nuts
- 8 oz/250 g blanched spinach or 3 lb/1.5 kg tender young spinach leaves
- salt and freshly ground black pepper

Vegetables

Braised Savoy cabbage

Verze sofegae

- 1 Savoy cabbage, weighing about 4 lb/2 kg
- 6 tablespoons finely chopped fresh pork fat (replace with butter or extra-virgin olive oil, if preferred)
- 1 sprig rosemary
- 1 clove garlic, peeled and lightly crushed
- salt
- ¹/₂ cup/125 ml dry white wine

Discard the tougher leaves of the cabbage; then take the rest apart leaf by leaf, cutting out the hard ribs and rinsing. Cut the leaves into thin strips. • Chop the pork fat and rosemary leaves together with a *mezzaluna* (half-moon cutter) or heavy kitchen knife. Sauté briefly in a saucepan over medium heat with the garlic, discarding the garlic when it starts to color. • Add the cabbage and a pinch of salt and cover. Cook over low heat, stirring frequently to prevent the cabbage from sticking and burning, for up to 1 hour. • Add the wine, then cover and continue cooking for another hour. • Serve hot.

Serves 6 • Prep: 10 min • Cooking: 2 hr • Level: 1

Cauliflower with tomato and fennel seeds

Cavolfiore in umido

Heat the oil in a large frying pan over high heat. Add the garlic and fennel seeds and cook for 2–3 minutes, or until aromatic. Add the tomato sauce and cook for about 5 minutes, or until the sauce has reduced slightly. • While the sauce is cooking, cut the cauliflower up into florets, removing the tough pieces of stalk or cutting into cubes. • Add the cauliflower to the tomato sauce and season with salt and pepper. Cover and cook until the florets are cooked but still crunchy, about 10 minutes.

Serves 4 • Prep: 10 min • Cooking: 15–20 min • Level: 1

- ¹/₄ cup/60 ml extra-virgin olive oil
- 2 cloves garlic, finely chopped
- 1 teaspoon fennel seeds
- 1 cup/250 ml tomato sauce or peeled and chopped tomatoes
- 1 medium cauliflower
- salt and freshly ground black pepper

Cauliflower with tomato and fennel seeds

Italian stuffed eggplants

CHEESE AND POTATO PIE

Tortino di patate

- 1¹/₂ lb/750 g firm waxy potatoes
- ¹/₂ cup/125 g butter
- 8 oz/250 g piece of Parmesan cheese, shavings
- salt and freshly ground black pepper
- 1 cup/250 ml milk

Wash the potatoes thoroughly. Boil them with their skins on for about 20 minutes, or until tender but still firm. • Peel while hot and set aside to cool. • Preheat the oven to 400°F/200°C/gas 6. • Cut the potatoes into ¹/₂-inch (1 cm) slices and arrange in layers in a deep ovenproof dish greased with butter. Dot each layer with the butter and sprinklings of Parmesan. Season with salt and pepper. • Pour in the milk. • Bake for 20–25 minutes, or until golden brown.

Serves 4 • Prep: 20 min • Cooking: 45 min • Level: 1

ITALIAN STUFFED EGGPLANTS

Melanzane ripiene

Preheat the oven to 350°F/180°C/gas 4. • Rinse the eggplants thoroughly under cold running water and slice them in half. Use a sharp knife to hollow out the flesh, taking care not to pierce the skins. • Dice the eggplant flesh and combine with the Mozzarella and garlic (if using). Drizzle with 2 tablespoons of oil and season with salt and pepper. Mix well. • Arrange the hollowed-out eggplant halves in a shallow ovenproof dish. Fill with the Mozzarella mixture. Spoon the chopped tomato over the top. • Bake for 25–30 minutes, or until golden brown. • Serve hot or at room temperature.

Serves 4 • Prep: 20 min • Cooking: 30 min • Level: 1

- 4 eggplants/aubergines
- 8 oz/250 g Mozzarella cheese, cut into small cubes
- 1 clove garlic, finely chopped (optional)
- 3 tablespoons extra-virgin olive oil
- salt and freshly ground black pepper
- 3 large ripe tomatoes, peeled and diced

Cheeses

Parmesan and Mozzarella are probably the best-known Italian cheeses. But many more types—such as Pecorino, Gorgonzola, Fontina, and Provolone—are now available in specialty stores and supermarkets. For desserts, Ricotta and Mascarpone are the most widely available cheeses.

Salads

ITALIAN SALAD

Insalata italiana

- 10 oz/300 g potatoes, peeled and boiled
- 8 oz/200 g beets/beetroot, boiled and peeled
- 8 oz/200 g green beans, boiled in salted water
- 1 tablespoon white wine vinegar
- ¹/₄ cup/60 ml extra-virgin olive oil
- salt and freshly ground black pepper
- 4 leaves basil (optional)

This salad is called Insalata Italiana *because it has the same colors—red, white, and green—as the Italian flag.*

Cut the potatoes and beets into cubes, and the beans into 2-inch lengths. Place the vegetables in a large salad bowl. • Mix the vinegar, oil, salt, and pepper in a small bowl. Pour over the vegetables just before serving. Garnish with the basil leaves, if using.

Serves 4 • Prep: 25 min • Level: 1

FENNEL AND PINE NUT SALAD

Insalata di finocchi e pinoli

Strip the tough, outer sections from the fennel bulbs. Rinse and slice thinly lengthwise. Place on a serving plate. • Sprinkle with the pine nuts and season with the oil, lemon juice, salt, and pepper. • Sprinkle with Parmesan and serve.

Serves 4 • Prep: 10 min • Level: 1

- 4 small round bulbs fennel
- ¹/₄ cup/25 g toasted pine nuts
- ¹/₄ cup/60 ml extra-virgin olive oil
- 2 tablespoons fresh lemon juice
- salt and freshly ground black pepper
- 3 oz/90 g Parmesan cheese, flaked

ITALIAN ORANGE SALAD

Insalata con le arance

- 4 ripe, juicy oranges
- 8–10 green or black olives, pitted/stoned and quartered
- 1 medium leek, white part only, trimmed and thinly sliced or ¹/₄ cup/60 g finely chopped chives
- 1 tablespoon finely chopped fresh parsley
- ¹/₄ cup/60 ml extra-virgin olive oil
- salt and freshly ground black pepper

Peel the oranges, removing all the white pith as well as the skin. • Slice them thinly or cut into small pieces. Place in a salad bowl and add the olives, leek, parsley, oil, salt, and pepper. • Toss well and let stand for 10 minutes, then toss again and serve.

Serves 4 • Prep: 15 min • Level: 1

GREEN SALAD WITH RASPBERRIES AND WILD RICE

Insalata di bosco

Cook the brown and red rice in a large pot of salted boiling water for 35–40 minutes, until tender. • Toss together the salad greens, watercress, arugula, and mint on a large platter. • Drain the rice, shaking well to remove excess moisture. Transfer to a bowl and mix well with the oil and 4 tablespoons of the vinegar. Spoon on top of the salad greens. Sprinkle with the carrots and raspberries. • Drizzle with the remaining 2 tablespoons balsamic vinegar and serve.

Serves 6 • Prep: 30 min • Cooking: 35–40 min. • Level: 1

- 1 cup/200 g brown rice
- ¹/₂ cup/100 g wild black or red rice
- ¹/₂ lb/250 g mixed salad greens (Belgium endive, dandelion greens, wild endive, leaf lettuce, chicory, corn salad, burnet)
- 2 bunches watercress, coarsely chopped
- 1 bunch arugula/rocket, coarsely chopped
- 15 leaves mint
- ¹/₄ cup/60 ml extra-virgin olive oil
- 4–6 tablespoons best-quality balsamic vinegar
- 4 carrots, finely grated
- 1 cup/250 g fresh raspberries

Italian salad

ROMAN CREAM CAKES

Maritozzi

- 1 oz/25 g fresh yeast or 2 packages (¹/₄ oz/7 g) active dry yeast
- 2²/₃ cups/650 ml lukewarm water
- 6 cups/900 g all-purpose/plain flour
- 7 large eggs + 4 large egg yolks
- ¹/₃ cup/80 ml extra-virgin olive oil
- 1 cup/200 g granulated sugar
- grated zest of 1 lemon
- ¹/₂ teaspoon vanilla extract
- 2 cups/500 ml light/single cream
- ¹/₄ cup/30 g confectioners'/icing sugar

There are two versions of this traditional Roman pastry. This is the simpler version, and it lends itself to a cream filling. The other version features raisins and pine nuts added to the dough before the final rising.

Dissolve the yeast in 1 cup (250 ml) of the warm water. Let stand 10 minutes, or until foamy. • Sift 2 cups (300 g) of flour into a large bowl and make a well in the center. Pour in the yeast mixture and enough warm water to form a firm dough. • Place the dough in a clean bowl. Cover with a clean cloth and let rise in a warm place for about 45 minutes, or until doubled in bulk. • While the dough is rising, lightly beat together 6 eggs and the egg yolks, oil, granulated sugar, lemon zest, and vanilla in a medium bowl. • Sift the remaining 4 cups (600 g) flour onto a work surface and make a well in the center. Knead in the egg mixture. Continue kneading as you gradually add the remaining water to form a soft dough. • Knead in the dough that has doubled in bulk. • Shape into small 2-inch (5-cm) long oval loaves. Arrange on greased baking sheets and cover with a kitchen towel. Let rest in a warm place for 45 minutes, or until doubled in bulk. • Preheat the oven to 350°F/180°C/gas 4. • Beat the remaining egg and brush over the loaves. • Bake for 15–20 minutes, or until golden brown. • Beat the cream in a medium bowl until stiff. Fit a pastry bag with a ¹/₂-inch (1-cm) star tip and fill with the cream. • Slice the cooled loaves horizontally and pipe in the cream. Sprinkle with the confectioners' sugar.

Makes 40 • Prep: 50 min + 90 min to rise • Cooking: 15–20 min • Level: 2

Maritozzi

pastries are a delicacy from Rome, where the windows of pasticcerie are piled high with them every morning. Romans eat them for breakfast along with a cup of strong black coffee or a cappuccino. Maritozzi are also good as a dessert.

Roman cream cakes

Light almond cake

CANNOLI

- 1¹/₃ cups/180 g all-purpose/plain flour
- 1 large egg, separated
- 3 tablespoons granulated sugar
- 1 tablespoon brandy
- 3–4 tablespoons dry white or Marsala wine
- 2 tablespoons butter, melted and cooled
- ¹/₈ teaspoon salt
- 3 tablespoons almond oil
- lard or oil for frying
- 8 oz/250 g Ricotta cheese
- ³/₄ cup/125 g confectioners'/icing sugar, + extra to dust
- 1 oz/30 g semisweet chocolate, finely chopped
- ¹/₄ cup/30 g very finely diced mixed candied peel
- 2 tablespoons finely chopped pistachios

Sift the flour into a bowl and add the egg yolk, granulated sugar, brandy, 3 tablespoons wine, butter, and salt. • Mix, adding more wine if needed, until the dough is smooth and elastic. • Shape into a ball, wrap in a clean cloth, and set aside for 1 hour. • Roll the dough out thinly and cut into 12 squares. • Rub 12 cannoli pastry tubes with almond oil and wrap the squares diagonally around the tubes, starting with one corner and finishing with the opposite corner. • Beat the egg white and use it to moisten the overlapping surfaces. This will stop them from unwrapping during cooking. • Deep fry, two to three at a time, in plenty of very hot lard, until deep brown, with small blisters on the surface. • Lift out with a slotted spoon and drain on paper towels. When cool enough to handle, slide carefully off the pastry tubes. • Strain the Ricotta into a bowl and beat in the ³/₄ cup (125 g) confectioners' sugar until creamy. • Fold in the chocolate and candied peel. • Fill the cases with the Ricotta and dip each end in the nuts. Sift with confectioners' sugar and serve.

Serves 4–6 • Prep: 25 min + 1 hr to rest • Cooking: 30–40 min • Level: 3

LIGHT ALMOND CAKE

Mantovana

This cake comes from the Tuscan town of Prato, not Mantua (in Italian, Mantova), as the name suggests. It is excellent with a cream or vanilla pastry cream filling.

Preheat the oven to 325°F/170°C/gas 3. • Butter and flour a 10-inch (26-cm) round cake pan. • Sift the flour, cornstarch, and baking powder into a large bowl. • Beat the egg yolks and granulated sugar in a large bowl with an electric mixer at high speed until pale and thick. • Use a large rubber spatula to fold the dry ingredients, lemon zest, and melted butter into the beaten yolk mixture. • With mixer at high speed, beat the egg whites and salt in a large bowl until stiff peaks form. • Use the spatula to fold them into the batter. • Spoon the batter into the prepared pan. Sprinkle with the almonds. • Bake for 35–40 minutes, or until a toothpick inserted into the center comes out clean. • Cool the cake in the pan for 15 minutes. Turn out onto a rack to cool completely. Dust with the confectioners' sugar.

Serves 6–8 • Prep: 20 min • Cooking: 35–40 min • Level: 1

- 1¹/₂ cups/225 g all-purpose/plain flour
- 1¹/₂ cups/225 g cornstarch/cornflour
- 2 teaspoons baking powder
- 4 large eggs, separated, + 4 large egg yolks
- 2 cups/400 g granulated sugar
- grated zest of 1 lemon
- 1¹/₄ cups/310 g butter, melted
- ¹/₈ teaspoon salt
- ¹/₂ cup/50 g almonds with skin on, chopped
- ¹/₂ cup/50 g almonds with skin removed, chopped
- confectioners'/icing sugar, to dust

Desserts

PEARS IN RED WINE

Pere al barolo

- 8 small pears or 4 large, firm cooking pears
- 1¼ cups/250 g granulated sugar
- 3 cups/750 ml full-bodied, dry red wine (preferably Barolo)
- 3 cloves
- 2 pieces lemon zest
- ¾-inch/2-cm stick of cinnamon (optional)

Preheat the oven to 350°F/180°C/gas 4. • Peel the pears carefully, leaving them whole with the stem still attached. • Transfer to a deep casserole into which they fit snugly, standing upright, stem-side up. Sprinkle with half the sugar. Pour in the wine and add the cloves, lemon zest and, if desired, the cinnamon. • Bake for about 1 hour, or until tender. The time will vary depending on how firm the pears are. Test by inserting a thin skewer deep into one to see if it is tender. They should be an attractive russet color. • Lift the pears carefully out of the wine and place upright in a serving dish or, better still, in individual glass dishes. • Reduce the cooking liquid over medium heat until it has thickened to a pouring syrup. Discard the cloves, lemon zest, and cinnamon and pour the syrup over the pears. • Serve at room temperature.

Serves 4 • Prep: 10 min • Cooking: 1 hr 20 min • Level: 1

APRICOT POCKETS

Tasche di albicocche

Preheat the oven to 400°F/200°C/gas 6. • Cook the wine, brown sugar, honey, and cinnamon in a saucepan over high heat until syrupy. • Cut out 6 large pieces of parchment paper to make the "pockets." • Place 2 halved apricots in the center of each sheet of paper, pour a little of the syrup over them, sprinkle with the crumbled amaretti, and decorate with the pine nuts and raisins. • Tie up the pockets with kitchen string. • Bake for 15 minutes. Unwrap the packages and serve hot or warm.

Serves 4 • Prep: 10 min • Cooking: 15 min • Level: 1

- 1 cup/250 ml white wine
- 6 tablespoons firmly packed brown sugar
- 2 tablespoons honey
- 1 teaspoon ground cinnamon
- 12 apricots, halved and pitted/stoned
- 10 crushed amaretti cookies
- 2 tablespoons pine nuts
- 2 tablespoons raisins

Pears in red wine

Zabaione

ZABAIONE

- 4 large egg yolks
- ¹/₄ cup/50 g granulated sugar
- ¹/₂ cup/125 ml dry Marsala wine, or dry sherry, or Vin Santo (a sweet Tuscan dessert wine)

Beat the egg yolks and sugar in a double boiler with an electric mixer at high speed until pale and very thick. • Gradually pour in the Marsala. • Place over barely simmering water and cook, stirring constantly with a wooden spoon, until very thick, about 10–15 minutes. • Serve right away or place plastic wrap directly on the surface and refrigerate until ready to serve.

Serves 4 • Prep: 5 min • Cooking: 10–15 min • Level: 1

LEMON RICE FRITTERS

Frittelle di riso

Cook the rice in the milk over low heat for about 1 hour, or until the grains have almost disintegrated. • Stir in the butter and remove from the heat. • Add the granulated sugar and zest. Add the eggs, one at a time, mixing until just blended after each addition. • Stir in the salt, flour, raisins, and rum and refrigerate for 1 hour. • Heat the oil in a nonstick frying pan until very hot. To test, drop a tiny piece of fritter into the oil. If bubbles form around it immediately, it is hot enough. • Use a tablespoon to drop spoonfuls of the fritter mixture into the oil. Fry, turning during cooking, for 3–4 minutes, or until until golden brown. • Drain on paper towels. Dust with the confectioners' sugar. Transfer to a heated serving dish and serve hot.

Serves 4–6 • Prep: 20 min + 1 hr to rest • Cooking: 1 hr 25 min • Level: 1

- 1 cup/200 g short-grain rice
- 2¹/₄ cups/500 ml whole milk
- 1 tablespoon butter
- 3 tablespoons granulated sugar
- grated zest of ¹/₂ lemon or orange
- 2 large eggs
- ¹/₈ teaspoon salt
- ¹/₄ cup/50 g all-purpose/plain flour
- ¹/₃ cup/50 g golden raisins, soaked in warm water for 15 minutes, drained and squeezed
- ¹/₄ cup/60 ml rum
- 1 cup/250 ml olive oil, for frying
- ²/₃ cup/100 g confectioners'/icing sugar

Cookies

ITALIAN PASTRY CREAM KISSES

Peschine

- 6 large eggs
- 4 cups/800 g granulated sugar
- grated zest of 1 lemon
- 3 lb/1.5 kg all-purpose/plain flour, or more as needed
- 1 cup/250 ml Sambuca
- 2 cups/500 ml milk + 2 tablespoons, to brush

Vanilla Pastry Cream
- 8 large egg yolks
- ¹/₂ cup/125 g granulated sugar
- ¹/₂ cup/125 g all-purpose/plain flour
- 1 quart/1 liter milk, boiling
- 1 teaspoon vanilla extract

- 1 cup/250 ml Alchermes liqueur
- raw sugar, to roll

These little pastries are made throughout Italy, but are especially popular in Tuscany, where they are made with Alchermes, a distinctive red liqueur dating back to the Middle Ages that is still widely used. Cherry liqueur can be substituted for the Alchermes.

Preheat the oven to 325°F/170°C/gas 3. • Butter two to three baking sheets. • Beat the eggs and granulated sugar in a large bowl with an electric mixer at high speed until pale and thick. • Use a large rubber spatula to fold in the lemon zest, and flour, alternating with the Sambuca and 2 cups (500 ml) milk. Make a fairly soft dough and shape into balls the size of walnuts. • Place on the prepared sheets, 1 inch (2 cm) apart. • Bake for 8–10 minutes, or until lightly browned. • Cool on a rack. • <u>Vanilla Pastry Cream</u>: Beat the egg yolks and sugar until pale and creamy. Stir in the flour, then gradually add the milk. Cook over medium heat until thick. Stir in the vanilla and set aside to cool. • While the cakes are still hot, poke a hole in the flat bottom of each one to make room for the filling. Let cool completely. • Brush with a little milk and fill with the pastry cream, sticking them together in pairs. • Dip in the liqueur to color. Roll in the raw sugar. • Let stand in a cool place for 4 hours before serving.
Makes about 36 pastries • Prep: 30 min • Cooking: 8–10 min • Level: 2

LADIES KISSES

Baci di dama

These little cakes can be found in most Italian pastry shops, both in this version and flavored with chocolate.

Preheat the oven to 300°F/150°C/gas 2. • Butter a baking sheet. • Beat the butter and superfine sugar in a large bowl with an electric mixer at high speed until creamy. • Use a large rubber spatula to fold in the hazelnuts, flour, and salt. Shape into balls the size of walnuts. • Place on the prepared sheet. • Bake for 25–30 minutes, or until lightly browned. Cool completely on a rack. • <u>Filling</u>: Melt the chocolate in a double boiler over barely simmering water. Remove from the heat. • Heat the cream in a small saucepan until warm. Stir the warm cream into the melted chocolate and continue mixing until cooled. • Spread the filling onto half the cookies. Join the halves together.
Makes 40–45 cookies • Prep: 20 min • Cooking: 40–45 min • Level: 1

- 7 tablespoons butter, softened
- ³/₄ cup/150 g superfine/caster sugar
- 1¹/₄ cups/150 g hazelnuts, toasted and finely ground
- ³/₄ cup/125 g all-purpose/plain flour
- ¹/₈ teaspoon salt

Filling
- 3 oz/90 g semisweet/plain chocolate
- 6 tablespoons heavy/double cream

Italian pastry cream kisses

FRANCE

French cuisine varies greatly from region to region. Generally speaking, a division can be made between northern French cooking, with its rich, butter-based sauces, and southern or Mediterranean cuisine, which is based on olive oil, garlic, and fresh herbs. The recipes in this chapter are almost all drawn from the southern regions of Provence, Côte d'Azur, and Languedoc.

Fish soup
(see page 68)

Olive and caper sauce
Walnut and anchovy sauce
Provençal garlic mayonnaise

Sauces

OLIVE AND CAPER SAUCE

Tapenade

- 2 lb/1 kg pitted black olives
- 2 tablespoons capers, rinsed and dried
- 4 anchovy fillets
- 1 clove garlic, peeled and left whole
- freshly ground black pepper
- 1/2 cup/125 ml extra-virgin olive oil
- juice of 1/2 lemon

The name for this sauce derives from the Provençal word tapeno, *which means "capers." Serve with boiled vegetables or fish, or spread on toast as an appetizer.*

Chop the olives, capers, anchovies, and garlic coarsely in a food processor. • Season with pepper and gradually stir in the oil followed by the lemon juice.

Serves 4 • Prep: 15 min • Level: 1

PROVENÇAL GARLIC MAYONNAISE

Aïoli

Eating eggs that are not completely cooked poses the possibility of salmonella food poisoning. The risk is greater for pregnant women, the elderly and very young, and people with impaired immune systems. If you are concerned about salmonella, use pasteurized eggs, which are available in some areas. Alternatively, for the sauces on this page, use store-bought mayonnaise, and season with garlic (for the Aioli) or garlic and saffron (for the Rouille).

Crush the garlic using a pestle and mortar or garlic crusher. • Place in a medium bowl and stir in the egg yolks and vinegar. • Add the oil in a thin, steady trickle, stirring constantly, until smooth and creamy. • Season with salt and pepper and drizzle with the lemon juice.

Serves 6 • Prep: 15 min • Level: 1

- 6 cloves garlic, peeled
- 2 large egg yolks
- 1 tablespoon white wine vinegar
- 2 cups/500 ml extra-virgin olive oil
- salt and freshly ground white pepper
- 1 tablespoon fresh lemon juice

WALNUT AND ANCHOVY SAUCE

Saussoun

- 3 oz/75 g salted anchovy fillets
- 2 cups/250 g finely ground walnuts
- 1/2 cup/125 ml extra-virgin olive oil
- 1 teaspoon cold water

Serve with boiled or grilled vegetables and salads, or spread on warm toast.

Desalt the anchovies carefully under a trickle of cold running water. Drain well and pat dry with paper towels. • Place the anchovies in a small bowl and crush with the back of a fork. Stir in the walnuts. • Add the oil in a thin, steady trickle, stirring constantly, until well-mixed. • Stir in the water.

Serves 4–6 • Prep: 15 min • Level: 1

SAFFRON AND GARLIC SAUCE

Rouille au safran

Traditionally, this sauce is served with Bouillabaisse (see page 80) or French Fish Soup (see page 68).

Use a mortar and pestle to crush the garlic with the salt. • Season with saffron. Add the egg yolks and beat with a wooden spoon. Set aside for 5 minutes. • Add the oil in a thin, steady trickle, stirring constantly, until smooth and creamy.

Serves 4–6 • Prep: 15 min • Level: 1

- 6 cloves garlic, peeled
- 1/2 teaspoon salt
- 1/2 teaspoon crumbled saffron threads
- 2 large egg yolks
- 1 cup/250 ml extra-virgin olive oil

Anchovies

Anchovies are a common ingredient in all Mediterranean cuisines. The salty bite of the anchovy is used in sauces, salads, pizzas, and pies, either for its own sake or to underline the character of another ingredient or the main flavor of the dish.

Soups

VEGETABLE SOUP WITH BASIL SAUCE

Soupe au pistou

- 2 cups/200 g canned/tinned and drained red kidney beans
- 2 cups/200 g canned/tinned and drained white kidney beans
- 1¹/₃ cups/125 g chopped green beans
- 2–3 medium potatoes, peeled and cut into cubes
- 2–3 medium carrots, cut into small cubes
- 2–3 zucchini/courgettes, cut into small cubes
- 3 tomatoes, finely chopped
- 1 medium onion, finely chopped
- 4 quarts/4 liters water
- salt and freshly ground black pepper
- 7 oz/200 g small soup pasta

Basil sauce
- 4 cloves garlic, peeled and left whole
- 1 bunch fresh basil, leaves only
- 1 cup/250 ml extra-virgin olive oil
- ³/₄ cup/90 g freshly grated Parmesan cheese

This fragrant soup is a summertime favorite in Provence. The basil sauce is almost identical to Italian pesto, which is hardly surprising since it originated just over the border, in Liguria.

Place the red and white kidney beans, green beans, potatoes, carrots, zucchini, tomatoes, and onion in a large saucepan with the water. Season with salt and pepper. • Bring to a boil and cook, stirring often, over low heat for 1 hour. • Add the pasta and cook for 15 minutes more. • <u>Basil Sauce</u>: Chop the garlic and basil finely in a food processor. Gradually pour in the oil and Parmesan, processing until smooth. • Spoon the basil sauce onto the soup. • Serve hot.

Serves 6 • Prep: 15 min • Cooking: 75 min • Level: 1

FRENCH FISH SOUP

Soupe de poisson

Serve this striking red soup with Provençal Garlic Mayonnaise (see page 66).

Heat the oil in a large saucepan over medium heat. Sauté the leeks and onion until lightly browned. • Add the tomatoes. Lower the heat and cook for 2–3 minutes, or until the tomatoes have softened. • Add the tomato paste, garlic, fennel, bay leaf, and orange zest. Season with salt and pepper. Pour in the water. • Add the fish, bring to a boil, and cook for 20 minutes. • Discard the bay leaf and orange zest. Transfer to a food processor and process until smooth. • Add the saffron and return to medium heat for 2–3 minutes, stirring often. • Serve hot.

Serves 4–6 • Prep: 20 min • Cooking: 30 min • Level: 2

- ¹/₃ cup/80 ml extra-virgin olive oil
- 2 leeks, trimmed and finely chopped
- 1 onion, finely chopped
- 4 tomatoes, peeled and finely chopped
- 1 tablespoon tomato paste
- 2 cloves garlic, finely chopped
- ¹/₄ teaspoon fennel seeds
- 1 bay leaf
- one ¹/₂-inch/1-cm piece of orange zest
- salt and freshly ground black pepper
- 2 quarts/2 liters water
- 2 lb/1 kg boneless fish, (red snapper, halibut, cod, sea bass), cleaned and cut into chunks
- ¹/₂ teaspoon crumbled saffron threads

Vegetable soup with basil sauce

Mussel soup with saffron

MUSSEL SOUP WITH SAFFRON

Soupe de moules au safran

- 5 lb/2.5 kg mussels in shell, soaked for 3 hours
- 2 cups/500 ml dry white wine
- 1 tablespoon finely chopped fresh thyme
- 1 bay leaf
- ¼ cup/60 ml extra-virgin olive oil
- 1 onion, finely chopped
- 2 cloves garlic, finely chopped
- 1 tomato, finely chopped
- ½ teaspoon crumbled saffron threads
- 1 tablespoon finely chopped fresh parsley
- salt and freshly ground black pepper
- 1 quart/1 liter water

Cook the mussels in a large saucepan with the wine, thyme, and bay leaf for 8–10 minutes, or until the shells have opened. • Discard any that do not open. • Shell the mussels and place the meat in a large deep serving dish. • Strain the stock into a separate bowl, taking care to remove any sand which may have settled on the bottom of the pan. • Heat the oil in a large saucepan over medium heat. Sauté the onion until lightly browned. Add the garlic, tomato, saffron, and parsley. Season with salt and pepper. • Pour in the mussel stock and water and bring to a boil over high heat. Cook for 15–20 minutes. • Pour over the mussels and serve hot.

Serves 6 • Prep: 15 min • Cooking: 30 min • Level: 1

CREAM OF CELERY SOUP

Crème de céleri

Heat the oil in a large saucepan over medium heat. Sauté the leeks for 5–7 minutes, or until lightly browned. • Add the celery and pour in the stock and water. • Continue cooking for about 25 minutes, or until the celery is tender. • Process in a food processor until smooth. • Season with salt and pepper and return to the heat for 5 minutes. • Place 1 tablespoon of croutons in the bottoms of six soup bowls and ladle the soup over the top. • Serve hot.

Serves 6 • Prep: 20 min • Cooking: 30 min • Level: 2

- 2 tablespoons extra-virgin olive oil
- 2 lb/1 kg leeks, white parts only, sliced
- 2 lb/1 kg celery, coarsely chopped
- 2 cups/500 ml beef stock or broth
- 2 cups/500 ml water
- salt and freshly ground black pepper
- 6 tablespoons croutons

Croutons

These crunchy cubes of fried bread are served with soups and salads. Buy them already made, or prepare them yourself by cutting the crusts off yesterday's bread and dicing it into ½-inch (1-cm) cubes. Fry the cubes in very hot oil until crisp and golden brown. Drain on paper towels.

Soups

TOMATO AND POTATO SOUP WITH FRESH BASIL

Soupe provençale

- ¹/₄ cup/60 ml extra-virgin olive oil
- 2 onions, finely chopped
- 3 cloves garlic, 2 finely chopped, 1 peeled and left whole
- 1¹/₂ lb/750 g potatoes, peeled and halved or quartered
- 1¹/₂ lb/750 g tomatoes, peeled and coarsely chopped
- bunch of fresh basil, leaves only, coarsely chopped
- salt and freshly ground black pepper
- water
- 6 slices firm-textured bread, toasted

Heat the oil in a large saucepan over medium heat. Sauté the onions until translucent. • Add the chopped garlic, potatoes, tomatoes, and half the basil. Season with salt and pepper. • Add enough water to cover the vegetables. Bring to a boil, then simmer over low heat for 1¹/₂ hours. • Add the remaining basil just before serving. • Rub the toast with the remaining garlic and place a slice in each soup bowl. • Ladle the soup over the top and serve hot.

Serves 6 • Prep: 20 min • Cooking: 1 hr 45 min • Level: 1

CREAM OF ZUCCHINI SOUP

Crème de courgettes

Place the zucchini, garlic, and thyme in a large deep saucepan. Pour in the stock. • Bring to a boil, lower the heat, and simmer for 8–10 minutes, or until the zucchini are tender. • Process the soup in a food processor until smooth. • Stir in the cream cheese until smooth and return to the heat for 2–3 minutes. • Season with salt and pepper. Sprinkle with the parsley and serve hot.

Serves 4 • Prep: 10 min • Cooking: 15 min • Level: 1

- 4 large zucchini/courgettes, sliced
- 1 clove garlic, finely chopped
- 1 tablespoon finely chopped fresh thyme
- 1 quart/1 liter stock or broth, boiling
- ¹/₄ cup/60 g cream cheese
- salt and freshly ground black pepper
- 1 tablespoon finely chopped fresh parsley

FRENCH ONION SOUP

Soupe à l'oignon

- ¹/₄ cup/60 ml extra-virgin olive oil
- 4 large onions, finely chopped
- 2 tablespoons all-purpose/plain flour
- 1¹/₂ quarts/1.5 liters water
- salt and freshly ground black pepper
- 4 slices firm-textured bread, toasted
- 4 oz/125 g freshly grated firm-textured cheese (Gruyère, Cheddar, Emmental)

Heat the oil in a large saucepan over medium heat. Sauté the onions until lightly browned. • Sprinkle with flour and continue cooking, stirring often, for 5 minutes. • Pour in the water and season with salt and pepper. • Bring to a boil and let simmer for 20 minutes. • Divide the toast among four ovenproof soup bowls. Sprinkle with the grated cheese and ladle the soup over the top. Place under a preheated broiler (grill) for 5–10 minutes, or until the cheese is lightly browned. Serve hot.

Serves 4 • Prep: 15 min • Cooking: 45 min • Level: 1

CHILLED TOMATO SOUP WITH FRESH HERBS

Soupe glacée à la tomate

Blanch the tomatoes in a large pot of boiling water for 30 seconds. Drain and slip off the peels. Cut in half and squeeze gently to remove the seeds. • Process the tomatoes, onion, garlic, herbs with the water and oil in a food processor until smooth. • Season with salt and pepper. • Refrigerate for at least 2 hours. Pour into individual bowls and serve chilled.

Serves 4 • Prep: 20 min + 2 hr to chill • Level: 1

- 1 lb/500 g ripe tomatoes
- 1 onion, quartered
- 1 clove garlic, peeled and left whole
- 2–3 tablespoons chopped fresh mixed herbs (basil, chervil, oregano, mint, tarragon, parsley, thyme)
- 2 cups/500 ml water
- ¹/₂ cup/125 ml extra-virgin olive oil
- salt and freshly ground black pepper

Appetizers

WARM GOAT CHEESE WITH BASIL DRESSING

Chèvre chaud au basilic

- large bunch fresh basil, leaves only
- ¹/₂ cup/125 ml extra-virgin olive oil
- 8 oz/250 g mixed salad greens
- juice of 1 lemon
- salt and freshly ground black pepper
- 4 small rounds goat cheese, each measuring about 2¹/₂ inches (6 cm) in diameter and at least ¹/₂ inch (1 cm) thick
- 4 slices firm-textured bread, toasted

Process the basil in a food processor until finely chopped. Gradually pour in ¹/₄ cup (60 ml) oil, processing until smooth. Transfer to a small bowl and let stand for 1 hour. • Arrange the salad greens on individual serving plates. Drizzle with the lemon juice and remaining ¹/₄ cup (60 ml) oil. Season with salt and pepper. • Heat a frying pan over medium heat. Cook the cheese for 5 minutes until soft and warmed through. • Arrange the cheese on top of the salad and serve with the toast. Drizzle with the basil dressing.

Serves 4 • Prep: 10 min + 1 hr • Level: 1

BAKED TOMATO AND EGGPLANT

Tomates et aubergines au four

Preheat the oven to 350°F/180°C/gas 4. • Oil a large baking dish. • Heat ¹/₄ cup (60 ml) oil in a large frying pan over medium heat. Fry the eggplant in small batches for 5–7 minutes, or until golden brown all over. Drain well and pat dry on paper towels. • Sauté the tomatoes for 5 minutes in the same pan. Add the garlic, shallot, and thyme. • Place a layer of eggplant in the bottom of the prepared dish and cover with a layer of tomato mixture. Repeat until all the eggplant and tomatoes are in the dish. • Bake for 25–30 minutes. • Top with the cheese and season with salt and pepper. Drizzle with the remaining ¹/₄ cup (60 ml) oil. Return to the oven and cook for 10 minutes more, or until the cheese is bubbling.

Serves 6 • Prep: 20 min • Cooking: 35–40 min • Level: 1

- ¹/₂ cup/125 ml extra-virgin olive oil
- 4 eggplants/aubergines, thickly sliced
- 8 large tomatoes, peeled and chopped
- 1 clove garlic, finely chopped
- 1 shallot, finely chopped
- 2 teaspoons finely chopped thyme
- 1 bay leaf
- 8 oz/200 g Mozzarella cheese, thinly sliced
- salt and freshly ground black pepper

Warm goat cheese with basil dressing

Olive loaf

OLIVE LOAF
Cake aux olives

- 1²/₃ cups/250 g all-purpose/plain flour
- 1 teaspoon baking powder
- 4 large eggs
- ¹/₂ cup/125 ml dry white wine
- ¹/₂ cup/125 ml extra-virgin olive oil
- 8 oz/200 g ham, diced
- 5 oz/150 g salt pork or lardons (fat bacon), diced
- 1¹/₂ cups/150 g thinly sliced pitted black olives
- 1¹/₄ cups/150 g freshly grated Parmesan cheese
- pinch of salt
- ¹/₈ teaspoon freshly ground black pepper

Preheat the oven to 350°F/180°C/gas 4. • Butter a 5 x 9-inch (13 x 23-cm) loaf pan. • Sift the flour and baking powder into a large bowl. Make a well in the center and add the eggs, one at a time, stirring until just blended after each addition. Add the wine and oil and stir until smooth. • Stir in in the ham, salt pork, olives, and cheese. Season with salt and pepper. • Pour the batter into the prepared pan. • Bake for about 1 hour, or until a toothpick inserted into the center comes out clean. • Cool the loaf in the pan for 15 minutes. Turn out onto a rack and let cool completely.

Serves 4 • Prep: 15 min • Cooking: 1 hr • Level: 1

HOT ANCHOVY TOASTS
Toasts chauds aux anchois

Preheat the broiler (grill). • Cover each piece of toast with a layer of tomatoes and top with a quarter of the anchovies and olives. Sprinkle with the cheese. • Drizzle with the oil. Season with pepper. • Broil (grill) the toasts about 5 inches (12 cm) from the heat source until the cheese is lightly browned and bubbling. • Serve hot.

Serves 2–4 • Prep: 10 min • Cooking: 10 min • Level: 1

- 4 slices firm-textured bread, lightly toasted
- 2 large ripe tomatoes, thinly sliced
- 4 anchovy fillets, chopped
- 20 black olives, pitted and coarsely chopped
- ³/₄ cup/90 g freshly grated Gruyère cheese
- 2 tablespoons extra-virgin olive oil
- freshly ground black pepper

Appetizers

TOMATO QUICHE
Flan de tomate

- 4 large tomatoes, peeled, seeded, and cut into small cubes
- 4 large eggs
- $^2/_3$ cup/150 ml milk
- salt and freshly ground black pepper
- $^2/_3$ cup/150 g heavy/double cream, whipped
- $1^1/_4$ cups/150 g freshly grated Gruyère cheese
- 2 cloves garlic, finely chopped
- 1 tablespoon finely chopped fresh parsley
- 4 leaves basil, torn
- 1 tablespoon finely chopped fresh thyme
- 9-inch/23-cm baked pie crust (store-bought or see recipe below)

Drain the tomatoes in a colander for 1 hour. • Preheat the oven to 400°F/200°C /gas 6. • Beat the eggs and milk in a large bowl until frothy. Season with salt and pepper. • Stir in the tomatoes, cream, cheese, garlic, parsley, basil, and thyme. • Pour the mixture into the pie shell. • Bake for 35–40 minutes, or until a toothpick inserted into the center comes out clean. • Serve hot or at room temperature.
Serves 4 • Prep: 15 min + 1 hr to drain • Cooking: 35–40 min • Level: 1

LEMON- AND HERB-MARINATED SARDINES
Sardines marinées au citron

Arrange the sardines on a large serving plate. Season with salt and pepper and drizzle with the lemon juice. Let stand for 10 minutes. • Drizzle with the oil and sprinkle with the herbs. • Marinate in the refrigerator for 8 hours before serving.
Serves 4 • Prep: 15 min + 8 hr to marinate • Level: 1

- 1 lb/500 g canned/tinned sardines in brine, drained and filleted
- salt and freshly ground black pepper
- 2–3 tablespoons fresh lemon juice
- 6 tablespoons extra-virgin olive oil
- 2–3 tablespoons finely chopped mixed fresh herbs (parsley, chervil, and chives)

Tomato quiche

Never-fail savory pie crust

Preheat the oven to 400°F/200°C/gas 6. Sift 1²/₃ cups (250 g) all-purpose/plain flour into a food processor. Add ¹/₂ cup (125 g) butter, at room temperature, and season with salt and pepper to taste. Process to fine crumbs, adding enough cold water (2–4 tablespoons) until the dough binds together into a smooth disk. Set aside for 30 minutes, then press into a 9-inch (24-cm) pan and bake for 10–15 minutes, or until pale golden brown.

Baked gnocchi, Niçoise-style

BAKED GNOCCHI, NIÇOISE-STYLE

Tian de gnocchis à la niçoise

- 2 lb/1 kg potatoes, scrubbed
- 3 large eggs, lightly beaten
- salt and freshly ground black pepper
- $^1/_2$ teaspoon freshly grated nutmeg
- 1 cup/150 g all-purpose/plain flour
- 1$^1/_4$ cups/150 g freshly grated Gruyère or Emmental cheese
- 2 cups/500 ml tomato sauce (homemade or store-bought)

Rather than using a store-bought sauce, make the recipe for Tomato Sauce on page 28. It's an Italian sauce, but then Nice is just across the border!

Preheat the oven to 400°F/200°C/gas 6. • Oil an ovenproof dish. • Bake the potatoes with their skins on for 40–50 minutes, or until tender. • Peel the hot potatoes and mash in a bowl. • Add the eggs and stir with a wooden spoon until well blended. Season with salt, pepper, and nutmeg. Gradually add the flour, mixing well. Let cool completely. • Lay out a clean cloth on a work surface and sprinkle with flour. • Use your hands to shape the mixture into balls the size of walnuts. Sprinkle with flour and flatten slightly with a fork. Let dry for 3–4 hours. • Cook the gnocchi in batches in a large pot of salted, boiling water for 4–5 minutes, or until they bob to the surface. • Drain well and place in the prepared dish. • Sprinkle with half the cheese and spoon the tomato sauce over the top. Sprinkle with the remaining cheese. • Lower the oven temperature to 325°F/170°C/gas 3. • Bake for 15–20 minutes, or until the cheese is golden brown.

Serves 6 • Prep: 20 min + 3–4 hr to dry gnocchi • Cooking: 65–80 min • Level: 2

Salads

FRISÉE SALAD WITH HERBS

Salade frisée aux herbes

- 1 tablespoon finely chopped fresh tarragon
- ¹/₄ cup/60 g finely chopped fresh basil
- ¹/₂ cup/60 g finely chopped fresh parsley
- ¹/₂ cup/125 ml vinaigrette
- 1 head frisée (curly endive), torn

Use store-bought vinaigrette for this salad or make your own by whisking ¹/₂ cup (125 ml) extra-virgin olive oil with 1–2 tablespoons red wine vinegar, 1 teaspoon Djion mustard, and salt and pepper to taste.

Mix the tarragon, basil, and parsley into the vinaigrette. • Place the lettuce in a large salad bowl. Toss the salad well with the vinaigrette and serve.

Serve 4–6 • Prep: 5 min • Level: 1

TOMATO SALAD

Salade de tomates

Place the tomatoes in a colander and sprinkle with salt. Let stand for 1 hour to drain. • Whisk the basil, tarragon, oil, and vinegar in a small bowl. Season with salt and pepper to taste. • Arrange the tomatoes in a large salad bowl. Scatter with the onions. Drizzle with the vinaigrette and serve.

Serves 6 • Prep: 10 min + 1 hr to drain tomatoes • Level: 1

- 10 firm-ripe tomatoes, thinly sliced
- salt
- 1 tablespoon finely chopped fresh basil
- 1 tablespoon finely chopped fresh tarragon
- ¹/₃ cup/80 ml extra-virgin olive oil
- 1 tablespoon white wine vinegar
- freshly ground black pepper
- 2 medium red onions, cut into rings

NIÇOISE SALAD

Salade niçoise

- 10 medium firm tomatoes, cut into 8 wedges
- salt
- 1 cup/90 g mixed salad greens, well-washed
- 1 red bell pepper/ capsicum, seeded and cut into thin strips
- 6 oz/200 g canned/ tinned tuna in oil, drained
- 3 stalks celery, finely chopped
- 3 shallots, finely chopped
- 7 black olives
- 7 anchovy fillets in oil
- 1 hard-cooked egg, peeled and cut into 6 wedges

Vinaigrette
- ¹/₂ cup/125 ml extra-virgin olive oil
- 2 tablespoons white wine vinegar
- salt and freshly ground black pepper

There are many variations on this classic salad. Feel free to experiment, but always keep the basic mix of tomato, tuna, eggs, and anchovies.

Place the tomatoes in a colander and sprinkle with salt. Let stand for 1 hour to drain. • Arrange the salad greens on the serving plate with the tomatoes around the edge. • Place the bell pepper, tuna, celery, and shallots in the center. • Wrap the olives up in the anchovy fillets and arrange on top. Garnish with the egg wedges. • <u>Vinaigrette</u>: Mix the olive oil, vinegar, salt, and pepper in a small bowl. Drizzle over the salad and serve.

Serves 6 • Prep: 15 min + 1 hr to drain tomatoes • Level: 1

BAKED ZUCCHINI SALAD

Salade de courgettes

Preheat the oven to 400°F/200°C/gas 6. • Place the zucchini in a large oiled baking dish. Season with salt and pepper and drizzle with ¹/₄ cup (60 ml) oil. • Bake for 40–45 minutes, turning frequently to brown. • Remove from the oven and let drain in a colander. • Arrange on a deep serving plate and drizzle them with the remaining ¹/₄ cup (60 ml) oil. Sprinkle with the parsley and garlic and toss gently. • Refrigerate until ready to serve.

Serves 6 • Prep: 15 min • Cooking: 40–45 min • Level: 1

- 3 lb/1.5 kg zucchini/ courgettes, peeled and thickly sliced
- salt and freshly ground black pepper
- ¹/₂ cup/125 ml extra-virgin olive oil
- 2 tablespoons finely chopped fresh parsley
- 2 cloves garlic, finely chopped

Salads

CAMARGUE RICE SALAD

Salade de riz camarguais

- 2 quarts/2 liters water
- 1¹/₄ cups/250 g short-grain rice (preferably red Camargue rice)
- 1 bay leaf
- 2 onions (1 whole, 1 thinly sliced)
- 6 tomatoes, peeled, seeded, and finely chopped
- 2 red bell peppers/capsicums, seeded and cut into strips
- ¹/₂ cup/50 g green olives
- ¹/₂ cup/50 g black olives
- 1 tablespoon white wine vinegar
- 6 tablespoons extra-virgin olive oil
- salt and freshly ground black pepper
- 6 anchovy fillets

Use rare red Camargue rice if you can find it. The Camargue is the coastline between Marseille and Montpellier on the French Riviera.

Bring the water to a boil in a large pot with the rice, bay leaf, and whole onion. • Lower the heat and simmer for 25–30 minutes, or until the rice is tender. • Drain well, discarding the bay leaf and onion. Let cool. • Stir together the rice, onion rings (reserving a few rings to garnish), tomatoes, bell peppers, and green and black olives in a large salad bowl. • Mix the vinegar and oil in a small bowl. Season with salt and pepper and drizzle over the salad. Toss the salad and scatter with the reserved onion rings and anchovies.

Serves 4–6 • Prep: 15 min • Cooking: 25–30 min • Level: 1

FRESH FAVA BEAN SALAD

Salade de fèves fraîches

Cook the fava beans in a large pot of salted boiling water with the parsley for 20–25 minutes, or until tender. • Remove the skin from each fava bean by pinching it between your thumb and index finger. • Mix the oil, shallot, vinegar, salt, and pepper in a small bowl. • Toss the fava beans, dressing, and basil in a large salad bowl. • Sprinkle with the cheese.

Serves 4–6 • Prep: 20 min • Cooking: 20–25 min • Level: 1

- 4 lb/2 kg fresh fava/broad beans, shelled
- 2–3 sprigs parsley
- ¹/₂ cup/125 ml extra-virgin olive oil
- 1 shallot, finely chopped
- 1 tablespoon white wine vinegar
- salt and freshly ground black pepper
- 3 tablespoons finely chopped fresh basil
- ¹/₄ cup/30 g freshly grated cheese (Gruyère, Parmesan)

Camargue rice salad

Prawn salad

GREEN BEAN AND TUNA SALAD

Salade de haricots verts et thon

- 1¹/₂ lb/750 g green beans or snow peas
- 2 tablespoons extra-virgin olive oil
- 1 tablespoon balsamic vinegar
- 1 medium onion, thinly sliced
- salt and freshly ground black pepper
- 1 cup/200 g canned/tinned tuna in oil, drained and broken up with a fork

Boil the green beans in a large pot of salted boiling water over medium heat for 5–10 minutes, or until tender. • Drain well and cut into short lengths. • Mix the oil, vinegar, and onion in a large salad bowl. Season with salt and pepper. • Add the warm green beans and tuna. Toss carefully and serve.

Serves 6 • Prep: 20 min • Cooking: 5–10 min • Level: 1

PRAWN SALAD

Salade tiède de langoustines à la provençale

Boil the asparagus in a large pot of salted, boiling water over medium heat for 6–7 minutes, or until just tender. Drain well and pat dry with paper towels. Cut into pieces about ¹/₂ inch (1 cm) long. • Mix the lemon juice and 6 tablespoons of oil in a small bowl. Season with salt and pepper. Set aside. • Arrange the salad greens, tomatoes, radishes, avocados, and asparagus on individual serving plates. • Heat the remaining 2 tablespoons oil in a large frying pan over medium heat. Sauté the prawns for 5 minutes, or until just cooked. Arrange the prawns on top of the salads. Drizzle with the oil and lemon dressing. Season with salt and pepper.

Serves 4 • Prep: 40 min • Cooking: 12 min • Level: 1

- 10–12 asparagus stalks
- juice of 1 lemon
- ¹/₂ cup/125 ml extra-virgin olive oil
- salt and freshly ground white pepper
- 8 oz/250 g mixed salad greens
- 2 large tomatoes, finely chopped
- 1 bunch radishes, trimmed and thinly sliced
- 3 avocados, peeled and cubed
- 30 large prawns (langoustines, lobsterettes, Dublin Bay prawns, Italian scampi) or substitute jumbo shrimp, shelled

Seafood

BOUILLABAISSE

- ¹/₂ cup/125 ml extra-virgin olive oil
- 2 medium onions, finely chopped
- 2 leeks, trimmed and finely sliced
- 1 lb/500 g tomatoes, peeled, seeded, and finely chopped
- 6 small potatoes, peeled
- 2 cups/500 ml dry white wine
- 6 cloves garlic, finely chopped, + 2 cloves, peeled and left whole
- 1 bunch common or wild fennel
- 2 bay leaves
- ¹/₂ teaspoon crumbled saffron threads
- salt and freshly ground black pepper
- 1¹/₂ quarts/1.5 liters fish stock or water
- 24 small clams, in shell
- 2 lb/1 kg mixed shellfish (scallops, shrimp, lobster, crab)
- 2 lb/1 kg fish fillets or boneless steaks (halibut, cod, sea bass, red snapper, grouper), cut into chunks
- 6–8 thick slices firm-textured bread

Serve the bouillabaisse with Aïoli (see page 66) or Rouille (see page 66).

Heat ¹/₄ cup (60 ml) oil in a large saucepan over low heat. Sauté the onions and leeks for 5–7 minutes, or until lightly browned. • Add the tomatoes, potatoes, wine, chopped garlic, fennel, bay leaves, saffron, and remaining ¹/₄ cup (60 ml) oil. Season with salt and pepper. Add the stock and simmer for 10 minutes. • Add the clams to the stock and cook until they begin to open, 5 minutes. Discard any that do not open. Add the remaining seafood and the chunks of fish and simmer gently for 10–15 minutes, or until the fish begins to flake. • While the fish is cooking, toast the bread in the oven until it dries out but is not too brown. Rub each piece of toast with garlic and set aside. • Ladle the fish stock into the soup bowls and place the toast on top of the soup. • Place the pieces of fish and seafood on a large heated serving platter and serve as a second course.

Serves 6–8 • Prep: 30 min • Cooking: 30–35 min • Level: 2

SOLE WITH ASPARAGUS AND LEMON SAUCE

Sole aux asperges

Cook the asparagus in a pot of salted, boiling water for 6–7 minutes, or until tender. • Trim the asparagus stalks so that they are a little longer than the width of the sole fillets. • Roll the sole fillets up around 12 asparagus stalks. • Place the shallots in a large frying pan. Arrange the sole rolls on top. • Pour in the wine, cover, and cook for 10–15 minutes over low heat, or until the sole is cooked. Carefully remove the fish and asparagus and set aside on a warmed serving platter. • Continue cooking, uncovered, until the sauce reduces by about half. • Cut the remaining asparagus into small pieces. • Add the butter to the pan, adding a few pieces at a time, beating with a wire whisk. • Add the remaining asparagus, mixed herbs, and lemon juice and cook over medium heat for 2–3 minutes, or until well combined. • Spoon the sauce over the sole fillets and serve hot.

Serves 6 • Prep: 25 min • Cooking: 21–23 min • Level: 2

- about 30 asparagus stalks
- 12 sole fillets, each weighing 2–3 oz/ 60–90 g
- 2 shallots, chopped
- 1 cup/250 ml dry white wine
- 1 cup/250 g butter, cut into pieces
- 5 tablespoons finely chopped mixed fresh herbs (parsley, basil, tarragon, chervil, etc.)
- juice of 1 lemon

Bouillabaisse

Provence's bouillabaisse is probably the most famous of the fish soups or stews that are made all around the Mediterranean basin. In Provence itself, there is an ongoing debate about how bouillabaisse should be made. Purists believe, for example, that potatoes should not be added to the famous stew, although almost everyone else puts them in. Some people add a few drops of pastis (an aniseed-flavored local liqueur) to accentuate the flavor of the wild fennel, while others insist that bouillabaisse without lobster is not the real thing. Certainly any dish that can provoke such passionate feelings and debate must be worth trying!

Seafood

TROUT PROVENÇAL-STYLE
Truite à la provençale

- ¹/₃ cup/80 ml extra-virgin olive oil
- 1 lb/500 g tomatoes, peeled, seeded, and finely chopped
- 1 red bell pepper/capsicum, seeded and cut into thin strips
- salt and freshly ground black pepper
- 4 medium trout, skinned and gutted
- 1 cup/100 g pitted black olives, coarsely chopped

Heat ¹/₄ cup (60 ml) oil in a large frying pan over medium heat. Sauté the tomatoes and bell pepper for 15–20 minutes, or until the bell pepper is tender and the tomatoes have reduced a little. Season with salt and pepper. Set aside in a warm oven. • Fry the trout in the remaining 2 tablespoons oil for 5 minutes on each side. • Arrange the trout on a large serving platter and spoon the sauce over the top. Garnish with the olives and serve.

Serves 4 • Prep: 15 min • Cooking: 25–30 min • Level: 1

SOLE WITH LEMON AND BUTTER
Sole meunière

Place the flour on a plate and dredge the sole in it until well coated. • Melt the butter in a large frying pan over medium heat. Fry the sole for 5 minutes on one side. Use a spatula to turn the fish over and cook for 5 minutes more. • Pour the lemon juice over the fish and cook for 1 minute. Season with salt, sprinkle with the parsley, and serve.

Serves 4 • Prep: 15 min • Cooking: 15 min • Level: 1

- ¹/₂ cup/75 g all-purpose/plain flour
- 4 sole, skinned and gutted
- ¹/₂ cup/125 g butter
- juice of 1 lemon
- salt
- 2 tablespoons finely chopped fresh parsley

Trout Provençal-style

Prawns with bell peppers

PRAWNS WITH RED BELL PEPPERS

Langoustines aux poivrons rouges

- 4 red bell peppers/ capsicums
- ¹/₄ cup/60 ml extra-virgin olive oil
- salt
- 1 teaspoon sugar
- 1 lb/500 g prawns (langoustines, lobsterettes, Dublin Bay prawns, Italian scampi) or substitute large shrimp, shelled
- freshly ground black pepper

Turn on the broiler (grill). Broil the bell peppers about 6 inches (18 cm) from the heat source for 8–10 minutes, or until the skins are blackened. Peel off the skins under cold running water. Remove the seeds. Cut into 1-inch (2.5 cm) squares. • Heat the oil in a large frying pan over medium heat and sauté the bell peppers for 5 minutes. Season with salt and sprinkle with sugar. • Add the prawns and cook, stirring often, for 5–10 minutes, or until the prawns are cooked. • Season with salt and pepper and serve.

Serves 4 • Prep: 25 min • Cooking: 20–25 min • Level: 2

MUSSELS WITH CREAM AND WHITE WINE

Moules marinières

Soak the mussels in a large bowl of cold water for 2–3 hours, changing the water often. Rinse well under cold running water to remove the final traces of sand. • Heat the oil in a large frying pan over medium heat. Sauté the onion, garlic, shallots, parsley (reserving 2 tablespoons), and bay leaves for 5 minutes. • Add the mussels and cook, covered, for 15 minutes, shaking the pan occasionally. Discard any mussels that have not opened. • Pour in the wine and cook until evaporated. • Stir in the cream and cook for 2–3 minutes. • Sprinkle with the reserved parsley and serve.

Serves 6–8 • Prep: 15 min + 2–3 hr to soak • Cooking: 25–30 min • Level: 1

- 6 lb/3 kg mussels, in shell
- ¹/₄ cup/60 ml extra-virgin olive oil
- 1 large onion, finely chopped
- 2 cloves garlic, finely chopped
- 2 shallots, finely chopped
- 1 bunch parsley, finely chopped
- 2 bay leaves
- 1 cup/250 ml dry white wine
- ¹/₂ cup/125 ml heavy/ double cream

Veal & Beef

PROVENÇAL POT ON THE FIRE

Pot-au-feu provençal

- 2 lb/1 kg beef tenderloin
- 2 lb/1 kg chicken
- 1 lb/500 g lamb shoulder roast
- 4 oz/125 g salt pork
- water
- 1 cup/250 ml dry white wine
- 2 cloves
- 2 medium onions
- 4 cloves garlic, finely chopped
- 3 turnips, halved
- 4 tomatoes, halved
- 1 lb/500 g carrots, scraped
- 2 leeks, trimmed
- 1 bouquet garni (celery, bay leaves, chervil, thyme)
- salt and freshly ground black pepper
- 6–8 slices firm-textured bread, toasted

Place the beef, chicken, lamb, and salt pork in a large pot with enough water to cover. Bring to a boil over medium heat. • Pour in the wine. Press a clove into each onion and add along with the garlic, turnips, tomatoes, carrots, leeks, and the bouquet garni. Season with salt and pepper. • Bring to a boil and skim off any foam. Cook over low heat for 2–3 hours, or until the meat is very tender. • Place the toast in individual soup bowls and ladle the bouillon over the top. Serve the meat and chicken, sliced, and vegetables on a large platter as a second course.

Serves 6–8 • Prep: 25 min • Cooking: 3 hr • Level: 1

Pot-au-feu

Pot-au-feu is the perfect one-pot winter dish. Serve the broth with the toast as a first course, then the well-cooked meat and vegetables as a second. Although pot-au-feu is a national dish, served all over France, every region has local variations. In Provence, for example, it is often served with a tomato sauce and an onion omelet.

VEAL WITH ASPARAGUS

Veau aux asperges

Melt the butter with the oil in a Dutch oven or large deep saucepan over medium heat. • Sauté the onions for 5 minutes, then add the veal and cook until browned all over, 20 minutes. Season with salt and pepper. • Pour in the stock and wine and add the bouquet garni. • Cook, covered, over low heat for 1½ hours. • Cook the asparagus in a large pot of salted, boiling water over medium heat for 6–7 minutes, or until tender. • Drain well and add to the veal with the cream. Cook for 5 minutes more. Season with salt and pepper. • Cut the veal into slices and place on a heated serving platter. Spoon the sauce over the top. Sprinkle with the parsley and serve.

Serves 6 • Prep: 20 min • Cooking: 2 hr • Level: 1

- 3 tablespoons butter
- 2 tablespoons extra-virgin olive oil
- 2 large onions, finely chopped
- 3 lb/1.5 kg veal or beef tenderloin
- salt and freshly ground black pepper
- 2 cups/500 ml meat stock or broth
- ²⁄₃ cup/150 ml dry white wine
- 1 bouquet garni (parsley, bay leaves, thyme)
- 1 lb/500 g asparagus stalks, trimmed
- 2 tablespoons heavy/double cream
- 1 tablespoon finely chopped fresh parsley

BEEF AND POTATO PIE

Hachis parmentier

Preheat the oven to 400°F/200°C/gas 6. • Peel the potatoes and place in a large bowl. Add half the butter and mash until smooth. Pour in the milk and stir until creamy. Season with salt, pepper, and nutmeg. • Melt the remaining butter in a large frying pan over medium heat. Sauté the onion until translucent. Add the beef. Season with salt and pepper and cook for 5 minutes. • Spread half the potato puree in a large oiled baking dish. Sprinkle with parsley and spoon in the beef. Spoon the remaining potato puree over the top. • Bake for 15–20 minutes, or until crispy on top.

Serves 4 • Prep: 20 min • Cooking: 30 min • Level: 1

- 2 lb/1 kg potatoes, boiled in their skins
- ¹⁄₃ cup/80 g butter
- 2 cups/500 ml milk
- salt and freshly ground black pepper
- ¹⁄₂ teaspoon freshly grated nutmeg
- 1 large onion, finely chopped
- 10 oz/300 g ground/minced beef
- 1 tablespoon finely chopped fresh parsley

Lamb & Rabbit

STUFFED LAMB SHOULDER

Épaule de mouton farcie

- 3 lb/1.5 g boneless lamb shoulder roast
- 8 oz/200 g salt pork or unsmoked bacon, cut into cubes
- 4 shallots
- 3 cloves garlic, peeled
- small bunch parsley
- 1 large egg, lightly beaten
- salt and freshly ground black pepper
- 2 teaspoons finely chopped fresh thyme
- 1/4 cup/60 ml extra-virgin olive oil

Sauce

- 3 medium onions, finely chopped
- 1 cup/250 ml dry white wine
- 5 cloves garlic, finely chopped
- 1 tablespoon finely chopped fresh parsley
- 8 firm-ripe tomatoes, peeled, seeded, and finely chopped
- 2 bay leaves
- salt and freshly ground black pepper
- 1 quart/1 liter water
- 1 tablespoon finely chopped fresh thyme

- 1 lb/500 g pasta, to serve

Place the lamb on a work surface, remove the netting or string, and trim off most external fat. Trim off about 8 oz (250 g) of meat. Spread out the shoulder so it lies flat, cut-side up. • Cook the salt pork in a large pot of boiling water for 10 minutes. Drain well. • Chop the 8 oz of lamb in a food processor with the salt pork, shallots, garlic, and parsley. • Transfer to a bowl and stir in the egg. Season with salt, pepper, and thyme. • Spoon the stuffing mixture onto the shoulder of lamb, stuffing the mixture into any pockets and crevices left by the bones. Roll the roast around the stuffing to form a cylinder and tie in four or five places and around the edges with kitchen string. • Heat the oil in a large Dutch oven (saucepan) over medium heat. Add the lamb shoulder, and

cook, turning occasionally until browned all over, about 20 minutes. • <u>Sauce</u>: When the meat is browned, add the onions and cook for 7–10 minutes. Pour in the wine and cook until evaporated. Add the garlic, parsley, tomatoes, and bay leaves. Season with salt and pepper. Continue cooking for 5 minutes. Add the water and thyme. • Cook, covered, over low heat for about 1¹/₂ hours, or until the meat is very tender. • Cook the pasta in a large pot of salted boiling water until al dente. Drain well. • Serve the meat sauce with pasta and cut the shoulder into thin slices and serve as a main course.

Serves 4–6 • Prep: 30 min • Cooking: 2 hr 25 min • Level: 2

Stuffed lamb shoulder

Bouquet garni

A bouquet garni is a bunch of carefully chosen fresh herbs, usually tied together with kitchen string or wrapped in cheesecloth, that is added to the dish during cooking and removed before serving. A classic bouquet garni could include bay leaves, celery, thyme, and parsley; but the choice of herbs should vary from dish to dish. For example, a simple mixture of sage and parsley is often enough for pork.

Lamb with eggplant

LAMB WITH EGGPLANT

Agneau aux aubergines

- ¹/₂ cup/125 ml extra-virgin olive oil
- 2 medium onions, finely chopped
- 1 clove garlic, finely chopped
- 1 tablespoon finely chopped fresh thyme
- 1 bay leaf
- 2¹/₂ lb/1.25 kg boneless lamb shoulder roast, cut into cubes
- 2 zucchini/courgettes, cut into cubes
- 8 firm-ripe tomatoes, cut into cubes
- ¹/₂ cup/125 ml dry white wine
- 6 firm-ripe eggplants/aubergines, thinly sliced lengthwise
- salt and freshly ground black pepper

Heat ¹/₄ cup (60 ml) oil in a large deep frying pan over low heat. Sauté the onions, garlic, thyme, and bay leaf until the onion is translucent. Add the lamb and sauté until browned. • Add the zucchini and tomatoes. Pour in the wine and cook over low heat for 2 hours. • Preheat the oven to 350°F/180°C /gas 4. • Heat the remaining ¹/₄ cup oil (60 ml) in a large frying pan. Fry the eggplant in batches for 5–7 minutes, or until golden brown on both sides. Drain on paper towels. • Line six to eight 4-oz (125 g) or similar small ramekins with slices of eggplant. Spoon the lamb sauce into the ramekins. Seal the tops of the ramekins with more slices of eggplant. • Bake for 30 minutes. • Invert onto serving plates and serve hot.

Serves 6–8 • Prep: 30 min • Cooking: 2 hr 45 min • Level: 2

RABBIT AND ZUCCHINI CASSEROLE

Lapin aux courgettes

This dish is equally good made with the same quantity of chicken instead of rabbit.

Melt the butter with the oil in a large Dutch oven or deep saucepan over medium heat. Sauté the rabbit and salt pork until browned. • Stir in the zucchini, garlic, onions, thyme, bay leaves, and tomatoes. Season with salt and pepper. • Cover and cook over low heat for about 1 hour, or until the rabbit is tender. Stir frequently to prevent the rabbit from sticking. Serve hot.

Serves 6 • Prep: 15 min • Cooking: 75 min • Level: 1

- 1 tablespoon butter
- 3 tablespoons extra-virgin olive oil
- 1 rabbit, weighing about 3 lb/1.5 kg, cut into 6 pieces
- 5 oz/150 g salt pork, cut into cubes
- 6 zucchini/courgettes, thickly sliced
- 6 cloves garlic, finely chopped
- 3 onions, quartered
- 1 small bunch thyme, finely chopped
- 2 bay leaves
- 6 medium tomatoes, peeled and coarsely chopped
- salt and freshly ground black pepper

Meat, Chicken & Eggs

BEEF CASSEROLE

Boeuf à l'étouffée

- ¹/₄ cup/60 ml extra-virgin olive oil
- 6 oz/150 g salt pork or bacon, diced
- 3 lb/1.5 kg chuck steak, cut into chunks
- 5 medium onions, finely chopped
- 2 cups/500 ml dry white wine
- 1 quart/1 liter water
- 2 stalks celery, diced
- 2 bay leaves
- 3 medium carrots, thinly sliced
- salt and freshly ground black pepper
- 1 tablespoon finely chopped fresh thyme
- 20 black pitted olives
- 20 green pitted olives
- 4 firm-ripe tomatoes, peeled, seeded, and finely chopped
- 6 cloves garlic, finely chopped
- grated zest of 1 small orange

Preheat the oven to 325°F/170°C/gas 3. • Heat the oil in a large Dutch oven (casserole) over medium heat. Sauté the salt pork until lightly browned. Add the beef and cook for 8–10 minutes, or until browned. • Stir in the onions and cook for 10 minutes more. • Drain off any excess fat. • Pour in one-third of the wine and cook until it has evaporated. Repeat twice until all the wine has been added. • Pour in the water, celery, bay leaves, and carrots. Season with salt and pepper. • Bring to a boil and cook, covered, for 5 minutes. Add the thyme, olives, tomatoes, garlic, and orange zest. • Bake, covered, for about 3 hours, or until the meat is very tender.

Serves 6–8 • Prep: 30 min • Cooking: 4 hr • Level: 2

CHICKEN PROVENÇAL

Poulet rôti à la provençale

Heat the oil in a large frying pan over medium-high heat. Sauté the chicken until lightly browned. • Season with salt and pepper. Remove the chicken from the pan and set aside. • In the same pan, sauté the onion, garlic, and tomatoes for 8–10 minutes, or until the tomatoes begin to break down. Season with salt. • Lower the heat and pour in the wine. Stir in the rosemary, thyme, and olives. Cook for 10 minutes. • Return the chicken to the pan and season with salt and pepper. • Cover and cook over low heat for 30 minutes, or until the chicken is very tender. • Serve hot.

Serves 6 • Prep: 30 min • Cooking: 1 hr • Level: 2

- ¹/₄ cup/60 ml extra-virgin olive oil
- 1 chicken, weighing about 3 lb/1.5 kg, cut into small chunks
- salt and freshly ground black pepper
- 1 onion, finely chopped
- 3 cloves garlic, finely chopped
- 6 firm-ripe tomatoes, peeled and coarsely chopped
- 2 cups/500 ml dry white wine
- 1 tablespoon finely chopped fresh rosemary
- 1 tablespoon finely chopped fresh thyme
- 1 cup/100 g black olives

Beef casserole

Provençal omelet

CHICKEN POT-AU-FEU

Poule au pot

- 1 chicken, weighing about 6 lb/3 kg
- 6 onions, 3 unpeeled
- 1 whole head garlic
- 1 bouquet garni or mixed herbs
- salt and freshly ground black pepper
- 6 carrots
- 6 leeks, white parts only, trimmed
- 6 turnips
- 1 cabbage, cut into 6 wedges
- 1 quart/1 liter chicken stock or broth
- 4 lb/2 kg potatoes, peeled

Place the chicken in 10 quarts (10 liters) water in a large pot over medium heat. • Broil the 3 unpeeled onions and garlic until they turn very dark brown. Add the onion and garlic to the chicken. Cook for 45–50 minutes over low heat. Add the bouquet garni. Season with salt and pepper. • Cook for 2 hours. Add the carrots, leeks, turnips, and remaining 3 onions. Simmer for 90 minutes more. • About 1 hour before the chicken is done, boil the cabbage in a large saucepan with 2 cups (500 ml) chicken stock over medium heat until tender. • About 30 minutes before the chicken is done, boil the potatoes in a large saucepan with 2 cups (500 ml) chicken stock until tender. • Remove the chicken from the pot and carve. Serve with the vegetables and stock.

Serves 7–8 • Prep: 1 hr • Cooking: 4½ hr • Level: 1

PROVENÇAL OMELET

Omelette provençale

Heat ¼ cup (60 ml) oil in a large frying pan over low heat. Sauté the onion for 5 minutes, or until translucent. Add the tomatoes and season with salt and pepper. • Cook for 15 minutes, then add the garlic and sugar. Cook for 5 minutes more. • Season the beaten eggs with salt and pepper and sprinkle with the parsley and basil. • Heat the remaining 2 tablespoons oil in another frying pan over medium heat. Pour in the beaten eggs. • When the bottom has set, slide a wooden spatula under the eggs to loosen them from the pan. Shake the pan with a rotating movement to spread if it can fit. Cook until nicely browned on the underside. • Spoon a layer of the tomato mixture over the top. • Roll up the omelet and top with the butter. • Serve hot.

Serves 4 • Prep: 15 min • Cooking: 30 min • Level: 2

- ⅓ cup/80 ml extra-virgin olive oil
- 1 medium red onion, halved and thinly sliced
- 4 firm-ripe tomatoes, finely chopped
- salt and freshly ground black pepper
- 2 cloves garlic, finely chopped
- ¼ teaspoon sugar
- 10 large eggs, lightly beaten
- 1 tablespoon finely chopped fresh parsley
- 1 tablespoon finely chopped fresh basil
- 1 tablespoon butter

Vegetables

SNOW PEAS WITH BACON

Pois au lard

- ¹/₄ cup/60 ml extra-virgin olive oil
- 2 onions, finely chopped
- ³/₄ cup/90 g diced bacon
- 4 cloves garlic, finely chopped
- 2 lb/1 kg snow peas/mange-tout peas
- 2 cups/500 ml beef stock or broth
- salt and freshly ground black pepper

Heat the oil in a large frying pan over medium heat. Sauté the onions and bacon for 5–7 minutes, or until lightly browned. • Add the garlic and let brown. • Stir in the snow peas and stock. Cook over low heat for 10–15 minutes, or until the snow peas are tender. • Season with salt and pepper and serve.

Serves 6 • Prep: 5 min • Cooking: 15–20 min • Level: 1

POTATO CROQUETTES

Croquettes de pommes de terre

- 2 lb/1 kg baking potatoes, peeled
- 1 teaspoon freshly grated nutmeg
- 3 cloves garlic, finely chopped
- 1 tablespoon finely chopped fresh parsley
- salt and freshly ground black pepper
- 4 large eggs + 3 large egg yolks
- 1 cup/125 g fine dry bread crumbs
- ¹/₂ cup/125 ml olive oil, for frying

Cook the potatoes in a large pot of salted boiling water for 20–25 minutes, or until tender. • Drain well and mash until smooth. • Place the potato puree, nutmeg, garlic, and parsley in a large saucepan over low heat. Season with salt and pepper. • Stir in 2 eggs and the egg yolks, one at a time, until just blended after each addition. Cook for 5 minutes, stirring often. • Remove from the heat and set aside to cool for 10 minutes. • Turn the potato mixture out onto a lightly floured work surface. Use your hands to shape the mixture into small croquettes. • Beat the remaining 2 eggs in a small bowl until frothy. • Place the bread crumbs in a separate small bowl. • Dip the croquettes first in the beaten eggs, then in the bread crumbs. • Heat the oil in a deep frying pan to very hot. Fry the croquettes in batches for 5–7 minutes, or until golden brown all over. Drain on paper towels and serve hot.

Serves 6 • Prep: 15 min • Cooking: 45 min • Level: 1

RATATOUILLE

Heat the oil in a large saucepan over medium heat. Sauté the onions for 5 minutes, or until translucent. • Stir in the eggplants and zucchini, followed by the bell peppers, tomatoes, bay leaf, thyme, and garlic. Season with salt and pepper. • Cook, covered, over low heat for 1 hour. Stir in the olives and garnish with basil. Serve hot.

Serves 6 • Prep: 15 min • Cooking: 65 min • Level: 1

- ¹/₂ cup/125 ml extra-virgin olive oil
- 2 onions, finely chopped
- 1 lb/500 g eggplants/aubergines, cut into small cubes
- 1 lb/500 g zucchini/courgettes, cut into small cubes
- 1 red or yellow bell pepper/capsicum, seeded and cut into thin strips
- 1 green bell pepper/capsicum, seeded and cut into thin strips
- 2 lb/1 kg tomatoes, peeled, seeded, and finely chopped
- 1 bay leaf
- 1 tablespoon finely chopped fresh thyme
- 2 cloves garlic, finely chopped
- salt and freshly ground black pepper
- ¹/₂ cup/50 g black olives
- 1 tablespoon finely chopped fresh basil

Ratatouille

This colorful vegetable dish hails from Provence and is made from a base of eggplants (aubergines), zucchini (courgettes), tomatoes, onions, and bell peppers (capsicums), simmered slowly with the best-quality olive oil. Like most other dishes from Provence, the ingredients for ratatouille vary from village to village. Ratatouille can be eaten hot with couscous or served cold with a crusty French loaf.

Vegetables

ARTICHOKES PROVENÇAL-STYLE

Artichauts à la provençale

- 6 artichokes
- 1 lemon
- ¹/₄ cup/60 ml extra-virgin olive oil
- 2 onions, finely chopped
- 2 cloves garlic, finely chopped
- 1 cup/250 ml dry white wine
- 1 teaspoon finely chopped fresh thyme
- 1 bay leaf
- salt and freshly ground black pepper

Remove the tough outer leaves from the artichokes by snapping them off at the base. Cut off the top third of the remaining leaves. Cut the artichokes in half and remove any fuzzy choke with a sharp knife. Rub with the lemon. • Heat the oil in a large frying pan over medium heat. Sauté the onions and garlic for 5 minutes, or until lightly browned. • Add the artichokes and pour in the wine. Cook for 7–10 minutes, stirring often. Season with salt and pepper. Add the thyme and bay leaf. • Cook, covered, over low heat for 40–45 minutes, or until the artichokes are tender. • Arrange the artichokes on a serving plate and spoon the sauce over the top.

Serves 6 • Prep: 20 min • Cooking: 1 hr • Level: 1

BELL PEPPERS WITH GARLIC

Poivrons à l'ail

Heat the oil in a medium frying pan over medium heat and sauté the onions and garlic for 5 minutes, or until lightly browned. • Add the bell peppers and season with salt and pepper. • Cover and cook over low heat for 25–30 minutes, or until the bell peppers are tender. Serve hot or at room temperature.

Serves 4 • Prep: 20 min • Cooking: 30–35 min • Level: 1

- ¹/₄ cup/60 ml extra-virgin olive oil
- 2 large onions, finely chopped
- 2 cloves garlic, finely chopped
- 4 medium red or green bell peppers/capsicums, seeded and cut into thin strips
- salt and freshly ground black pepper

Artichokes Provençal-style

Potato bouillabaisse

POTATO BOUILLABAISSE

Bouillabaisse de pommes de terre

- ¹/₄ cup/60 ml extra-virgin olive oil
- 5 oz/150 g bacon, diced
- 1¹/₂ cups/150 g black olives
- 4 cloves garlic, peeled and left whole
- 1 bay leaf
- 3 lb/1.5 kg potatoes, peeled
- 1 quart/1 liter meat or vegetable stock or broth

Heat the oil in a large saucepan over high heat. Brown the bacon for 5 minutes with the olives, bay leaf, and garlic. • Drain the bacon, olives, garlic, and bay leaf thoroughly on paper towels. • Chop the potatoes into chunks if they are large, or leave whole if they are small. Add the potatoes and continue cooking over low heat for 5 minutes. • Bring the stock to a boil in a large saucepan and pour over the potatoes. Cook for 15–20 minutes, or until the potatoes are tender. • Serve hot or at room temperature.

Serves 6 • Prep: 15 min • Cooking: 30–40 min • Level: 1

ZUCCHINI COOKED WITH TOMATOES

Courgettes et tomates

Place the tomatoes in a colander and sprinkle with salt. Let stand for 1 hour to drain off the excess water. • Heat the oil in a large frying pan over medium heat. Add the garlic, tomatoes, and zucchini and cook for 10–15 minutes, or until softened. • Season with salt and pepper and sprinkle with the thyme. Serve hot.

Serves 6 • Prep: 15 min + 1 hr to drain • Cooking: 10–15 min • Level: 1

- 2 lb/1 kg firm-ripe tomatoes, quartered and seeded
- salt
- ¹/₄ cup/60 ml extra-virgin olive oil
- 1 clove garlic, finely chopped
- 6 zucchini/courgettes, cut into ¹/₂-inch/1-cm thick slices
- freshly ground black pepper
- 1 tablespoon finely chopped fresh thyme

Vegetables

Eggplant and tomato mix

EGGPLANT AND TOMATO MIX

La Bohémienne

- ¹/₄ cup/60 ml extra-virgin olive oil
- 3 lb/1.5 kg eggplants/aubergines, cut into small cubes
- ¹/₂ cup/125 ml milk
- 2 lb/1 kg firm-ripe tomatoes, peeled, seeded, and finely chopped
- 1 bay leaf
- 1 teaspoon granulated sugar
- 6 anchovy fillets
- 8 cloves garlic, finely chopped
- salt and freshly ground black pepper

La Bohémienne is a very old dish from Provençe. It is a mixture of tomato, eggplant, milk, and anchovies. Serve hot or at room temperature.

Heat the oil in a large frying pan over medium heat. Sauté the eggplants for 5–7 minutes, or until tender. Drain well, reserving the oil, and drain on paper towels. Set aside. • Bring the milk to a boil in a small saucepan. • Reheat the oil in a Dutch oven or large deep saucepan over medium heat. Add the tomatoes and bay leaf. Cook until the tomatoes have softened. • Stir in the sugar, anchovies, and garlic. • Cook over low heat for 5–8 minutes. Remove from the heat and pour in the hot milk. Season with salt. • Stir the sautéed eggplants into the tomato mixture. Season with pepper. • Cook over low heat for 15–20 minutes, or until well blended.

Serves: 6 • Prep: 30 min • Cooking: 40–50 min • Level: 1

BAKED CABBAGE OMELET

Tian de chou vert

Peel away the tough outer leaves of the cabbage. Cut into quarters and rinse well. • Cook the cabbage in a large pot of salted boiling water for 9–11 minutes, or until the leaves are tender. • Drain well and cut into thin strips. • Preheat the oven to 400°F/200°C/gas 6. • Use a fork to beat the eggs in a large bowl until frothy. Beat in the crème fraîche until well blended. • Season with salt and pepper. Add the cabbage and mix well. • Grease an ovenproof dish with the oil. Pour in the egg mixture and sprinkle with the Gruyère. • Bake for 15–20 minutes, or until golden brown. Serve hot.

Serves: 6 • Prep: 20 min • Cooking: 24–31 min • Level: 1

- 1 cabbage, weighing about 4 lb/2 kg
- 2 large eggs
- ²/₃ cup/150 ml crème fraîche or sour cream
- salt and freshly ground black pepper
- 1 tablespoon extra-virgin olive oil
- ³/₄ cup/90 g freshly grated Gruyère cheese

Swiss chard gratin

SWISS CHARD GRATIN

Gratin de blettes

- 2 lb/1 kg Swiss chard
- 2 tablespoons butter
- 2 tablespoons all-purpose/plain flour
- ¹/₄ cup/60 ml milk
- salt and freshly ground black pepper
- ¹/₄ teaspoon freshly grated nutmeg
- ¹/₂ cup/60 g freshly grated firm cheese

Prepare the Swiss chard by stripping the leaves off the stalks. Cook the leaves for 4 minutes in a pot of salted boiling water. Drain well and set aside. • Peel the stalks, removing the tough strands of fiber as much as possible. Cut into ¹/₂-inch (1-cm) pieces. • Cook in a pot of salted boiling water for 5–7 minutes, or until slightly softened. Drain well and set aside. • Preheat the oven to 400°F/200°C/gas 6. • Melt the butter in a small saucepan over low heat. Stir in the flour. • Bring the milk to a boil and gradually pour into the flour mixture, beating constantly to make sure no lumps form. Continue cooking until the sauce has thickened. Season with salt, pepper, and nutmeg. • Finely chop the Swiss chard greens. Stir into the stalks and arrange in an ovenproof dish. Pour the white sauce over and sprinkle with the cheese. • Bake for 20–25 minutes, or until the cheese is nicely browned.

Serves 4 • Prep: 20 min • Cooking: 1 hr • Level: 2

LEEK GRATIN

Gratin de poireaux

Cook the leeks in a large pot of salted boiling water for 5–7 minutes, or until tender. • Drain well, pressing with a fork to remove excess water, and set aside. • Preheat the oven to 400°F/200°C/gas 6. • Beat the cream and nutmeg in a large bowl with an electric mixer at high speed until soft peaks form. Season with salt and pepper. • Spread 3 tablespoons of the cream in an ovenproof dish. Arrange the cooked leeks on top and spread with the remaining cream. Sprinkle with the Gruyère. • Bake for 25–30 minutes, or until lightly browned and the cheese is bubbling.

Serves 6 • Prep: 25–30 min • Cooking: 55–60 min • Level: 2

- 14 leeks, white parts only, halved lengthwise
- 1 cup/250 ml heavy/double cream
- 1 teaspoon freshly grated nutmeg
- salt and freshly ground black pepper
- ³/₄ cup/90 g freshly grated Gruyère cheese

Desserts

FLOATING ISLANDS
Îles flottantes

Vanilla Custard
- 1 cup/200 g granulated sugar
- 8 large egg yolks
- 2 quarts/2 liters milk
- 2 vanilla beans, halved, or 1 teaspoon vanilla extract

- 16 large eggs, separated
- ¼ teaspoon salt
- 4 cups/800 g granulated sugar
- 2 tablespoons lukewarm milk
- 1 cup/100 g candied fruit, cut into small cubes
- 1 tablespoon dark rum
- ½ cup/125 ml water
- ½ cup/50 g flaked almonds

Prepare the vanilla custard following the instructions below. The custard should be very liquid. • Beat the egg whites and salt with an electric mixer at high speed until soft peaks form. Gradually add 2 cups (400 g) of sugar, beating until stiff peaks form. • Bring 3 quarts (3 liters) of water to a boil in a large saucepan. Lower the heat to very low and pour in 1 cup (250 ml) cold water to stop the boiling. • Use 2 tablespoons to form balls of meringue about the size of golf balls. Plunge them into the water to poach for 2 minutes. Use a slotted spoon to turn them over and poach for 2 minutes on the other side. Remove from the water and place on a kitchen towel. • Heat the candied fruit in the rum in a small saucepan for 2–3 minutes. Remove from heat and, if the fruit is sticking together, divide it into single pieces. • Dissolve the remaining 2 cups sugar in the water in a heavy-bottomed saucepan over medium heat. Increase the heat to high and boil the mixture until it darkens. • Pour the custard into a large serving dish. Place the meringues on top and drizzle with the caramel. Sprinkle with the candied fruit and almonds.

Serves 8–10 • Prep: 45 min • Cooking: 45 min • Level: 3

UPSIDE-DOWN APPLE TART
Tarte Tatin

Preheat the oven to 350°F/180°C/gas 4. • Heat the granulated sugar and water in a small saucepan over low heat until caramelized. • Spoon the caramel into a 9-inch (24-cm) round cake pan. • Sprinkle with 1 tablespoon of brown sugar and dot with the butter. • Arrange the apples in the prepared pan and sprinkle with the remaining brown sugar. • Roll the pastry out very thinly on a lightly floured surface. Cover the apples with the pastry, sealing the edges. • Bake for 40–45 minutes, or until golden brown. • Invert the cake onto a serving plate and let cool. • Serve hot or at room temperature.

Serves 6 • Prep: 25 min • Cooking: 40–45 min • Level: 2

- ½ cup/100 g granulated sugar
- 1 tablespoon cold water
- 1¼ cups/250 g firmly packed dark brown sugar
- ½ cup/125 g butter, cut up
- 6 apples, peeled, cored and quartered
- Pastry for one 9-inch (24-cm) or 10-inch (26-cm) pie crust

MAKING FLOATING ISLANDS

1. To make the vanilla custard, beat the egg yolks and sugar in a large bowl. Heat the milk in a large saucepan to almost boiling, then gradually pour into the egg mixture.

2. Beat the mixture for 2 minutes, then pour it back into the saucepan. Cook over low heat, stirring constantly, until the custard thickens a little. Stir in the vanilla and remove from heat.

3. Beat the custard for 2–3 minutes more. Strain into a large bowl.

4. With an electric mixer at high speed, beat the egg whites and salt until soft peaks form. Gradually add the sugar and beat until stiff, glossy peaks form.

5. Bring 3 quarts (3 liters) of water to a boil in a large saucepan. Pour in 1 cup (250 ml) cold water to stop it boiling. Lower heat to very low. Use two tablespoons to shape the meringue. Drop into the pan of water and cook on both sides. Drain on a kitchen towel.

6. Heat the remaining sugar in a large saucepan with ½ cup (125 ml) of water until caramel forms. Place the custard in a large serving dish. Arrange the meringues on top. Sprinkle with the candied fruit and drizzle with the caramel.

Desserts

CHOCOLATE SOUFFLÉ

Soufflé au chocolat

Chocolate Sauce
- 5 oz/150 g semisweet/plain chocolate, coarsely chopped
- 1 tablespoon butter
- $^1/_3$ cup/80 ml milk

Soufflé
- $^1/_2$ cup/75 g all-purpose/plain flour
- $1^2/_3$ cups/400 ml milk
- 5 oz/150 g semisweet/plain chocolate, coarsely chopped
- 8 large eggs, separated
- $^1/_2$ cup/100 g granulated sugar
- $^1/_8$ teaspoon salt
- confectioners'/icing sugar, to dust

<u>Chocolate Sauce</u>: Melt the chocolate and butter in a double boiler over barely simmering water. • Bring the milk to a boil in a small saucepan. Remove from the heat and gradually beat into the melted chocolate. • <u>Soufflé</u>: Preheat the oven to 450°F/230°C/gas 8. • Butter an 8-inch (20-cm) soufflé mold. • Sift the flour into a small bowl. • Bring the milk to a boil in a small saucepan. • Place the chocolate in a saucepan over medium heat and pour in $^3/_4$ cup (180 ml) milk, beating until smooth. Do not let it boil. • Pour in the remaining milk and bring to a boil for 30 seconds. Remove from the heat and set aside. • Beat 4 egg yolks with the granulated sugar in a large bowl with an electric mixer at high speed until pale and thick. With mixer at low speed, gradually beat in the flour, followed by the chocolate mixture. • Return to the saucepan and bring to a boil over medium heat for 1 minute. Transfer to a large bowl and let cool. • Beat the remaining 4 egg yolks into the chocolate mixture. • With mixer at high speed, beat the egg whites with the salt in a large bowl until stiff peaks form. • Use a large rubber spatula to fold the egg whites into the chocolate mixture. • Pour the batter into the prepared mold. • Bake for 25–30 minutes, or until risen. Sprinkle with confectioners' sugar. Serve with the chocolate sauce poured over the top.

Serves 4–6 • Prep: 45 min • Cooking: 1 hr • Level: 1

Soufflé

A freshly risen soufflé served straight from the oven is one of the most impressive desserts to present to your guests. The height is created by the beaten egg whites and the rim of the mold, which allows the soufflé to rise above the dish.

Chocolate soufflé

Old-fashioned madeleines with lavender honey

OLD-FASHIONED MADELEINES WITH LAVENDER HONEY

Madeleines à l'ancienne

- ¹/₂ cup/75 g all-purpose/plain flour
- ¹/₈ teaspoon salt
- 3 large eggs
- grated zest of 1 lemon
- ¹/₄ cup/60 ml lavender honey
- ¹/₂ cup/125 g butter, melted
- confectioners'/icing sugar, to dust

Preheat the oven to 425°F/220°C/gas 7. • Butter a madeleine pan. • Sift the flour and salt into a large bowl. • Beat the eggs and lemon zest in a large bowl with an electric mixer at high speed until pale and thick. Add the honey and beat until creamy. • Use a large rubber spatula to gradually fold in the dry ingredients, followed by the butter. • Spoon the batter into the prepared pan. • Bake for 15–20 minutes, or until a toothpick inserted into the centers comes out clean. • Cool the madeleines in the pan for 5 minutes. Turn out onto a rack and let cool completely. Dust with the confectioners' sugar.

Makes about 15 madeleines • Prep: 15 min • Cooking: 15–20 min • Level: 1

STRAWBERRIES WITH RED WINE

Fraises au vin rouge

Place one-quarter of the strawberries in a large salad bowl. Pour in the wine and water and dust with the confectioners' sugar. Drizzle with the orange liqueur and add the oranges. • Refrigerate for at least 2 hours. • Refrigerate the remaining strawberries. • Just before serving, stir in the remaining strawberries. • Serve in individual serving dishes.

Serves 6 • Prep: 20 min + 2 hr to chill • Level: 1

- 2 lb/1 kg strawberries, hulled
- 3 cups/750 ml excellent-quality dry red wine
- 3–4 tablespoons water
- ¹/₄ cup/30 g confectioners'/icing sugar
- ¹/₄ cup/60 ml orange liqueur
- 2 oranges, very finely sliced

Madeleines

Madeleines are baked in special shell-shaped molds. They are associated with the small town of Commercy in Lorraine and probably originated in the 18th century when Louis XV first tasted them at the local château and named them after the pastry cook, Madeleine Paulmier.

SPAIN

From Catalonia in the north to Andalusia in the south, the eastern coast of Spain has many regional cuisines, with specialties that include some of the best-loved Spanish dishes, such as gazpacho and paella. A combination of fresh and plentiful seafood, the exotic influence of Moorish cuisines, and a respect for fine food that is in many ways still untouched by the bustle of the modern world, bring unique flavors to the foods of the Spanish Mediterranean.

Meatballs with chopped almonds (see page 102)

Appetizers

MEATBALLS WITH CHOPPED ALMONDS

Albondigas con picada de almendras

- 8 oz/250 g ground/minced veal
- 4 oz/150 g ground pork
- 1/2 cup/60 g finely chopped bacon
- 1 medium onion, finely chopped
- 2 large eggs, lightly beaten
- 1 cup/60 g fresh bread crumbs
- salt
- 1/3 cup/70 g finely ground almonds
- 1/4 cup/60 ml extra-virgin olive oil
- 1 medium tomato, peeled and coarsely chopped
- 1 quart/1 liter water
- 2 1/2 cups/375 g peas

Mix the veal, pork, bacon, half the onion, eggs, bread crumbs, and salt in a large bowl. • Place the almonds in another large bowl. Form the meat mixture into balls the size of walnuts. Roll the meatballs in the almonds until well coated. • Heat the oil in a large frying pan over medium heat. Sauté the remaining onion for 8–10 minutes, or until lightly browned. • Add the tomato and cook for 5 minutes. • Pour in the water and season with salt. Add the peas and meatballs. Cover and cook for 20 minutes, or until the meatballs are cooked through. • Serve hot.

Serves 6 • Prep: 20 min • Cooking: 30 min • Level: 2

POTATO OMELET

Tortillas de patatas

Serve this tapa *straight from the pan or leave it to cool and serve at room temperature.*

Heat the oil in a large deep frying pan over medium heat. • Arrange the potatoes, overlapping slightly, in the pan. Cook, covered, for 12–15 minutes, or until the potatoes are tender but not browned. • Pour off the excess oil, leaving about 1 tablespoon in the pan. • Beat the eggs in a medium bowl until frothy. Season with salt. • Pour the eggs over the potatoes. • Cook for 8–10 minutes, or until the omelet is golden brown on the bottom and set on top. • Transfer to a serving plate and cut into wedges to serve.

Serves 4–6 • Prep: 20 min • Cooking: 20–35 min • Level: 1

- 3/4 cup/180 ml extra-virgin olive oil
- 4 medium potatoes, peeled and thinly sliced
- 5 large eggs
- salt

CHEESE AND SESAME PUFFS

Buñuelos de queso y sésamo

- 1/2 cup/75 g all-purpose/plain flour
- 1/2 teaspoon baking powder
- 1/2 teaspoon paprika
- salt and freshly ground black pepper
- 2 large eggs
- 1 cup/125 g freshly grated firm-textured cheese, such as Cheddar
- 1/2 cup/60 g coarsely chopped ham
- 6 tablespoons toasted sesame seeds
- 2 cups/500 ml olive oil, for frying

Stir the flour, baking powder, paprika, salt and pepper into a medium bowl. • Add the eggs, one at a time, mixing until just blended after each addition. • Stir in the cheese and ham. • Use a teaspoon to shape the mixture into balls. Refrigerate for at least 4 hours. • Roll the balls in the sesame seeds. • Heat the oil in a large frying pan to very hot. • Fry the balls in batches for 5–7 minutes, or until puffed and golden brown. • Drain on paper towels and serve hot.

Serves 6 • Prep: 20 min + 4 hr to chill • Cooking: 20 min • Level: 1

Cheese and sesame puffs

TOMATO ANCHOVY BREAD

Pan con tomates y anchoas

- 1 small loaf firm-textured white bread, sliced
- 12 oz/350 g cherry tomatoes, chopped
- ¹/₄ cup/60 ml extra-virgin olive oil
- salt
- 2 oz/50 g anchovy fillets

Place the bread on individual serving plates.
• Sprinkle with the tomatoes. Drizzle with the oil and season with salt. Garnish with the anchovies.

Serves 6 • Prep: 10 min • Level: 1

CROQUETTES OF SALT COD

Croquettes de bacalao

- 6 tablespoons extra-virgin olive oil
- 1 carrot, finely chopped
- 1 leek, white part only, trimmed and finely chopped
- 4 cloves garlic, finely chopped
- 1 medium tomato, finely chopped
- 1 bay leaf
- ¹/₂ cup/125 ml dry sherry
- 1 quart/1 liter water
- 1 lb/500 g salt cod, cut into small pieces
- 1²/₃ cups/400 ml milk
- ²/₃ cup/100 g all-purpose/plain flour
- ¹/₃ cup/50 g cornstarch/corn flour
- 3 large eggs, separated
- salt and freshly ground white pepper
- 1 tablespoon finely chopped fresh parsley
- 1 cup/125 g fine dry bread crumbs
- 2 cups/500 ml olive oil, for frying

Soak the salt cod in a large bowl of cold water for 2–3 days, changing the water every few hours. This will remove the excess salt. • Drain well and set aside. • Heat ¹/₄ cup (60 ml) oil in a large frying pan over medium heat. Sauté the carrot, leek, 3 cloves garlic, tomato, and bay leaf for 5–7 minutes, or until lightly browned. • Pour in the sherry and water. Bring to a boil, then simmer over medium heat for 10 minutes. • Lower the heat and add the salt cod. Cook for 2 minutes. • Remove from the heat and transfer the cod to a food processor. • Add the milk, flour, cornstarch, and 3 egg yolks and process until smooth. Season with salt and pepper. • Heat the remaining 2 tablespoons oil in a large saucepan over medium heat. Sauté the remaining 1 clove garlic and parsley until aromatic. • Add the cod mixture and cook, stirring constantly, until the mixture is thick, 4 minutes. • Remove from the heat and let cool completely. • Beat the egg whites in a small bowl until frothy. • Place the bread crumbs in a small bowl. • Use your hands to shape the cod mixture into small croquettes. Dip first in the beaten egg whites, then in the bread crumbs. • Heat the oil in a deep frying pan to very hot. • Fry the croquettes in batches for 5–7 minutes, or until golden brown and crispy. • Drain well on paper towels. Serve hot.

Serves 8 • Prep: 25 min + 2–3 days to soak • Cooking: 40 min • Level: 1

MIXED VEGETABLE SOUP

Sopa de vehículos mezclados

- 3 red onions, finely chopped
- 2 cloves garlic, finely chopped
- 2 leeks, white parts only, trimmed and finely chopped
- ²/₃ cup/150 ml extra-virgin olive oil
- 2 cups/500 g chopped tomatoes
- ¹/₂ teaspoon red pepper flakes
- ²/₃ cup/80 g shelled peas
- 3¹/₂ oz/100 g green beans
- 3¹/₂ oz/100 g young spinach leaves, washed and finely chopped
- salt and freshly ground black pepper
- 4 thick slices whole wheat bread

Sauté the onions, garlic, and leeks in ¹/₄ cup (60 ml) oil in a Dutch oven (casserole) over low heat until the onions and leeks have softened. • Add the tomatoes and red pepper flakes and cook until the tomatoes have broken down, about 10 minutes. • Add the peas, green beans, and spinach. Season with salt and pepper. Cook for 10 minutes more. • Use a slotted spoon to remove the vegetables and reserve the liquid. • Place the slices of bread in individual serving bowls and spoon over the vegetables. • Drizzle with the remaining oil and pour over the liquid.

Serves 4 • Prep: 30 min • Cooking: 35 min • Level: 2

COOL GARLIC AND ALMOND SOUP

Ajo blanco

Process the almonds and garlic in a food processor until smooth. Season with salt. • Add the bread crumbs and pour in the oil. Process until the mixture has a mayonnaise-like consistency. • Pour in the vinegar and water and process again until well blended. • Season with salt. • Pour into individual serving bowls and garnish with the grapes.

Serves 6 • Prep: 15 min • Level: 1

- 1 cup/150 g almonds, blanched and peeled
- 2 cloves garlic, peeled and left whole
- salt
- 2 cups/120 g fresh bread crumbs, soaked in ¹/₄ cup/60 ml water
- ¹/₃ cup/80 ml extra-virgin olive oil
- ¹/₂ cup/125 ml white distilled vinegar
- 1 quart/1 liter water
- 1 cup/250 g seedless white grapes, to garnish

GARBANZO BEAN AND TOMATO SOUP

Sopa de garbanzos y tomates

- ¹/₄ cup/60 ml extra-virgin olive oil
- 1 clove garlic, finely chopped
- 2 cups/500 g chopped tomatoes
- 1³/₄ cups/430 g canned garbanzo beans/chickpeas, drained
- 1 quart/1 liter vegetable stock or broth
- salt and freshly ground black pepper
- 1 tablespoon finely chopped fresh thyme

Heat the oil in a large saucepan over medium heat. Sauté the garlic until it is pale gold. • Add the tomatoes and cook until the tomatoes have broken down, about 10 minutes. • Add the garbanzo beans and pour in the stock. Season with salt and pepper and stir in the thyme. Cook for 10 minutes more. • Serve hot in individual serving bowls.

Serves 4 • Prep: 15 min • Cooking: 25 min • Level: 2

GARLIC SOUP

Sopa de ajo

Heat the oil in a large saucepan over medium heat. • Sauté the garlic for 5–7 minutes, or until translucent. • Pour in the water and bring to a boil. • Add the bread and eggs. Season with salt. • Cook for 10 minutes. • Pour the mixture into a food processor and process until smooth. • Serve hot.

Serves 4 • Prep: 20 min • Cooking: 15–20 min • Level: 1

- ¹/₂ cup/125 ml extra-virgin olive oil
- 6 cloves garlic, finely chopped
- 5 cups/1.25 liters water
- 6 slices white sandwich bread, crumbled
- 4 large eggs, lightly beaten
- salt

GAZPACHO

- 2–3 thick slices day-old firm-textured bread
- 2 tablespoons extra-virgin olive oil
- 1½ teaspoons sherry wine vinegar or 1 tablespoon white wine vinegar
- ⅛ teaspoon salt

- 4–6 large tomatoes, peeled and coarsely chopped
- 1 red bell pepper/ capsicum, seeded and coarsely chopped
- 1 large cucumber, peeled and coarsely chopped

- 1 hard-cooked egg, shelled and coarsely chopped
- 3 cloves garlic, peeled
- ¼ cup/60 ml cold water (optional)
- salt and freshly ground black pepper
- croutons, to serve

Gazpacho is a classic Andalusian dish. There are probably as many versions as there are cooks!

Soak the bread in the oil, vinegar, and salt for 15 minutes. • Process the tomatoes, bell pepper, cucumber, egg, garlic, and bread mixture in a food processor until smooth. • If the soup is too dense, add the water. • Season with salt and pepper and serve with croutons.

Serves 4 • Prep: 20 min • Level: 1

Salads

FAVA BEAN SALAD WITH SPANISH HAM AND MINT

Ensalada de habas baby con jamón serrano y perfume de menta

- 1³/₄ lb/750 g fresh fava/broad beans, shelled
- 1 cup/250 ml extra-virgin olive oil
- ¹/₄ cup/60 ml sherry wine vinegar or ¹/₃ cup/80 ml white wine vinegar
- ¹/₂ teaspoon tarragon mustard
- salt and freshly ground black pepper
- 1 bunch mint, finely chopped
- 1 small onion, finely chopped
- 1 large tomato, cut into cubes
- 2 hard-cooked eggs, quartered
- 4 slices jamón serrano or prosciutto/Parma ham, coarsely chopped

Cook the fava beans in a large pot of salted boiling water for 20–25 minutes, or until tender. • Remove the skin from each fava bean by pinching it between your thumb and index finger. • Drain and let cool completely. • Mix the oil, vinegar, and mustard in a small bowl. Season with salt and pepper. • Toss the fava beans, mint, onion, and tomato in a large salad bowl. • Pour the dressing over and toss well. • Top with the eggs and jamón serrano and serve.

Serves 4 • Prep: 20 min • Cooking: 20–25 min • Level: 1

ORANGE SALAD

Ensalada de naranjas

Plump the raisins in lukewarm water for 15 minutes. Drain well and pat dry with paper towels. • Mix the oil, vinegar, and sugar in a small bowl. Season with salt and pepper. • Cut the oranges into ¹/₄-inch (5-mm) thick slices. • Arrange the oranges on a large serving plate. Place the onion rings on top and sprinkle with the raisins. • Drizzle with the dressing and serve.

Serves 4 • Prep: 20 min + 15 min to plump • Level: 1

- 1 tablespoon golden raisins/sultanas
- ¹/₄ cup/60 ml extra-virgin olive oil
- 1 tablespoon red wine vinegar
- ¹/₄ teaspoon sugar
- salt and freshly ground black pepper
- 2 large oranges, peeled and seeded
- 2 small red onions, sliced

POMEGRANATE SEED SALAD

Ensalada con granadas

Cut the pomegranate into quarters, reserving the seeds and juice. • Mix the oil, vinegars, and pomegranate juice in a small bowl. Season with salt and pepper. • Place the salad greens, onion, and scallions in a large salad bowl. • Drizzle with the oil mixture and toss well. • Garnish with the pomegranate seeds.

Serves 4 • Prep: 15 min • Level: 1

- 1 pomegranate
- ¹/₃ cup/80 ml extra-virgin olive oil
- 2 teaspoons sherry wine vinegar
- 1 tablespoon red wine vinegar
- salt and freshly ground black pepper
- 8 oz/200 g mixed salad greens
- 1 red onion, finely chopped
- 2 scallions/spring onions, finely chopped

Oranges

When the Moors arrived in Spain, they planted vast groves of lemon and orange trees along the southeastern coastline. Oranges are synonymous with Spain and, in particular, the Valencia area where groves stretch as far as the horizon. The southern Spanish climate allows orange trees to flourish unhindered by frost. Throughout the Andalusia region, the freshest oranges are used for salads, desserts, and many other novel culinary purposes. Oranges are a main feature in the famed alcoholic punch, sangria, along with red wine, lemon, and sugar.

SUMMER POTATO SALAD WITH VINAIGRETTE

Ensalada de patatas en vinagreta de Verano

- 2 lb/1 kg waxy potatoes
- 1 medium onion, thinly sliced
- ¼ cup/60 ml cold water
- 1 tablespoon white wine vinegar
- salt
- 6–8 oz/250 g canned tuna in olive oil, drained and crumbled
- 2 medium cucumbers, thinly sliced
- 1 cup/100 g black and green olives
- 2 tablespoons extra-virgin olive oil
- 1 medium tomato, thinly sliced
- 1 hard-cooked egg, shelled and sliced into quarters
- 4 anchovies or 8 anchovy fillets
- 1 yellow bell pepper/capsicum, seeded and cut into thin strips

Cook the potatoes in their skins in a large pot of salted boiling water for 20 minutes, or until tender. • Peel the potatoes and let cool completely. • Cut into bite-sized pieces. • Place the onion in a large bowl with the water, vinegar, and 1 teaspoon salt. Let stand 30 minutes. Drain well. • Place the potatoes, tuna, cucumbers, olives, and onion in a large salad bowl. Season with salt and oil. • Toss carefully and garnish with the tomato, egg, anchovies, and bell pepper.

Serves 4 • Prep: 20 min + 30 min to stand • Cooking: 20–25 min • Level: 1

SPINACH WITH RAISINS AND PINE NUTS

Espinacas con pasas y piñones

Cook the spinach in a large pot of salted boiling water for 1–2 minute(s), or until just wilted. • Drain well, squeezing out excess water. • Melt the butter in a large saucepan over medium heat. Sauté the raisins and pine nuts for 5–7 minutes, or until toasted. • Add the spinach and cook for 5 minutes, stirring constantly, until the butter has been absorbed. Season with salt. • Serve hot.

Serves 6 • Prep: 5 min • Cooking: 15–20 min • Level: 1

- 4 lb/2 kg spinach, well-washed and chopped
- 2 tablespoons butter
- ¾ cup/135 g raisins
- ¾ cup/135 g pine nuts
- salt

Summer potato salad with vinaigrette

Vegetables

PISTO

- ¹/₄ cup/60 ml extra-virgin olive oil
- 2 medium potatoes, peeled and cut into small cubes
- 1 large onion, finely chopped
- 1 red bell pepper/capsicum, seeded and cut into small chunks
- 1 green bell pepper/capsicum, seeded and cut into small chunks
- 1 eggplant/aubergine, cut into small cubes
- 1 large zucchini/courgette, cut into small cubes
- 4 large tomatoes, coarsely chopped
- salt and freshly ground black pepper
- ¹/₄ cup/60 ml water (optional)

This is another classic dish. Variations are served all over Spain. It can be served as a side dish with meat or fish, or on its own as a light lunch. In many regions, 2–3 lightly beaten eggs are stirred into the pan when the vegetables are almost cooked.

Heat the oil in a large frying pan over medium heat. Sauté the potatoes for 8–10 minutes, or until lightly browned. • Add the onion and bell peppers and cook, stirring, for 8–10 minutes, or until the onion is lightly browned. • Add the eggplant and zucchini and cook, stirring, for 5 minutes. • Stir in the tomatoes. • Season with salt and pepper. • Cook, adding the water if needed, for 10–15 minutes more, or until the vegetables are tender.

Serves 4–6 • Prep: 10 min • Cooking: 35–40 min • Level: 1

POTATOES WITH PEPPERS

Patatas con pimientos

Cook the potatoes in salted boiling water for 20 minutes, or until tender. • Drain well, and cut into bite-sized pieces (or leave whole if small). • Heat the oil in a large frying pan over medium heat. Sauté the potatoes for 5 minutes, or until lightly browned. • Grind the garlic, red pepper flakes, and cumin using a pestle and mortar until crushed. • Transfer to a small bowl and add the paprika and vinegar • Add the garlic mixture and bell pepper to the potatoes. Cook, stirring often, for 10 minutes. • Season with salt and serve hot.

Serves 4 • Prep: 15 min • Cooking: 25 min • Level: 1

- 1¹/₂ lb/750 g new potatoes
- ¹/₃ cup/80 ml extra-virgin olive oil
- 2 cloves garlic, chopped
- ¹/₂ teaspoon red pepper flakes
- ¹/₂ teaspoon cumin seeds
- ¹/₄ teaspoon paprika
- 2 tablespoons white wine vinegar
- 1 green bell pepper/capsicum, seeded and thinly sliced
- salt

ONIONS WITH HONEY

Cebollas con miel

- 20 small white onions, trimmed
- 3 tablespoons extra-virgin olive oil
- 3 tablespoons honey
- 1 teaspoon freshly ground cumin seeds
- salt and freshly ground black pepper

Plunge the onions into a large pot of salted boiling water and leave for 1 minute. Drain in a colander, reserving the boiling water, and slip off their skins. • Return the onions to the pot with the reserved water and simmer for 20 minutes, or until tender. • Drain the onions, reserving about 2 tablespoons of the cooking water. Place the onions and reserved water in a large frying pan with the oil, honey, and cumin. Season with salt and pepper. • Cook, stirring often, over medium-high heat for 5–10 minutes, or until the liquid is all absorbed and the onions are tender and golden.

Serves 4 • Prep: 10 min • Cooking: 25–30 min • Level: 1

SAUTÉED SWISS CHARD WITH RAISINS AND PINE NUTS

Acelgas rehogadas

Plump the raisins in a small bowl of lukewarm water for 10 minutes. Drain well and pat dry with paper towels. • Cook the Swiss chard in salted boiling water for 10–15 minutes, or until tender. • Drain well and squeeze out excess moisture. • Heat the oil in a large frying pan and sauté the garlic, pine nuts, and raisins for 3–4 minutes. • Add the Swiss chard and sauté for 5–10 minutes, or until the flavors have been absorbed by the vegetables. • Serve hot or at room temperature.

Serves 4 • Prep: 15 min • Cooking: 20–25 min • Level: 1

- 2–3 tablespoons raisins
- 1¹/₂ lb/750 g Swiss chard, coarsely chopped
- ¹/₃ cup/80 ml extra-virgin olive oil
- 2 cloves garlic, finely chopped
- 2–3 tablespoons pine nuts
- salt and freshly ground black pepper

Vegetables

FAVA BEANS, CATALAN-STYLE

Habes a la catalana

- 1 tablespoon butter
- 1 tablespoon extra-virgin olive oil
- 3 oz/90 g bacon, diced
- 3 oz/90 g blood sausage, morcilla, or black Catalan sausage, sliced
- 1 medium onion, finely chopped
- 3 cloves garlic, finely chopped
- $^1/_2$ cup/125 g chopped tomatoes
- 1 teaspoon finely chopped fresh mint
- $^1/_2$ teaspoon cayenne pepper
- 1 cup/250 ml dry white wine
- 8 lb/4 kg fresh fava/broad beans, shelled
- salt
- 1 teaspoon sugar

Heat the butter and oil in a large frying pan over medium heat. Sauté the bacon, sausage, onion, garlic, tomatoes, mint, and cayenne pepper until aromatic. • Pour in the wine and add the fava beans. Season with salt and sugar. • Cover and cook for 20–25 minutes, or until the fava beans are tender.

Serves 6 • Prep: 10 min • Cooking: 25–35 min • Level: 1

ALMERIAN HUNTERS' BREAKFAST

Migas de Almeria

Crumble the bread into a large bowl. Drizzle with the water and let stand for 12 hours. • Heat the oil in a large frying pan over medium heat. Sauté the bacon and salami for 5–7 minutes, or until well browned. • Transfer to a plate and set aside. • Sauté the garlic in the same pan until transparent. • Season with the cayenne pepper and add the bread crumb mixture. Cook for 2–3 minutes, until aromatic. • Add the bacon and salami and cook for 5 minutes more. • Serve hot.

Serves 4 • Prep: 15 min + 12 hr to stand • Cooking: 20 min • Level: 1

- 2 lb/1 kg day-old bread
- $^1/_3$ cup/80 ml water
- $^1/_3$ cup/80 ml extra-virgin olive oil
- 8 oz/200 g bacon, diced
- 4 oz/125 g salami, diced
- 2 cloves garlic, peeled and lightly crushed
- 1 teaspoon cayenne pepper
- salt

Fava beans Catalan-style

Rice

SEAFOOD RICE

Arroz a la marinera

- ¹/₄ cup/60 ml extra-virgin olive oil
- 1 medium onion, finely chopped
- 5 cloves garlic, finely chopped
- 1 medium tomato, coarsely chopped
- 6 oz/200 g canned tuna in oil, drained and crumbled
- 4 oz/90 g shrimp, peeled
- 1 lb/500 g clams, in shell
- 10 oz/300 g squid or cuttlefish, cut into rings
- 1 lb/500 g mussels, in shell
- 1 cup/200 g short-grain rice
- 1 quart/1 liter fish stock
- 1 dried red chile, finely chopped
- 1 teaspoon finely chopped fresh parsley
- 4–6 threads saffron, crumbled
- salt

Heat the oil in a large frying pan over medium heat. • Sauté the onion, garlic, and tomato for 8–10 minutes, or until the onion is lightly browned. • Add the tuna, shrimp, clams, squid, mussels, and rice. Sauté over high heat for 3–4 minutes. • Discard any mussels that do not open. Lower the heat to medium. Pour in the stock and bring to a boil. Add the chile, parsley, and saffron and season with salt. • Cook for 20–25 minutes, or until the fish and seafood are tender. • Serve hot.

Serves 6 • Prep: 15 min • Cooking: 30–35 min • Level: 2

SAFFRON RICE

Arroz al azafran

Saffron, the most expensive spice in the world, was reintroduced to Europe via Spain in the 8th century by the Moors. They planted the precious plant in Andalusia and Valencia. Some of the best saffron in Europe is still grown in these parts, and it is a vital ingredient in many local dishes. If possible, buy saffron in threads (also called strands)—they should be intact and a deep red color—to make sure you are getting the real thing.

Preheat the oven to 425°F/220°C/gas 7. • Melt the butter in a medium ovenproof Dutch oven (casserole) over medium heat. • Sauté the onion for 8–10 minutes, or until lightly browned. • Add the rice and toast it for a few seconds. • Pour in the stock and water and bring to a boil. • Add the parsley and saffron and season with salt and pepper. • Remove from the heat and cover with aluminum foil. • Bake for 15 minutes. • Remove from the oven and let stand for 10 minutes before serving.

Serves 2–4 • Prep: 23–25 min + 10 min to stand • Cooking: 25 min • Level: 1

- 2 tablespoons butter
- 1 small onion, finely chopped
- 1 cup/200 g short-grain rice
- 1 cup/250 ml beef stock or broth
- 1 cup/250 ml water
- 2 tablespoons finely chopped fresh parsley
- 4–6 saffron threads, crumbled
- salt and freshly ground black pepper

Rice

The coastal area of southeastern Spain was irrigated and cultivated for the growth of rice by the Moors. Today this region prides itself on the variety and quality of the rice dishes produced. Paella would never have become the famous Spanish dish it is today had it not been for the rice grown here. If you can find Spanish rice, then use it for its authenticity in these recipes. Other types of short-grain rice, such as Italian arborio, will work equally well.

Emperor's black ink rice

EMPEROR'S BLACK INK RICE

Arroz negre de l'emperador

- $^1/_3$ cup/80 ml extra-virgin olive oil
- 2 medium onions, finely chopped
- 1 small fresh green chile pepper, finely chopped
- 4 cloves garlic, finely chopped
- 2 firm-ripe tomatoes, peeled and coarsely chopped
- $1^1/_2$ lb/750 g squid or cuttlefish, cleaned and ink sacs reserved
- 2 cups/400 g short-grain rice
- 1 quart/1 liter fish stock, made with very little salt

Heat the oil in a large frying pan over medium heat. Sauté the onions and bell pepper for 8–10 minutes, or until the onions are lightly browned. • Stir in 1 clove of garlic and the tomatoes. Cook for 10–15 minutes, or until the liquid has reduced. • Stir in the squid and reserved ink sacs, which will color the mixture. • Add the rice and stir over high heat for 2–3 minutes. • Pour in the fish stock and bring to a boil. Lower the heat and simmer for 5 minutes more. • Add the remaining garlic and cook for 15 minutes more, or until the rice is tender.

Serves 6 • Prep: 15 min • Cooking: 40–45 min • Level: 2

RICE WITH CHORIZO SAUSAGE

Arroz con chorizo

Heat the oil in a large frying pan over medium heat. Sauté the onion for 8–10 minutes, or until lightly browned. • Add the sausage and sauté for 5–7 minutes, or until browned. • Add the rice and stir over high heat for 2–3 minutes. • Pour in the stock and add the peas. Bring to a boil and simmer, covered, for 15 minutes. • Stir in the tomatoes, olives, and parsley. • Cover and cook for 5–7 minutes, or until the rice is tender. • Season with salt and pepper. • Serve hot.

Serves 4 • Prep: 15 min • Cooking: 40–50 min • Level: 2

- $^1/_4$ cup/60 ml extra-virgin olive oil
- 1 small onion, finely chopped
- 1 lb/500 g chorizo sausage, sliced
- 1 cup/200 g short-grain rice
- $1^2/_3$ cups/400 ml meat stock or broth
- 2 cups/250 g peas
- 2 cups/500 g peeled and chopped tomatoes
- $^1/_3$ cup/30 g black olives
- 2 tablespoons finely chopped fresh parsley
- salt and freshly ground black pepper

Rice

PAELLA, VALENCIA-STYLE

Paella Valenciana

- ¹/₄ cup/60 ml extra-virgin olive oil
- 3 cloves garlic, peeled and lightly crushed
- 1 roasting chicken (or rabbit), boned and cut into small chunks, weighing about 1 lb/500 g
- 3 cups/600 g short-grain rice
- 1¹/₂ quarts/1.5 liters boiling water
- 2 lb/1 kg snails, clams, or shrimp, cleaned
- 2 artichoke hearts, cleaned and chopped
- 8 oz/200 g green beans, cut into short lengths
- 1³/₄ cups/200 g peas
- 1 lb/500 g mussels, in shell
- 1 lb/500 g eel or tuna, cleaned and chopped
- salt and freshly ground black pepper
- 1 bay leaf
- 8–10 threads saffron, crumbled

This is a traditional recipe from the coastal regions in southeastern Spain. Paella lends itself to an endless array of variations, so if you don't like snails or eel, substitute other meat or seafood that you do like.

Preheat the oven to 400°F/200°C/gas 6. • Heat the oil in a paella pan or large frying pan about 18 inches (45 cm) in diameter over medium heat. Sauté the garlic for 2–3 minutes. • Discard the garlic. • Brown the chicken in the same pan for 5 minutes. • Add the rice and stir until well coated with oil. • Pour in the water and bring to a boil. • Add the snails, artichokes, green beans, peas, mussels, and eel. Season with salt and pepper. Add the bay leaf and saffron. • Continue cooking over medium-high heat until the liquid has almost all been absorbed. Discard any clams or mussels that do not open. The rice grains should still be slightly crunchy and there should still be some liquid in the pan. • Bake in the oven, uncovered, for 10 minutes. • Cover the pan with foil or parchment paper and let stand for 10 minutes. Remove the bay leaf before serving.

Serves 6–8 • Prep: 25 min + 10 min to stand • Cooking: 30 min • Level: 2

VEGETABLE PAELLA

Paella de verduras

For a vegetarian paella, replace the chicken stock with the same quantity of vegetable stock.

Soak the garbanzo beans in cold water overnight. • Preheat the oven to 400°F/200°C/gas 6. • Cook the garbanzo beans, covered, in the stock with the onion, bay leaf, and peppercorns for 90 minutes. • Strain the garbanzo beans, reserving the stock and discarding the bay leaf and peppercorns. Mash the beans. Add the wine to the stock and bring to a boil. • Heat the oil in a paella pan or large frying pan about 18 inches (45 cm) in diameter. • Add the garlic, potatoes, zucchini, green beans, mushrooms, artichokes, peas, bell peppers, carrot, spinach, mashed garbanzo beans, and parsley and sauté over medium-high heat for 5–7 minutes. • Add the tomatoes, paprika, and saffron followed by the rice. Stir for 2–3 minutes, then pour in the stock and wine mixture. • Continue cooking over medium-high heat until liquid has almost all been absorbed. The rice grains should still be slightly crunchy and there should still be some liquid in the pan. • Bake in the oven, uncovered, for 10 minutes. • Cover the pan with foil or parchment paper and let stand for 10 minutes before serving.

Serves 6–8 • Prep: 30 min + 12 hr to soak • Cooking: 2 hr 10 min • Level: 2

- 1 cup/100 g dry garbanzo beans/chickpeas
- 1¹/₂ quarts/1.5 liters chicken stock or broth
- 1 small onion, cut in half
- 1 bay leaf
- 8–10 peppercorns
- ¹/₂ cup/125 ml white wine
- ¹/₃ cup/80 ml extra-virgin olive oil
- 3 cloves garlic, finely chopped
- 2–3 medium potatoes, peeled and cut into small cubes
- 1 zucchini/courgette, sliced
- 8 oz/250 g green beans, cut into short pieces
- 12 mushrooms, chopped
- 4 artichoke hearts, sliced
- 1 cup/125 g peas
- 2 green bell peppers/capsicums, seeded and chopped
- 1 carrot, sliced
- 8 oz/250 g spinach, coarsely chopped
- 2 tablespoons finely chopped fresh parsley
- 3–4 tomatoes, chopped
- 2 teaspoons paprika
- 8–10 threads saffron, crumbled
- 3 cups/600 g short-grain rice
- salt

MAKING CLASSIC PAELLA

1. Remove the peppercorns and bay leaves. Mash the cooked garbanzo beans (chickpeas) as you strain the stock. The garbanzo bean mash should be added with the vegetables.

2. Brown any meats, then sauté all the vegetables in a paella pan or large frying pan for 5–7 minutes, or until they cook down a little.

3. Add the rice and stir to coat well with the oil. Pour in the hot stock and wine mixture, and cook until only a little liquid remains in the pan.

4. Place the pan in a preheated oven and cook for 10 minutes. Remove from the oven, cover with parchment paper or foil, and let stand for 10 minutes before serving.

Paella Valencia-style

Seafood

FRIED ANCHOVIES

Anchoas fritas

- 10 oz/300 g anchovies, cleaned and gutted
- 2 cups/500 ml milk
- 1/2 cup/75 g all-purpose/plain flour
- 1 cup/250 ml olive oil, for frying
- salt

These anchovies also make an excellent starter. These quantities are enough for 2 people as a main dish or for 4 people as an appetizer.

Soak the anchovies in the milk in a medium bowl for 30 minutes. • Drain well and pat dry with paper towels. • Dip in the flour, making sure they are well covered. • Heat the oil in a large deep frying pan to very hot. • Fry the anchovies for 5–7 minutes, or until golden brown and crispy. • Drain on paper towels. • Season with salt and serve hot.

Serves 2–4 • Prep: 15 min + 30 min to soak • Cooking: 5–7 min • Level: 1

SQUID WITH PEAS

Calamar con guisantes

Cut the squid into 1-inch (2-cm) rings. • Place the squid in a large frying pan with about 1/2 inch (1 cm) of boiling water. Add the oil and cook over medium heat for 10–12 minutes, or until the water has evaporated and the squid has softened. • Add the onions and continue cooking, stirring often, for 20 minutes. • Stir in the tomatoes and cook for 5 minutes. • Add the peas and enough boiling water to keep the pan moist and cook for 10 more minutes, or until the peas are tender. • <u>Sauce</u>: Stir together the garlic, parsley, flour, oil, and water in a small saucepan over medium heat for 4–5 minutes, or until dense. • Serve the squid with the sauce passed on the side.

Serves 4 • Prep: 20 min • Cooking: 45 min • Level: 2

- 1 1/2 lb/750 g squid or cuttlefish, cleaned
- 1 tablespoon extra-virgin olive oil
- 2 medium onions, finely chopped
- 2 medium tomatoes, finely chopped
- 6–7 cups/1 kg peas
- 1 cup/250 ml boiling water

Sauce
- 1 clove garlic, finely chopped
- 2 tablespoons finely chopped fresh parsley
- 1 tablespoon all-purpose/plain flour
- 1/4 cup/60 ml extra-virgin olive oil
- 1/3 cup/80 ml water

FISH BAKED IN SALT WITH MEDITERRANEAN HERBS

Pescados al sal con aromas mediterraneos

- 4-lb/2-kg firm-textured fish, such as snapper, porgy, or sea bream, gutted and cleaned
- 1 bunch mint
- 1 bunch common or wild fennel leaves
- 8 lb/4 kg coarse salt
- 1 cup/250 g pine needles (optional)
- 1/4 cup/60 ml water
- 1 cup/250 ml anisette

Preheat the oven to 475°F/250°C/gas 9. • Line a large baking dish with aluminum foil. • Stuff the fish with a few sprigs of mint and fennel. • Cover the bottom of the pan thickly with salt. Cover with mint, fennel, and pine needles, if using. • Place the fish on top and cover with the remaining herbs. • Cover completely with the remaining salt. • Drizzle with the water and anisette. • Seal the baking dish with foil. • Bake for 45 minutes. • Remove the foil and bring to the table. Break the crust of salt in front of your guests. • Serve hot.

Serves 6 • Prep: 20 min • Cooking: 45 min • Level: 2

SARDINES IN SPICY MARINADE

Sardinas en escabeche

Dip the sardines in the flour, making sure they are well covered. • Heat the oil in a large frying pan over medium heat. Fry the sardines for 5 minutes on both sides, or until golden brown. • Drain well on paper towels and place in an earthenware dish. • In the same skillet, sauté the garlic and red pepper flakes for 5–7 minutes. • Pour in the vinegar and let it reduce. • Add the bay leaf and rosemary. Season with salt and pepper. • Pour in the water and bring to a boil. Cook for 5 minutes. • Pour the sauce over the sardines and let marinate for 1 hour before serving.

Serves 4 • Prep: 15 min + 1 hr to marinate • Cooking: 20 min • Level: 1

- 24 large sardines, gutted and cleaned
- 2/3 cup/100 g all-purpose/plain flour
- 1/2 cup/125 ml extra-virgin olive oil
- 5 cloves garlic, finely chopped
- 1 teaspoon red pepper flakes
- 1 tablespoon white wine vinegar
- 1 bay leaf
- 1 sprig rosemary
- salt and freshly ground black pepper
- 1 cup/250 ml water

Seafood

SHRIMP WITH CHOCOLATE

Gambas con chocolate

- ¹/₂ cup/125 ml extra-virgin olive oil
- 2 medium onions, finely chopped
- 1 bay leaf
- 1 teaspoon finely chopped fresh thyme
- 1 small ham bone (optional)
- 2 lb/1 kg firm-ripe tomatoes, diced
- 1 quart/1 liter water
- 12 shrimp, each weighing about 2 oz/ 60 g, peeled
- salt and freshly ground black pepper
- 3 cloves garlic, very finely chopped
- ¹/₂ cup/50 g finely chopped toasted almonds
- 4 oz/125 g semisweet/plain chocolate, melted

Try this modern Spanish dish for a mouthwateringly tasty experience. Use a good-quality dark chocolate.

Heat 2 tablespoons of oil in a medium saucepan over medium heat. Sauté the onions, bay leaf, thyme, and ham bone, if using, for 8–10 minutes, or until the onions are lightly browned. • Stir in the tomatoes. Lower the heat and cook, covered, for 15 minutes. • Pour in the water and let it reduce by half. • Strain the sauce. • Season with salt and pepper. • Heat the remaining 6 tablespoons oil in a large frying pan over medium heat. Fry the shrimp for 8–10 minutes, or until cooked. • Remove from the pan, reserve the oil, and arrange the shrimp in a serving dish, covering with the sauce. • Mix the garlic, almonds, and chocolate in a small bowl. Pour in ¹/₄ cup (60 ml) of the reserved oil and spoon over the shrimp.

Serves 4 • Prep: 20 min • Cooking: 35 min • Level: 2

FISH STEW

Caldereta de pescado

Heat the oil in a large saucepan over medium heat. Sauté the leeks and onion for 8–10 minutes, or until lightly browned. • Stir in the tomatoes, potatoes, fennel, and bell pepper. • Add the fish and eel. Pour in the wine and cook until reduced by half. • Pour in the stock and cook over high heat for 10 minutes. • Add the saffron, garlic, and almonds. Season with salt and pepper. • Serve hot.

Serves 6 • Prep: 20 min • Cooking: 25–30 min • Level: 1

- ¹/₄ cup/60 ml extra-virgin olive oil
- 2 leeks, white parts only, finely chopped
- 1 medium onion, finely chopped
- 3 sun-dried tomatoes, finely chopped
- 1 lb/500 g potatoes, peeled and cut into small cubes
- 1 sprig wild fennel
- 1 red bell pepper/capsicum, seeded and coarsely chopped
- 6 lb/3 kg firm-textured fish, such as snapper or bream, cleaned, filleted, deboned, and thinly sliced
- 2 lb/1 kg eel or swordfish, cleaned and thinly sliced
- 1 cup/250 ml dry white wine
- 1 quart/1 liter fish stock
- 4 saffron threads
- 3 cloves garlic, finely chopped
- ¹/₄ cup/40 g almonds, coarsely chopped
- salt and freshly ground black pepper

Shrimp with chocolate

HAKE WITH GREEN BEANS

Merluza con judías verdes

- ¹/₄ cup/60 ml extra-virgin olive oil
- 5 cloves garlic, finely chopped
- 4 hake or cod steaks, each weighing about 8 oz/200 g, cleaned
- ¹/₄ cup/30 g all-purpose/plain flour
- 1 cup/250 ml fish stock
- 8 oz/200 g green beans, cut into small lengths
- 1 tablespoon finely chopped fresh parsley
- salt and freshly ground black pepper

Heat the oil in a large frying pan over medium heat. • Sauté the garlic for 5 minutes, or until translucent. • Dip the fish in the flour, making sure the steaks are well covered. • Add the fish to the skillet and cook for 5 minutes on each side. Remove from the pan and set aside. • Pour in the stock and add the green beans. • Cook for 10–12 minutes, or until the beans are tender. • Return the hake to the pan and cook for 3–4 minutes, or until the fish is warmed through. Add the parsley and season with salt and pepper. • Serve hot.

Serves 4 • Prep: 20 min • Cooking: 35–40 min • Level: 1

SAFFRON FISH STEW

Estofado de pescado con azafràn

Soak the mussels in a large pot of cold salted water. Let stand for 1 hour. • Drain well and sauté in a large frying pan over high heat until they have all opened. Remove the mussels and discard the shells. • Heat the oil in a large saucepan over medium heat. Sauté the onion for 5–7 minutes, or until translucent. • Add the garlic, bell pepper, and ham and cook for 2 minutes. • Stir in the tomatoes, bay leaf, and oregano. Cook for 10–15 minutes, or until the sauce has thickened. • Add the fish to the sauce and pour in the wine and stock. Season with salt and add the saffron. • Bring to a boil, stirring often. • Add the mussels, shrimp, and crabmeat. Cover and cook for 5 minutes. • Season with salt and pepper and transfer to a large serving dish. Garnish with the parsley and lemon.

Serves 4 • Prep: 20 min + 1 hr to stand • Cooking: 30–35 min • Level: 2

- 15 mussels in shell
- ¹/₄ cup/60 ml extra-virgin olive oil
- 1 medium onion, finely chopped
- 3 cloves garlic, finely chopped
- 1 red bell pepper, seeded and finely chopped
- 2 tablespoons finely chopped ham
- 1 cup/250 ml chopped tomatoes
- 1 bay leaf
- ¹/₄ teaspoon dried oregano
- 1 lb/500 g swordfish steaks, well-washed and cut into small chunks
- ¹/₂ cup/125 ml dry white wine
- 2 cups/500 ml fish stock
- salt
- 3 saffron threads
- 12 shrimp, shelled and cleaned
- 8 oz/250 g crabmeat
- salt and freshly ground black pepper
- 3 tablespoons finely chopped fresh parsley
- 1 lemon, quartered

Mediterranean seafood

Covering almost 1 million square miles (2.5 million square km), the Mediterranean is the world's largest inland sea. It is home to a huge variety of fish and seafood, including tuna, sardines, anchovies, hake, flounder, sole, turbot, red mullet, grouper, sea bream, and many others. Many parts of the rocky coastlines are well-stocked with crabs, lobsters, prawns, shrimp, clams, and mussels. Every country has its own very active fishing industry, which is causing grave concern about overfishing in many areas.

Oxtails, Jumilla-style

OXTAILS, JUMILLA-STYLE

Rabo di toro de Jumilla

- 2 cups/500 ml water
- 2 bay leaves
- 3 large oxtails
- salt and freshly ground black pepper
- ¹/₄ cup/60 ml extra-virgin olive oil
- 2 lb/1 kg onions, finely chopped
- 2 cups/500 ml dry red wine
- 2 lb/1 kg potatoes, cut into cubes

This recipe takes its name from Jumilla, a town near Alicante in the Southeast of Spain.

Bring the water and bay leaves to a boil in a large saucepan. • Season the oxtails with salt and pepper. • Heat the oil in a large frying pan over medium heat. Sauté the oxtails for 10–15 minutes, or until well browned. • Remove from the pan and place in the saucepan of boiling water. • Sauté the onions in the same pan for 8–10 minutes, or until lightly browned. Add the onions to the water. • Add the wine, cover, and cook for 2¹/₂–3 hours, or until the meat is tender. • About 20 minutes before the oxtails are cooked, sauté the potatoes in the pan used to cook the oxtails until tender. • Place the potatoes on a serving dish with the oxtails and spoon the sauce over the top.

Serves 6–8 • Prep: 15 min • Cooking: 3¹/₂ hr • Level: 1

CHICKEN WITH ALMONDS AND SAFFRON

Pollo en pepitoria

Heat the oil in a large deep frying pan over medium heat. • Brown the chicken for 10–12 minutes, or until golden brown. Remove from the pan. • In the same pan, sauté the onion for 8–10 minutes, or until lightly browned. • Pour in the wine and cook until it has evaporated. Return the chicken to the pan. • Pour in 3 cups (750 ml) stock. Cover and cook over medium heat for 20 minutes, or until the chicken is almost tender. • Process the egg yolks, almonds, garlic, saffron, parsley, and the remaining 1 cup (250 ml) chicken stock in a food processor until smooth. • Add this mixture to the chicken and cook for 10 minutes more. • Serve hot.

Serves 4 • Prep: 20 min • Cooking: 50 min • Level: 1

- ¹/₄ cup/60 ml extra-virgin olive oil
- 1 chicken, weighing about 2 lb/1 kg, cut into small chunks
- 1 large onion, finely chopped
- 2 cups/500 ml dry white wine
- 1 quart/1 liter chicken stock or broth
- 2 hard-cooked egg yolks
- ³/₄ cup/120 g whole almonds
- 2 cloves garlic, peeled and left whole
- 4–6 saffron threads
- small bunch parsley

FREE-RANGE CHICKEN WITH OLIVES

Pollo a la vinegreta de olivas

- ¹/₂ cup/125 ml extra-virgin olive oil
- 2 medium onions, finely chopped
- 2 leeks, white parts only, finely chopped
- 1 bay leaf
- 1 teaspoon finely fresh chopped thyme
- 1 teaspoon finely chopped fresh oregano
- ³/₄ cup/180 ml sherry vinegar
- 1 quart/1 liter water
- 1 free-range chicken, weighing about 6 lb/3 kg, cut into 12 pieces
- 1 cup/100 g green olives
- 1 cup/100 g black olives

Heat ¹/₄ cup (60 ml) oil in a saucepan over medium heat. Sauté the onions, leeks, bay leaf, thyme, and oregano for 8–10 minutes, or until the onions and leeks are lightly browned. • Pour in the vinegar, water, and remaining ¹/₄ cup (60 ml) oil. • Add the chicken to the saucepan. • Cover and cook over low heat for 50 minutes, or until tender. • Add the olives 5 minutes before the chicken is cooked. Remove the bay leaf. Bone the chicken and serve hot with beans.

Serves 4–6 • Prep: 20 min • Cooking: 1 hr • Level: 1

MARINATED RABBIT

Conejo escabechado

This recipe is equally delicious made with chicken instead of rabbit.

Heat 2 tablespoons of oil in a large frying pan over medium heat. Sauté the onion, leek, and carrot for 8–10 minutes, or until lightly browned. • Add the red pepper flakes, garlic, bay leaf, rosemary, thyme, vinegar, sherry, remaining ¹/₄ cup (60 ml) oil, and the rabbit. • Cover and cook for 25–30 minutes, or until the rabbit is tender. Season with salt and pepper. • Remove from the heat and let cool completely. • Transfer to a serving plate and marinate in the refrigerator for 12 hours before serving. • Serve at room temperature.

Serves: 4 • Prep: 20 min + 12 hr to marinate • Cooking: 40 min • Level: 1

- ¹/₃ cup/80 ml extra-virgin olive oil
- 1 medium onion, finely chopped
- 1 leek, white part only, finely chopped
- 1 carrot, finely chopped
- 1 teaspoon red pepper flakes
- 4 cloves garlic, finely chopped
- 1 bay leaf
- 1 tablespoon finely chopped fresh rosemary
- 1 tablespoon finely chopped fresh thyme
- ¹/₄ cup/60 ml white distilled vinegar
- ¹/₄ cup/60 ml dry sherry
- salt and freshly ground black pepper
- 1 rabbit, weighing about 2 lb/1 kg, cut into 8 pieces

Free-range chicken with olives

Poultry & Meats

LAMB SHOULDER WITH DRIED FRUIT

Paletilla de cordero lacada con frutos secos

- 1 bone-in lamb shoulder roast, weighing about 4 lb/2 kg
- fresh rosemary leaves
- freshly ground black pepper
- $^2/_3$ cup/150 g butter
- $^1/_2$ cup/125 ml brandy
- $^1/_2$ cup/125 ml port
- $^1/_2$ cup/125 g prunes
- $^1/_2$ cup/125 g dried apricots
- 3 tablespoons honey

Preheat the oven to 450°F/230°C/gas 8. • Score the lamb shoulder in four places, taking care not to cut it all the way through, only to cleave the bone. Rub the surface and interior with the rosemary and sprinkle with pepper. • Place the lamb in a baking dish and dot with the butter. • Bake the lamb for 10 minutes, then turn it. • Bake for 10 minutes more, then drizzle with the brandy and port, and turn it. • Bake for 5 minutes more and add the prunes and apricots. Drizzle with the honey. • Return to the oven and continue cooking, basting frequently, for 30–35 minutes, or until the juices run clear. Transfer to a serving plate and spoon the prunes and apricots over the top. • Reduce the sauce a little and pour over the meat. • Serve hot.

Serves 4–6 • Prep: 15 min • Cooking: 1 hr • Level: 2

DUCK WITH PEAR SAUCE

Pato con salsa di pera

Season the duck with salt and pepper. • Sauté the pears and onion in the butter in a Dutch oven (casserole) over medium heat until lightly browned. • Increase the heat to high and add the seasoned duck, turning until browned all over. • Pour in the wine and cook for 2 minutes. • Pour in the stock and season with salt and pepper. Cook over low heat for 40–50 minutes, or until the stock has reduced by half and the duck is tender. • Remove the duck from the pan and set aside. • Process the sauce and cooking juices in a food processor or blender until smooth. • Carve the duck and serve hot with the sauce.

Serves 4 • Prep: 35 min • Cooking: 1 hr • Level: 2

- 1 duck, weighing 3 lb/1.5 kg, cleaned and boned
- salt and freshly ground white pepper
- 8 firm ripe pears, quartered
- 1 red onion, finely chopped
- $^1/_4$ cup/60 g butter, cut in chunks
- $^1/_2$ cup/125 ml dry white wine
- 1 quart/1 liter chicken stock or broth

Dining Spanish-style

Spaniards love fine food and are prepared to dedicate a great deal of time and money to eating well. A typical day begins with a light breakfast, usually just a café solo (an espresso) and a pastry. Work stops at 1:00 P.M., when many people gather in bars for an aperitif and an endless array of snacks, or tapas. The tapas custom started in Andalusia to highlight the flavors of the region's sumptuous aperitifs, including the famous amontillado sherry. The tapas hour is followed by the main meal of the day, la comida. This is the time for a relaxing lunch, comprising, at the very least, an appetizer and a main course. Many Spaniards still enjoy a siesta, or short sleep, after lunch before returning to work around 4:00 P.M. The working day ends at around 8:00 P.M., and the festivities begin again with a second tapas hour and supper at around 10:00 P.M.

Poultry & Meats

VEAL IN MUSHROOM–WINE SAUCE

Fricando

- 1¼ lb/650 g veal, thinly sliced
- salt
- ⅓ cup/50 g all-purpose/plain flour
- ¼ cup/60 ml extra-virgin olive oil
- 1 medium onion, finely chopped
- 1 medium tomato, coarsely chopped
- 1 cup/250 ml dry white wine
- 2 tablespoons dried mushrooms (soaked in warm water for 15 minutes)

Season the veal slices with salt. Dredge in the flour. • Heat the oil in a large frying pan over medium heat. Fry the veal slices for 5–7 minutes, or until the meat is cooked. • Transfer to a plate and cover to keep warm. • Sauté the onion and tomato in the same oil for 8–10 minutes, or until the onion is lightly browned. • Pour in the wine and season with salt. Add the mushrooms and their liquid and cook for 5 minutes. • Add the veal slices and cook for 5 minutes more, or until the veal is heated through. • Serve hot.

Serves 4–6 • Prep: 15 min • Cooking: 30 min • Level: 1

MARINATED PORK CHOPS

Chuletas de cerdo marinado

Mix the wine, orange zest and juice, onion, and thyme in a small bowl. • Place the pork chops in a baking dish and cover with the wine mixture. • Cover with aluminum foil and refrigerate for 12 hours. • Drain well, reserving the liquid. • Turn on the broiler (grill). • Broil the chops 4 to 6 inches (10–15 cm) from the heat source for 8–10 minutes on each side, or until the meat is well cooked. • Transfer the chops to a serving plate and cover to keep warm. • Strain the reserved liquid into a small saucepan and bring to a boil. Add the bouillon cube and simmer over low heat for 10 minutes. • Remove from the heat and stir in the cream. • Season the chops with salt and pepper. Spoon the sauce over the top and serve hot.

Serves 4 • Prep: 15 min + 12 hr to marinate • Cooking: 30 min Level: 1

- 1 cup/250 ml dry white wine
- grated zest and juice of 2 oranges
- 1 small onion, finely chopped
- 1 tablespoon finely chopped fresh thyme
- 4 large bone-in pork chops
- 1 bouillon/stock cube
- ½ cup/125 ml heavy/double cream
- salt and freshly ground black pepper

Veal in mushroom–wine sauce

Stuffed pork loin

STUFFED PORK LOIN

Lomo relleno

- 3 lb/1.5 kg boneless pork loin
- 1 cup/250 g prunes
- 3/4 cup/90 g diced bacon
- salt and freshly ground black pepper
- 1/4 cup/60 ml extra-virgin olive oil
- 2 medium red onions, finely chopped
- 3 cloves garlic, peeled
- 1 bay leaf
- 1 tablespoon finely chopped fresh thyme
- 1 tablespoon all-purpose/plain flour
- 2 cups/500 ml dry white wine
- 3 quarts/3 liters beef stock or broth

Preheat the oven to 400°F/200°C/gas 6. • Use a long sharp knife to cut a 1-inch (2-cm) round hole in the center of the pork loin. Fill with the prunes. • Arrange half of the bacon in a large baking dish. • Place the pork on top and season with salt and pepper. Top with the remaining bacon and drizzle with the oil. • Roast for 40–45 minutes, or until browned all over, turning occasionally. • Remove the pork from the baking dish and add the onions, garlic, bay leaf, and thyme. Let brown in the juices, then return the pork to the dish. • Continue until the juices run clear. Remove the pork from the dish. • Skim the fat from the cooking juices and pour into a medium saucepan. Add the flour, stirring constantly. Pour in the wine. • Cook for 5–10 minutes, or until reduced and thickened. • Pour in the stock. Bring to a boil and cook for 1 hour over low heat. • Strain the sauce. • Slice the pork loin and arrange on a large serving plate. Spoon the sauce over the top.

Serves 4 • Prep: 20 min • Cooking: 2 hr • Level: 2

CHICKEN WITH SPANISH HAM

Pollo con jamón serrano

Jamón serrano is a cured ham, similar to Italian prosciutto or Parma ham. It is popular all over Spain, where it is served thinly sliced as a tapa. *It is also diced and used to add flavor to many cooked dishes.*

Use a rolling pin to flatten the chicken breasts. • Mix the butter, garlic, and oregano in a small bowl. Season with salt and pepper. • Use a thin metal spatula to spread half the butter mixture evenly over the chicken. • Place four slices of jamón serrano on top of each chicken breast. • Use your fingertips to roll up the chicken breast tightly. Use toothpicks to secure the rolls. • Spread the remaining butter mixture over the rolls. • Turn on the broiler (grill). • Broil the chicken rolls 4 to 6 inches (10–15 cm) from the heat source for 15–20 minutes, turning them often, or until the chicken is cooked. • Transfer to serving plates and remove the toothpicks before serving.

Serves 4 • Prep: 15 min • Cooking: 15–20 min • Level: 1

- 4 boneless, skinless chicken breasts
- 1/2 cup/125 g butter
- 2 cloves garlic, finely chopped
- 1 teaspoon dried oregano
- salt and freshly ground black pepper
- 16 slices jamón serrano or prosciutto/Parma ham

Desserts

CATALONIAN CREAM

Crema catalana

- ¹/₃ cup/50 g cornstarch/cornflour
- 1 quart/1 liter milk
- grated zest of 1 lemon
- 1 teaspoon ground cinnamon
- 9 large egg yolks
- 1¹/₄ cups/250 g granulated sugar

Far a delicious caramel topping, mix ¹/₄ cup (50 g) of sugar with 2 tablespoons of cold water over low heat until caramelized. Drizzle the caramel over the chilled custards just before serving.

Dissolve the cornstarch in ¹/₂ cup (125 ml) milk in a small bowl. Set aside. • Bring the remaining 3¹/₂ cups (825 ml) milk, lemon zest, and cinnamon to a boil in a large saucepan over medium heat. • Beat the egg yolks and sugar with an electric mixer at high speed until pale and thick. • Slowly pour the boiling milk into the eggs and sugar. Return to the heat and gradually add the cornstarch mixture, stirring constantly. • Bring to a boil and cook 2–3 minutes over low heat, stirring constantly. • Remove from the heat and pour into individual ramekins. • Chill in the refrigerator for at least 2 hours before serving.

Serves 8 • Prep: 30 min • Cooking: 10 min • Level: 1

BAKED APPLES STUFFED WITH RICE AND MILK

Manzanas asadas rellenas de arroz con leche

Preheat the oven to 400°F/200°C/gas 6. • Butter a large baking dish. • Soak the rice in the milk in a large saucepan for 2 hours. • Bring the rice mixture to a boil over medium heat. Lower the heat and simmer for 10–15 minutes, or until tender. • Add the ¹/₂ cup (100 g) sugar and bring to a boil. • Remove from the heat and set aside. • Cut the tops off the apples and reserve. Core the apples and use a teaspoon to hollow out the insides. • Arrange the apples in the baking dish. Drizzle with the Marsala and water. • Bake for 30–40 minutes, or until softened, basting them often with their own juice. • Stuff with the rice and sprinkle with cinnamon. • Replace the tops and dust with the extra sugar. Return to the oven for 10–15 minutes, or until golden brown.

Serves 6 • Prep: 20 min + 2 hr to soak • Cooking: 40–55 min • Level: 1

- 2 cups/400 g short-grain rice
- 1 quart/1 liter milk
- ¹/₂ cup/100 g granulated sugar + extra to dust
- 6 large apples
- 6 tablespoons Marsala wine
- 2 tablespoons cold water
- ¹/₂ teaspoon ground cinnamon

Catalonian cream

Desserts

FRIED MILK FRITTERS

Latte frita

- 3 cups/750 ml milk
- ½ cup/100 g granulated sugar
- grated zest of 1 lemon
- ½ teaspoon vanilla extract
- ¾ cup/125 g semolina flour
- ½ cup/75 g all-purpose/plain flour
- 2 large eggs
- ¼ cup/30 g confectioners' sugar, to dust

Cook the milk with the granulated sugar and lemon zest in a large saucepan over low heat. Bring to a boil and gradually add the semolina, stirring constantly. • Simmer for 15 minutes, stirring all the time, making sure that the mixture does not stick to the pan bottom. • Stir in the vanilla. • Pour the mixture onto a 11 x 7-inch (28 x 18-cm) baking sheet. Let cool completely. • Sift the flour onto a medium plate. • Beat the eggs in a small bowl until frothy. • Cut the milk mixture into squares. Dip in the flour until well coated, then pass through the beaten eggs. • Heat the oil in a large deep frying pan until very hot. • Fry the fritters in small batches for 4–5 minutes, or until golden brown all over, turning them during cooking. • Drain well and pat dry on paper towels. • Dust with the confectioners' sugar and serve.

Makes 22–33 fritters • Prep: 20 min + 1 hr to cool • Cooking: 40 min • Level: 3

EGG YOLK NOUGAT

Turron de yema

Finely chop the almonds finely in a food processor and transfer to a medium bowl. Add enough water to prevent any oil from forming. • Whisk the egg yolks and ½ cup (100 g) of sugar in a double boiler until pale and creamy. Cook over low heat, stirring constantly, until the mixture lightly coats a metal spoon or registers 160°F/70°C on an instant-read thermometer. Immediately plunge the pan into a bowl of ice water and stir until the egg mixture has cooled. • Add the egg mixture to the almonds, stirring until well blended. • Stir the remaining 1½ cups (300 g) sugar, lemon zest, and cinnamon in a small saucepan over medium heat. • Cook for 8–10 minutes, or until golden in color. Add the almond paste and cook, stirring constantly, until the mixture has lost its stickiness, 10 minutes. • Pour the mixture into a 11 x 7-inch (28 x 18-cm) baking tray and freeze for at least 2 hours. • Remove from the freezer and use a toffee hammer to break up the nougat.

Makes 1 tray of nougat • Prep: 30 min + 2 hr to freeze • Level: 2

- 2¾ cups/400 g almonds, blanched and peeled
- 2 teaspoons cold water
- 8 large egg yolks
- 2 cups/400 g granulated sugar
- grated zest of 1 lemon
- ½ teaspoon ground cinnamon

GOOD FRIDAY FRITTERS

Buñuelos de Viernes Santo

- 1¾ cups/430 ml milk
- ½ cup/100 g granulated sugar
- 1 teaspoon ground aniseeds + extra to dust
- ½ teaspoon vanilla extract
- 1½ cups/225 g all-purpose/plain flour
- grated zest of 1 lemon
- ½ teaspoon ground cinnamon
- 4 large eggs
- 4 apples, peeled, cored, and finely chopped
- 2 cups/500 ml olive oil, for frying

Bring the milk, 3 tablespoons of sugar, and aniseeds to a boil in a medium saucepan. Stir in the vanilla. • Sift the flour into a large bowl. • Stir in the lemon zest and cinnamon and make a well in the center. • Pour in the boiling milk mixture and stir until smooth. • Add the eggs, one at a time, until just blended after each addition. • Add the apples. • Heat the oil in a large frying pan to very hot. • Fry tablespoons of the batter in batches for 5–7 minutes, or until golden brown all over. • Drain well on paper towels. • Dust with the remaining sugar and aniseeds.

Serves: 4–6 • Prep: 15 min • Cooking: 20 min • Level: 2

PINE NUT COOKIES

Panellets

Preheat the oven to 400°F/200°C/gas 6. • Butter a large baking sheet. • Mix the sugar, almonds, and water until a smooth marzipan dough is formed. • Cut the dough into small slices and use your hands to shape them into balls the size of walnuts. • Brush with the beaten egg. • Roll in the pine nuts, making sure that the nuts stick. • Place the cookies on the prepared baking sheet. • Bake for 10–15 minutes, or until risen and lightly browned. • Cool the cookies completely on the baking sheet.

Makes 15 cookies • Prep: 20 min • Cooking: 10–15 min • Level: 1

- 2½ cups/500 g granulated sugar
- 5 cups/500 g finely ground almonds
- about ½ cup/125 ml water
- 1 large egg, lightly beaten
- 1 cup/180 g pine nuts

NORTH AFRICA

Full-flavored and often fiery, the cuisines of Morocco, Tunisia, and Algeria combine Middle Eastern and African traditions with those of the northern Mediterranean. With its culinary roots in the nomadic Berber people who invented couscous more than 2,000 years ago, the region has absorbed the flavors of Arabia, Turkey, Spain, France, and the New World to create its own inimitable cuisines.

Grilled salad
(see page 132)

SPICY CARROT APPETIZER

Ommok houria

- 1 lb/500 g carrots, cut into thin strips
- ¹/₄ cup/60 ml extra-virgin olive oil
- 3 cloves garlic, finely chopped
- 2 teaspoons caraway seeds
- 1 teaspoon freshly ground coriander seeds
- 1 teaspoon finely chopped fresh sweet red chile pepper
- 1 tablespoon harissa (see page 133)
- 1 tablespoon white wine vinegar or fresh lemon juice
- salt
- 3 tablespoons capers, to garnish

Lightly boiled carrots are braised in a mixture of harissa and other spices in this traditional Tunisian dish. The spices combine beautifully to counterbalance the natural sweetness of the carrots.

Cook the carrots in a large pot of salted boiling water for 8–10 minutes, or until crunchy-tender. Drain well, reserving 1 cup (250 ml) of the cooking water. • Heat the oil in a large frying pan over medium heat. Sauté the garlic for 5 minutes, or until pale gold. • Add the carrots, reserved water, caraway seeds, coriander, chile, harissa, and vinegar. Season with salt. • Cook over high heat for 8–10 minutes, or until the sauce has reduced. • Remove from heat and let cool. Serve at room temperature, garnished with the capers.

Serves 6 • Prep: 10 min • Cooking: 25 min • Level: 1

GRILLED SALAD

Slata mechouia

Grilled bell peppers and tomatoes are basic ingredients in countless preparations in Mediterranean cuisines. This unusual recipe comes from Tunisia.

Grill the bell peppers, tomatoes, garlic, and chile pepper, if using, on the barbecue or under a broiler (grill) for 12–15 minutes, or until the skins of the bell peppers are blackened. • Seal the bell peppers in a paper bag for 5 minutes to make it easier to remove the skins. Peel the bell peppers and tomatoes while still hot. Cut away the tough parts and remove the seeds. • Use a fork to coarsely mash the bell peppers, chile pepper, tomatoes, and garlic. Add mashed hard-cooked eggs, celery, parsley, capers, and cilantro. • Mix the oil and lemon juice in a small bowl. Drizzle over the vegetables. • Garnish with the remaining hard-cooked egg and olives.

Serves 6 • Prep: 20–25 min • Cooking: 12–15 min • Level: 2

- 6 green bell peppers/capsicums
- 4 large ripe tomatoes
- 4 cloves garlic, peeled and left whole
- 1 fresh red chile pepper, finely chopped (optional)
- 4 hard-cooked eggs, 3 mashed + 1 cut into quarters
- 2 stalks celery, finely chopped
- sprig parsley, finely chopped
- 1 tablespoon capers
- 1 tablespoon finely chopped fresh cilantro/coriander
- 3 tablespoons extra-virgin olive oil
- 1 tablespoon fresh lemon juice
- 1 cup/100 g black olives, to garnish

PRESERVED LEMONS

Lamoun makbouss

- about 2 lb/1 kg lemons, preferably organic
- 1 cup/250 g coarse salt, such as kosher salt

Preserved lemons are stored for about a month before use. They will produce enough juice to marinate, enriching their already full flavor. Serve with chicken, fish, or other meat tajines and also with vegetables, rice, and couscous.

Soak the lemons in cold water for 3–4 days, changing the water daily. • Without slicing all the way through, cut each lemon vertically into four. Open them out carefully, salt generously, then press the quarters back together to make whole lemons. • Insert the lemons into two sterilized 1 quart (1 liter) preserving jars, packing them tightly together. Seal the jars. • Store in a cool dark place for one month.

Makes 2 lb/1 kg lemons • Prep: 30 min + 3–4 days to soak + 1 month to preserve • Level: 2

HONEY AND ONION SAUCE

Sauce de miel et oignons

Serve this recipe with toast or bread as an appetizer, or as a sauce with fried fish or meat.

Bring the onions and water to a boil in a medium saucepan over medium heat • Add the ras-al-hanout and season with salt. • Cover and simmer for 20 minutes. • Lower the heat and continue cooking for 15–20 minutes more, or until the liquid has evaporated and the onions have broken down. • Uncover and cook for 5 minutes over high heat, stirring constantly, until the sauce has reduced to a paste. • Add the oil and honey and cook for 5 minutes more. • Serve hot.

Serves 6 • Prep: 5 min • Cooking: 45–50 min • Level: 1

- 8 medium onions, finely chopped
- 1¹/₂ cups/375 ml water
- 2 teaspoons ras-al-hanout (see page 145)
- salt
- 5 tablespoons extra-virgin olive oil
- 2 tablespoons honey

Brik with tuna

Harissa

Harissa is a fiery red paste made with chile pepper, garlic, coriander, caraway seeds, salt, and olive oil. It also often includes nuts. It is used both as a flavoring ingredient and as a condiment with meat, fish, and vegetables.

BRIK WITH TUNA

Brik bel thon

- ¹/₂ cup/100 g canned tuna packed in olive oil, drained
- 1 onion, finely chopped
- 1 tablespoon finely chopped fresh parsley
- 10 capers, chopped
- 6 sheets ouarka dough or phyllo dough, cut into 8-inch/20-cm squares
- 4 large eggs
- ¹/₂ cup/125 ml olive oil, for frying
- 1 lemon, thinly sliced, to garnish

The dough for this dish from Tunisia and Algeria is the same as Moroccan ouarka dough. This is a difficult dough to make. Phyllo dough makes an excellent substitute.

Use a fork to crumble the tuna into a medium bowl. Stir in the onion, parsley, and capers. • Place a sheet of dough on a lightly floured work surface. Place half a second sheet of dough on top. Fold to make a square. • Use a tablespoon to place a quarter of the tuna filling in the center of the dough. Carefully break an egg over. Fold the dough over diagonally to form a triangle. Seal the edges well by folding them over repeatedly. • Heat the oil to very hot in a large frying pan. • Fry the brik in batches for 5–7 minutes, or until golden brown all over. • Drain on paper towels, garnish with the lemon slices, and serve hot.

Serves: 4 • Prep: 20 min • Cooking: 15 min • Level: 1

BRIOUATS

Briouats are Moroccan pastries made with thin sheets of ouarka (or phyllo) dough. They are stuffed with a variety of fillings and then folded into triangles or rolled into cigar shapes.

Place the cheese, butter, 7 eggs, and thyme in a saucepan. Season with salt and pepper. Cook over medium heat for 5–7 minutes, or until thickened. • Cut the dough into 4-inch (10-cm) wide sheets. • Place a spoonful of the filling about 1 inch (2.5 cm) from the top edge of each sheet. Fold over one of the corners to form a triangle over the filling, fold this triangle down over the remaining strip of dough, then fold it across, and then down again, leaving a final triangle of dough to fold onto the parcel which now consists of three layers of pastry. Brush the edges with the beaten yolk and seal. • Heat the oil to very hot in a large frying pan. • Fry the briouats for 5–7 minutes, or until lightly browned. • Drain on paper towels and serve hot.

Serves 6 • Prep: 20 min • Cooking: 20 min • Level: 2

- 1²/₃ cups/400 g Jbena cheese or goat cheese
- ¹/₄ cup/60 g butter, melted
- 7 large eggs + 1 large egg yolk, lightly beaten
- 2 teaspoons finely chopped fresh thyme
- salt and freshly ground black pepper
- 10 sheets of ouarka dough or phyllo dough
- 1 cup/250 ml olive oil, for frying

Soups

NORTH AFRICAN FISH SOUP

Chorba belhaut

- 2 lb/1 kg mixed firm-textured fish, cleaned, boned, and cut into small pieces
- 1½ tablespoons fresh lemon juice
- 4–6 threads saffron, crumbled
- ⅛ teaspoon salt
- ¼ cup/60 ml extra-virgin olive oil
- 3 large red bell peppers/capsicums, seeded and cut into thin strips
- 2 onions, finely chopped
- 4 cloves garlic, chopped
- 4 large ripe tomatoes, finely chopped
- 1 stalk celery, chopped
- 1 carrot, finely chopped
- 4 sprigs fennel
- 1 bay leaf
- grated zest of 1 orange
- 2 quarts/2 liters water
- ¼ cup/50 g bulgur
- 20 capers
- ¼ teaspoon ground cumin

Place the fish in a large bowl and drizzle with the lemon juice. Add half the saffron and salt. Stir well and set aside for 15 minutes. • Heat the oil in a large saucepan over medium heat. • Sauté the bell peppers for 8–10 minutes, or until slightly softened. Transfer to a plate and set aside. • In the same pan, cook the onions, garlic, tomatoes, celery, carrot, fennel, bay leaf, and orange zest for 5 minutes. • Pour in the water and bring to a boil. Add the fish and simmer for 15–20 minutes, or until cooked. Remove the fish from the pan and cover with a serving plate to keep warm. • Return the stock to a boil and add the bulgur. Cook for 15–20 minutes. • Remove from the heat, and stir in the capers, remaining saffron, and cumin. • Place the fish in individual soup bowls and ladle the soup over the top. Serve hot.

Serves 6–8 • Prep: 30 min + 15 min to marinate fish • Cooking: 45–55 min • Level: 1

FAVA BEAN SOUP

Soupe de fève

- 2 lb/1 kg dried fava/broad beans, soaked overnight and drained
- 1 lb/500 g potatoes, peeled and cubed
- 2 cloves garlic, chopped
- cold water
- salt and paprika
- 2 teaspoons harissa (see page 133)
- 2 teaspoons ground cumin
- 1½ tablespoons fresh lemon juice
- ⅓ cup/80 ml extra-virgin olive oil

Use a clean kitchen towel to gently rub and remove the skins from the fava beans. • Place the fava beans, potatoes, and garlic in a large saucepan of cold water over medium heat. Bring to a boil, lower the heat, and simmer, covered, for 50–60 minutes, or until the beans are very tender. Season with salt and paprika. • Puree the beans in their liquid in a blender. Cook over low heat for 15–20 minutes, or until the soup is thick. • Add the harissa, cumin, and lemon juice. Drizzle with the oil. Serve hot or at room temperature.

Serves 6–8 • Prep: 15 min + overnight to soak beans • Cooking: 70–80 min • Level: 1

FRAGRANT MUTTON SOUP

Harira

This delicious soup is made with mutton, beans, and a harmonious array of spices. It is a traditional starter during the holy month of Ramadan and is usually accompanied by something sweet, such as dried dates or figs. It is a very popular dish, and variations are served right across North Africa, usually decorated with vermicelli, rice, or m'hamssa (large-grain couscous).

Place the mutton, butter, onions, celery, ½ tablespoon parsley, ½ tablespoon cilantro, cinnamon, saffron, and ginger in a large saucepan. Season with salt and pepper. Stir over medium heat until the butter has melted. • Pour in 1 quart (1 liter) of water. Bring to a boil and cook for 25–30 minutes, or until reduced by half. • Stir in the garbanzo beans and lentils. • Cook over medium heat for 70–80 minutes, or until the lentils are tender. • Stir in the tomatoes, 2 quarts (2 liters) of water, and the remaining parsley and cilantro. Bring to a boil, lower the heat, and simmer for 10 minutes more. • Add the vermicelli or rice, if using. • Mix the flour and the remaining 2 cups (500 ml) of water, stirring constantly, to prevent lumps from forming. • Remove from the heat and add the flour mixture, stirring constantly. • Return to the heat and cook for 15 minutes more, stirring constantly. The soup should not be too thick. Stir in the lemon juice. Serve hot.

Serves 6–8 • Prep: 15 min + overnight to soak beans • Cooking: 125–145 min • Level: 2

- 1 lb/500 g boneless mutton or lamb, cut up into small chunks
- 2 tablespoons clarified butter
- 2 onions, finely chopped
- 1 stalk celery, finely chopped
- 1 tablespoon finely chopped fresh parsley
- 1 tablespoon finely chopped fresh cilantro/coriander
- 1 stick cinnamon
- 4–6 threads saffron, crumbled
- ⅛ teaspoon ground ginger
- salt and freshly ground black pepper
- 3½ quarts/3.5 liters cold water
- 2 cups/200 g dried garbanzo beans/chickpeas, soaked overnight and drained
- 2½ cups/250 g brown lentils
- 2 lb/1 kg firm-ripe tomatoes, peeled and coarsely chopped
- ½ cup/100 g vermicelli or rice (optional)
- 3 tablespoons all-purpose/plain flour
- 2 tablespoons fresh lemon juice

MARINATED FISH WITH TOMATOES AND OLIVES

Poisson avec chermoula

Chermoula

- 5 cloves garlic, finely chopped
- 1 small onion, finely chopped
- 15 leaves cilantro/ coriander, finely chopped
- 1 teaspoon freshly ground cumin
- 2 teaspoons paprika
- 1/3 cup/80 ml extra-virgin olive oil
- 3 tablespoons fresh lemon juice
- 1/8 teaspoon salt

- 1 white-fleshed fish, weighing about 3 lb/1.5 kg, such as sea bass or bream, cleaned
- 1/4 cup/30 g finely chopped fresh parsley
- 1 1/2 lb/750 g firm-ripe tomatoes, thinly sliced
- 2 cups/200 g pitted green olives

Chermoula is a mix of herbs and spices used to marinate or stuff fish. Recipes vary from village to village and even from family to family.

Chermoula: Mix the garlic, onion, cilantro, cumin, paprika, oil, lemon juice, and salt in an oval dish into the which the fish will fit snugly. • Add the fish, ensuring that some of the sauce penetrates the belly. Cover with aluminum foil and marinate for 2 hours. • Preheat the oven to 425°F/220°C/ gas 7. • Arrange the parsley in an overproof baking dish and place the fish on top. Cover completely with the tomato slices. Spoon the chermoula over the top. • Bake for 25 minutes, then arrange the olives around the sides of the fish. • Bake for 10–15 minutes more, or until very well cooked. • Serve hot.

Serves 6 • Prep: 15 min + 2 hr to marinate • Cooking: 35–40 min • Level: 1

SHRIMP IN TOMATO SAUCE

Crevettes en sauce de tomate

This recipe is from Algeria, although there is also a Tunisian version that includes a pinch of freshly ground cumin seeds.

Cook the oil, tomatoes, garlic, paprika, chile pepper, and bay leaves in a large saucepan over medium heat for 10–15 minutes, or until the sauce has reduced. Add the shrimp and water. • Cook for 12–15 minutes, or until the shrimp are tender. Season with salt and pepper. • Serve hot, garnished with the parsley.

Serves 6–8 • Prep: 15 min • Cooking: 20–30 min • Level: 1

- 1/4 cup/60 ml extra-virgin olive oil
- 10 oz/300 g firm-ripe tomatoes, halved, seeded, and coarsely chopped
- 3 cloves garlic, finely chopped
- 1 tablespoon paprika
- 1 fresh chile pepper, sliced, or 1/2 red bell pepper/capsicum, sliced into thin strips
- 2 bay leaves
- 2 lb/1 kg shrimp, peeled
- 1/2 cup/125 ml water
- salt and freshly ground black pepper
- 1 tablespoon finely chopped fresh parsley

Marinated fish with tomatoes and olives

Stuffed sardines

STUFFED FISH

Hout mehchi

- 1¹/₂ cups/300 g short-grain rice
- 2 cups/400 g walnuts, toasted and coarsely chopped (reserve 10 whole to garnish)
- ¹/₂ teaspoon saffron threads
- ¹/₂ teaspoon ground ginger
- 2 teaspoons butter, softened
- 1 tablespoon ground cinnamon
- 1 tablespoon orange-flower water
- salt and freshly ground black pepper
- 1 white-fleshed fish, weighing about 3 lb/1.5 kg, such as sea bass, grouper, or bream, cleaned
- 1 tablespoon vegetable oil
- 3 large onions, finely chopped
- ¹/₂ cup/125 ml water
- juice of ¹/₂ lemon
- ¹/₄ cup/40 g slivered almonds, toasted

These ingredients and seasonings are especially typical of North African cuisine. The preparation is simple, but the flavors are complex and refined.

Cook the rice in a large saucepan of salted boiling water for 15–25 minutes. Drain well. • Mix the rice, walnuts, ¹/₈ teaspoon saffron, ¹/₈ teaspoon ginger, butter, 1 teaspoon cinnamon, and orange-flower water in a large bowl. Season with salt and pepper. • Stuff the fish with the filling and stitch the opening in the fish's belly with thread. • Heat the oil in a Dutch oven (casserole) over medium heat. • Sauté the onion for 8–10 minutes, or until lightly browned. Add the remaining spices. • Pour in the water and lemon juice. Place the fish on top. • Cover and cook over very low heat for 35–40 minutes, or until the fish is cooked. • Transfer the fish to a serving plate. Spoon the onion sauce over the top and sprinkle with the reserved walnuts and the almonds.

Serves 4 • Prep: 25–35 min • Cooking: 45–55 min • Level:2

STUFFED SARDINES

Sardine mehchi

Fried sardines are a standard item on the menus of restaurants all along the Algerian coast. Ask your local fish market to clean the sardines for you.

Mix the egg, garlic, parsley, cilantro, harissa, cumin, salt, pepper, and lemon juice in a large bowl. • Spoon some filling into each sardine. • Dredge the sardines in the flour, shaking off any excess. • Heat the oil in a large frying pan to very hot. • Fry the sardines in batches for 8–10 minutes, or until crispy. • Serve hot or at room temperature, seasoned with salt and garnished with lemon quarters.

Serves 6 • Prep: 10 min • Cooking: 36–40 min • Level: 1

- 1 large egg, lightly beaten
- 3 cloves garlic, finely chopped
- ¹/₄ cup/30 g finely chopped fresh parsley
- ¹/₄ cup/30 g finely chopped fresh cilantro/coriander
- 1 tablespoon harissa (see page 133)
- ¹/₂ teaspoon freshly ground cumin
- salt and freshly ground black pepper
- 1 tablespoon fresh lemon juice
- 2 lb/1 kg medium fresh sardines, heads cut off and gutted
- ²/₃ cup/100 g all-purpose/plain flour, or more if needed
- 1 cup/250 ml olive oil, for frying
- lemon quarters, to garnish

Poultry, Lamb & Eggs

Poultry pie

Bisteeya

- 3 tablespoons extra-virgin olive oil
- 4 large onions, finely chopped
- 2 chickens, weighing about 5 lb/3 kg in total, cut into chunks
- 1 tablespoon finely chopped fresh parsley
- $1/2$ teaspoon ground cinnamon + extra, to dust
- 8–10 threads saffron, crumbled
- $1/2$ teaspoon freshly grated nutmeg
- $1/2$ cup/100 g + 1 tablespoon granulated sugar
- salt and freshly ground black pepper
- 1 cup/250 ml water
- 8 large eggs + 1 large egg yolk, lightly beaten
- $2^1/2$ cups/250 g almonds, toasted and coarsely chopped
- 23 sheets ouarka or phyllo dough
- $2/3$ cup/150 g butter, melted

A specialty of the imperial cities of Morocco, a poultry pie is offered on virtually any formal occasion, during holidays, and at parties. Its taste— sweet and salty at the same time—is a key feature of the most refined Moroccan cuisine.

Butter a deep 12-inch (30-cm) round baking pan. • Heat the oil in a large frying pan over medium heat. • Sauté the onions and chicken for 8–10 minutes, or until lightly browned. • Add the parsley, $1/8$ teaspoon cinnamon, saffron, nutmeg, and 1 tablespoon of sugar. Season with salt and pepper. • Cook over high heat, turning the chicken occasionally, until aromatic. • Pour in the water, bring to a boil, and cook over very low heat for 40–45 minutes, or until the meat comes away easily from the bones. • Remove the chicken from the saucepan and set aside, in a warm oven. • Reduce the sauce for 10–15 minutes more. • Gradually add the beaten whole eggs to the sauce, stirring constantly, and cook for 2–3 minutes. Remove from heat. • Stir together the

almonds and remaining $1/2$ cup (100 g) sugar in a small bowl. • Preheat the oven to 300°F/150°C/gas 2. • Bone the chicken. • Place eight sheets of ouarka or phyllo, in the prepared pan, brushing every other sheet with melted butter. Cut away the overhanging dough as you layer it in the pan. • Reinforce with two more sheets of dough brushed with melted butter. • Spoon the sauce over the top and sprinkle with half the almond mixture. • Cover with two more dough sheets. • Top with the chicken meat and the remaining almond mixture. Cover with two more dough sheets. Brush with some beaten egg yolk. • Cover with another eight sheets, brushing every other one with butter. Cover with the remaining sheet. Fold this top sheet under the pie. • Bake for 20 minutes. Turn carefully and bake the other side for 15–20 minutes, or until golden brown. Dust with the cinnamon and serve.
Serves 6–8 • Prep: 40 min • Cooking: 100–120 min • Level: 3

Poultry pie

Lamb tajine with dates

LAMB TAJINE WITH DATES

Sikbadj

- $^1/_3$ cup/80 g butter
- 4 lb/2 kg boneless leg of lamb, cut into small pieces
- 5 onions, finely chopped
- 2 cloves garlic, finely chopped
- 1 teaspoon ground ginger
- 1 teaspoon ground turmeric
- salt
- $1^1/_2$ cups/375 ml water
- 2 lb/1 kg pitted dates
- 3 tablespoons honey
- 1 teaspoon ground cinnamon
- 1 tablespoon sesame seeds, toasted

Melt the butter in a large saucepan over medium heat. • Sauté the lamb, onions, and garlic for 8–10 minutes, or until lightly browned. • Add the ginger, turmeric, and salt. Pour in the water, cover, and cook over low heat for 35–40 minutes, or until the lamb is tender. • Stir in the dates, honey, and cinnamon. • Uncover and cook over low heat for 12–15 minutes more, or until the sauce has reduced. • Serve sprinkled with the sesame seeds.

Serves 4–6 • Prep: 10 min • Cooking: 1 hr • Level: 1

EGGS WITH SPICY SAUSAGE

Ojja bil mergez

- 6 large eggs
- 1 tablespoon harissa (see page 133)
- 1 teaspoon caraway seeds
- salt and freshly ground black pepper
- 3 tablespoons extra-virgin olive oil
- 6 mergez or spicy lamb sausages, cut into $1^1/_2$-inch/4-cm slices
- 3 fresh red chile peppers, thinly sliced
- 2 tablespoons tomato paste

This highly flavored egg-based dish is from Tunisia, where it is made with mergez, *a very spicy lamb sausage. There is also a version with shrimp.*

Beat the eggs, harissa, caraway seeds, salt, and pepper in a large bowl until frothy. • Heat the oil in a large frying pan over medium heat. • Brown the mergez. Add the chiles and cook for 5–7 minutes, or until the chiles have softened slightly. Add the tomato paste. • Pour in the beaten egg mixture. • Cook over low heat, stirring often, until the eggs are cooked but are still soft. • Serve hot.

Serves 6 • Prep: 10 min • Cooking: 15–20 min • Level: 1

CHICKEN TAJINE WITH PRUNES

Tajine de poulet aux pruneaux

Place the chicken, onions, butter, cinnamon, saffron, salt, pepper, and water in a large saucepan. • Cover and cook over low heat for 40–45 minutes, stirring occasionally. • Remove the chicken from the saucepan and cover with a serving plate to keep warm. • Add the prunes to the liquid and continue cooking for 10–15 minutes, or until the prunes have softened. Add the honey and lemon juice and cook over low heat until reduced by half. • Return the chicken to the saucepan and cook for 10 minutes more. • Serve sprinkled with the sesame seeds and almonds and serve hot.

Serves 4–6 • Prep: 15 min • Cooking: 60–70 min • Level: 1

- 1 large chicken, cut into 6–8 pieces
- 3 large onions, chopped
- $^1/_3$ cup/80 g butter
- 1 stick cinnamon
- $^1/_4$ teaspoon saffron threads
- salt and freshly ground black pepper
- $1^1/_2$ cups/375 ml water
- 1 cup/250 g pitted prunes
- 2 tablespoons honey
- 2 tablespoons fresh lemon juice
- 1 tablespoon sesame seeds
- $^3/_4$ cup/120 g almonds

Couscous

Couscous with seven vegetables

Couscous aux sept legumes

- 1 lb/500 g couscous
- 2 cups/500 ml water
- ²/₃ cup/60 g dried garbanzo beans/ chickpeas, soaked overnight and drained
- ¹/₈ teaspoon saffron threads
- 2 large onions, finely chopped
- 3 tomatoes, peeled and chopped
- 1¹/₂ quarts/1.5 liters water
- 3 tablespoons extra-virgin olive oil
- 2 tablespoons butter
- ¹/₂ medium Savoy cabbage, finely shredded
- 3 carrots, thinly sliced
- 1 yellow summer squash, thinly sliced
- 3 zucchini, thinly sliced
- 1²/₃ cups/60 g fresh fava/broad beans
- ¹/₄ cup/45 g raisins
- sprig parsley, finely chopped
- sprig cilantro/coriander, finely chopped
- ¹/₂ teaspoon dried ground chile pepper

This recipe, and the others on this page, explain how to make couscous beginning with the raw grains and cooking them in a traditional cooker made up of two earthenware or metal pots, called a couscoussière. The bottom pot holds the stew, while the top pot, which has a perforated bottom, holds the couscous. The steam rising from the stew cooks the couscous. However, in most parts of Europe and America, couscous is available in its "instant" form, which requires only the addition of hot water and time to soak. If using instant couscous, follow the instructions on the package and make the stew on its own in a heavy-bottomed saucepan or casserole.

If using regular (not instant) couscous, prepare as explained in the note below. • Place the garbanzo beans in the bottom pot of a couscoussière or a two-tiered vegetable steamer with the saffron, onions, tomatoes, and remaining 1 cup (250 ml) water. Bring to a boil and add the oil and butter. • Cover and cook for 30 minutes over very low heat. • Place the couscous in the top pot of the couscoussière and steam for 25 minutes. Remove from heat and work as explained in the note below. • Add the cabbage and carrots to the garbanzo bean mixture. Bring to a boil and cook for 20 minutes. • Stir in the yellow squash, zucchini, fava beans, raisins, parsley, coriander, and chile pepper. Remove the couscous from heat and work as explained in the note below. Cook for 20 minutes. • Spoon the couscous onto a serving plate. Make a well in the center and arrange the vegetable stew on top.
Serves 6 • Prep: 30 min • Cooking: 95 min • Level: 2

Fish couscous

Couscous au poisson

If using regular (not instant) couscous, prepare as explained in the note on below. • Place the heads and tails of the fish, the turnips, some outer cabbage leaves, and 1 stalk celery in a saucepan. Pour in 2 quarts (2 liters) cold water. • Add ¹/₈ teaspoon red pepper and season with black pepper. • Bring to a boil and cook for 15–20 minutes. • Strain the stock and set aside. • Heat the oil in the lower section of a couscoussière or a two-tiered vegetable steamer. • Sauté the onions for 8–10 minutes, or until lightly browned. • Pour in the fish stock, carrots, remaining celery, saffron, cumin, and coriander. Add the remaining water and bring to a boil. • Place the couscous in the top pot of the couscoussière and steam for 25 minutes. • Remove from heat and work as explained in the note below. • Add the tomatoes, zucchini, and remaining cabbage to the mixture in the bottom pot of the couscoussière. Season with salt and cook the stew and couscous for 20 more minutes. • Remove the couscous from heat and work as explained in the note below. • Add the fish to the bottom pan, cover with the top couscous pan and cook for 15–20 more minutes. • Remove the couscous from the heat and add the butter. • Spoon the couscous onto a serving plate. Make a well in the center and arrange the fish stew on top.
Serves 6 • Prep: 30 min • Cooking: 90–100 min • Level: 2

- 1 lb/500 g couscous
- 4 quarts/4 liters + 1 cup (250 ml) water
- 1 white-fleshed fish, weighing about 4 lb/2 kg, such as bream or snapper, cleaned and cut into thick slices (reserve the heads and tails for the stock)
- 2 turnips, peeled and chopped
- 1 small Savoy cabbage, finely shredded (reserve some outer leaves whole)
- 2 stalks celery, chopped
- 1 teaspoon red pepper flakes
- freshly ground black pepper
- 3 tablespoons extra-virgin olive oil
- 3 large onions, finely chopped
- 2 carrots, finely chopped
- 6–8 threads saffron, crumbled
- 1 teaspoon freshly ground cumin
- 1 teaspoon freshly ground coriander
- 1 lb/450 g firm-ripe tomatoes, peeled and chopped
- 3 zucchini/courgettes, thinly sliced
- ¹/₃ cup/80 g butter
- salt

Cooking couscous

If you are able to buy uncooked (not instant) couscous, do try to prepare it according to the traditional method. To begin, rinse 1 lb (500 g) couscous 2 or 3 times, then place it in a large dish and add 1 cup (250 ml) of lightly salted water. Rub the grains with your hands for a few minutes, then place in the couscoussière (or a steamer) and steam for 25 minutes. Remove from the heat and place in a large dish. Add another 1 cup (250 ml) of warm water and stir with a wooden spoon until cool enough to rub with your hands. Return to the couscoussière and cook for another 25–30 minutes. Remove from the heat and work in 2 tablespoons of butter or oil. Serve with the stew.

LAMB COUSCOUS

Couscous à l'agneau

- 1 lb/500 g couscous
- 2 cups/500 ml water
- ¹/₄ cup/60 ml sunflower oil
- 2 large onions, finely chopped
- 1¹/₂ lb/750 g boneless lamb, cut into small pieces
- 1 teaspoon finely chopped ginger
- freshly ground black pepper
- 4–6 threads saffron, crumbled
- 2 fresh chile peppers, finely chopped
- 2 cups/200 g dried garbanzo beans/chick-peas, soaked overnight and drained

- 2 firm-ripe tomatoes, peeled and chopped
- 2 quarts/2 liters water
- 2 turnips, peeled and chopped
- ¹/₂ head Savoy cabbage, shredded
- 1 yellow summer squash, chopped
- 2 zucchini/courgettes, finely chopped
- 1 eggplant/aubergine, cut into cubes
- 1 bunch parsley, finely chopped
- 1 bunch cilantro/coriander, finely chopped
- 2 tablespoons butter

If using regular (not instant) couscous, prepare as explained in the note on page 140. • Heat the oil in the bottom pot of a couscoussière or two-layered vegetable steamer. • Sauté the onion, lamb, ginger, pepper, saffron, and chile peppers for 8–10 minutes, or until lightly browned. • Add the garbanzo beans and tomatoes. Pour in the remaining 1 cup (250 ml) water and bring to a boil. • Place the couscous in the top pot of the couscoussière and steam for 25 minutes. • Cook the lamb mixture and couscous over low heat for another 25 minutes. • Remove the couscous from heat and work as explained in the note on page 140. • Add the turnip and cabbage to the lamb mixture in the bottom pan. Cook for 25 minutes more. • Remove the couscous from heat and work again as explained. • Add the yellow squash, zucchini, eggplant, parsley, and cilantro to the meat in the bottom pot. • Cook the stew and couscous for 25 minutes more. • Remove the couscous from the heat and add the butter. • Spoon the couscous onto a serving plate. Make a well in the center and arrange the stew on top. • Serve hot.

Serves 4–6 • Prep: 30 min • Cooking: 90–100 min • Level: 2

Chicken tajine
with preserved lemon

Tajines

SPINACH TAJINE WITH LAMB

Tajine sebnakh

- 6 tablespoons extra-virgin olive oil
- 2 lb/1 kg fresh spinach, coarsely chopped
- salt and freshly ground black pepper
- 1 teaspoon ground cinnamon
- 12 oz/300 g boneless lamb, cut into small cubes
- 1 large onion, finely chopped
- 1 cup/100 g cooked cannellini beans or garbanzo beans/chickpeas
- 1½ cups/375 ml water
- 4–6 threads saffron, crumbled
- 1¼ cups/150 g freshly grated firm cheese, such as Parmesan
- ½ cup/50 g coarsely grated day-old bread
- 6 large eggs, lightly beaten

Preheat the oven to 350°F/180°C/gas 4. • Butter a baking dish. • Heat 3 tablespoons oil in a large frying pan. • Sauté the spinach with the salt, pepper, and cinnamon over high heat for 8–10 minutes. Set aside. • Heat the remaining oil in a separate pan over medium heat. Sauté the lamb and onion for 8–10 minutes, or until lightly browned. • Add the beans and spinach and pour in the water. Season with salt and pepper and sprinkle with saffron. • Simmer over low heat for 15–20 minutes, or until the sauce has reduced. • Mix in the cheese, bread, eggs, and season with salt. • Spoon the mixture into the baking dish. • Bake for 15–20 minutes. • Serve hot.

Serves 6 • Prep: 15 min • Cooking: 40–50 min • Level: 2

CHICKEN TAJINE WITH PRESERVED LEMON

Djouaz el djedi be' zitoun ouellim

Arrange the chicken in a tajine or large Dutch oven (casserole). • Scoop the flesh from the preserved lemons and cut the zest into thin strips. • Top the chicken with the garlic, preserved lemon flesh, cinnamon, and ginger. Let marinate for 20 minutes. • Add the oil and butter. • Sauté the chicken over high heat for 8–10 minutes, turning often, until golden brown. • Remove the chicken from the tajine and set aside. • In the same tajine, sauté the onion, parsley, and cilantro for 5 minutes. Return the chicken to the tajine and pour in the water. Season with salt and sprinkle with saffron. • Cover and cook over low heat for 25–30 minutes, stirring occasionally. Add more water if the chicken begins to dry out. • Add the preserved lemon zest and olives. Cook for 10 minutes more. • Serve hot.

Serves 4–6 • Prep: 15 min + 20 min to marinate • Cooking: 50–55 min • Level: 1

- 3 lb/1.5 kg chicken, cut into 8 pieces
- 1 Preserved Lemon, quartered (see page 132)
- 1 clove garlic, finely chopped
- 2 teaspoons ground cinnamon
- 1 teaspoon diced fresh ginger
- 2 tablespoons vegetable oil
- 2 tablespoons clarified butter
- 1 large onion, finely chopped
- 1 tablespoon finely chopped fresh parsley
- 1 tablespoon finely chopped fresh cilantro/coriander
- 1 cup/250 ml water
- salt
- 6–8 threads saffron, crumbled
- 15 green olives

TAJINE OF SAVOY CABBAGE

Tajine de chou vert

- 1 Savoy cabbage, finely shredded
- 1 tablespoon extra-virgin olive oil
- 2 cloves garlic, finely chopped
- 1 teaspoon sweet paprika (optional)
- salt and freshly ground black pepper
- 1 Preserved Lemon (see page 132), cut into small pieces
- juice of 1 lemon
- 2 tablespoons water

Vary the vegetable in this tajine according to the season and what you have on hand. Chard, turnips, and broccoli all work well.

Place the cabbage in the tajine or saucepan with the oil, garlic, and paprika, if using. Season with salt and pepper. • Add the preserved lemon, lemon juice, and water. • Cook over very low heat for 35–40 minutes, or until the sauce has reduced by half. • Serve hot.

Serves 6 • Prep: 10 min • Cooking: 35–40 min • Level: 1

Tajines

This dish takes its name from a special cooking pot with a distinctive cone-shaped cover. It is used to cook meat, fish, and vegetables gently in an aromatic stew of herbs and spices. The tajine was probably first devised for toasting barley and wheat. Over time it has evolved into a method of cooking and a tradition handed down over the generations.

Tajines, Stews & Rice

DUCK AND FIG TAJINE

Tajine de canard aux figues

- ¹/₃ cup/80 g butter
- 1 duck, weighing about 4 lb/2 kg, cut into 8 pieces
- 2 onions, finely chopped
- 2 cloves garlic, finely chopped
- 1 teaspoon chopped fresh ginger
- 1 teaspoon ground turmeric
- salt
- 1¹/₂ cups/375 ml water
- 2 tablespoons honey
- 1 teaspoon ground cinnamon
- 1³/₄ lb/850 g fresh figs, chopped, or 1²/₃ cups/400 g dried figs, quartered

This recipe calls for fresh figs, but when figs are out of season, dried may be used. To use, soak in lukewarm water for about 15 minutes and add an extra 5 minutes or so to the cooking time.

Melt the butter in a tajine or saucepan over medium heat. • Sauté the duck, onions, and garlic for 8–10 minutes, or until nicely browned. • Add the ginger, turmeric, and salt. Pour in the water. • Cover and cook over very low heat for 40–45 minutes, or until the duck is tender. • Add the honey and cinnamon and cook for 10 minutes. • Stir in the figs and cook for 5 more minutes.

Serves 6 • Prep: 10 min • Cooking: 65–70 min • Level: 1

LIBYAN STEW

Sharba

This spicy stew is a good example of Libyan cuisine, with its predilection for hot spices.

Heat the oil in a large saucepan over medium heat. • Sauté the onion and beef for 8–10 minutes, or until lightly browned. Add the parsley and cinnamon. • Pour in the water, tomato paste, and salt. • Bring to a boil and cook over low heat for 10 minutes. Add the barley, lower the heat, and cook for 40–45 minutes, or until the barley is tender. • Add the lemon juice and serve hot.

Serves 4 • Prep: 10 min • Cooking: 58–65 min • Level: 1

- 2 tablespoons extra-virgin olive oil or clarified butter
- 1 large onion, finely chopped
- 8 oz/250 g boneless beef or lamb, cut into small pieces
- 1 tablespoon finely chopped fresh parsley
- ¹/₂ teaspoon ground cinnamon
- 2 cups/500 ml water
- 1 teaspoon tomato paste/puree
- salt
- ¹/₂ cup/100 g pearled barley
- 1 tablespoon fresh lemon juice

Libyan stew

Rice with squid

Ras-al-hanout

This spice blend is favored in Moroccan and Tunisian cuisines. It is made from allspice, nutmeg, ginger, turmeric, saffron, peppercorns, cinnamon, and cardamom and is used with vegetables and rice dishes.

RICE WITH SQUID
Riz avec calmar

- 2 cups/400 g long-grain rice
- 4–6 threads saffron, crumbled
- 3 tablespoons extra-virgin olive oil
- 1 ¼ lb/625 g squid, cleaned and cut into bite-size pieces
- 2 large onions, chopped
- 3 cloves garlic, chopped
- 1 tablespoon finely chopped fresh parsley
- 3 bay leaves
- 4 tomatoes, chopped
- 1 tablespoon paprika
- 1 tablespoon ras-al-hanout
- 1 teaspoon ground cumin
- salt and freshly ground black pepper
- 2 tablespoons tomato paste

The spices in the ras-al-hanout give this dish a special almost sweet flavor that goes perfectly with the saffron rice.

Cook the rice in salted boiling water for 15–20 minutes, or until tender. • Drain and mix in the saffron. • Heat the oil in a large saucepan over medium heat. • Sauté the squid, onions, garlic, parsley, bay leaves, tomatoes, paprika, ras-al-hanout, cumin, salt, pepper, and tomato paste for a few minutes. • Lower the heat and cook for 30 minutes, or until the squid is tender. • Spoon the squid stew onto the center of a serving plate and serve with the rice around the edges.

Serves 6 • Prep: 10 min • Cooking: 40 min • Level: 1

RICE WITH VEGETABLES
Riz avec légumes

This Algerian dish is simple but flavorful. Vary the vegetables according to the season and your personal preference.

Place the rice, peas, tomatoes, carrots, zucchini, onions, and garlic in a large saucepan. • Add the water, salt, pepper, and saffron. • Bring to a boil, then lower the heat, and cover and cook for 15–20 minutes, or until the water has been completely absorbed. • Spoon the rice and vegetables onto a serving dish. • Garnish with the parsley and serve hot. Pass the yogurt on the side.

Serves 6 • Prep: 10 min • Cooking: 15–20 min • Level: 1

- 3 cups/600 g short-grain rice
- 2 cups/250 g peas
- 4 firm-ripe tomatoes, coarsely chopped
- 2 carrots, coarsely chopped
- 3 zucchini/courgettes, coarsely chopped
- 2 onions, finely chopped
- 2 cloves garlic, finely chopped
- 2 quarts/2 liters water
- salt and freshly ground black pepper
- 4–6 threads saffron, crumbled
- 1 tablespoon finely chopped fresh parsley
- ½ cup/125 ml plain yogurt

FRIED PASTRY SPIRALS

Pâtisserie marocaine

- ¹/₂ oz/15 g fresh yeast or 1 (¹/₄-oz/7-g) package active dry yeast
- ¹/₄ cup/60 ml lukewarm water
- 1 tablespoon granulated sugar
- 3¹/₃ cups/500 g all-purpose/plain flour
- ¹/₈ teaspoon salt
- 2 cups/500 ml water
- 1 quart/1 liter olive oil, for frying
- 1¹/₃ cups/300 ml honey

These spirals of fried dough are one of the gems of Moroccan cuisine. They are handsome to behold and have been compared to the stuccoes of the Alhambra. There is also an Algerian version, with the addition of ¹/₂ teaspoon turmeric to the dough and a sugar syrup in place of the honey.

Mix the yeast, lukewarm water, and sugar in a small bowl. Set aside for 10 minutes, or until frothy. • Sift the flour and salt onto a clean work surface. Make a well in the center and pour in the yeast mixture. Use your hands to work the yeast mixture into the dry ingredients, gradually adding enough water to make a soft dough. • Cover with a clean cloth and let rest in a warm place for about 40 minutes, or until doubled in bulk. • Spoon the dough into a pastry bag fitted with a ³/₄-inch (2-cm) plain nozzle. • Heat the oil to very hot in a large deep frying pan. • Squeeze a thin stream of dough into the oil to form pinwheels or flowers. • Fry the dough for 5–7 minutes, or until golden brown. • Use a slotted spoon to remove the fried dough from the oil. Drain well on paper towels. • Dip in the honey and serve.

Serves 6 • Prep: 20 min + 40 min to rise • Cooking: 20–28 min • Level: 2

GAZELLE HORNS

Kaab ghozal

Tea is often accompanied by these delicious pastries, whose name actually means "ankles of gazelle."

Preheat the oven to 400°F/200°C/gas 6. • Butter and flour two baking sheets. • Very finely chop the almonds with the confectioners' sugar in a food processor. Add the orange-flower water and butter. Process to form a smooth paste. Set aside in a cool place. • Dough: Sift the flour onto a clean work surface and make a well in the center. Use your hands to work in the melted butter and enough cold water to make a firm dough. • Divide the almond paste into 40 portions. Shape into small 2¹/₂-inch (6-cm) long sausages, tapering the ends. • Divide the dough in two and roll into two rectangles about 5 x 2 inches (13 x 5-cm) wide. Place the pieces of almond paste lengthwise on one half of both rectangles, spacing them ³/₄ inch (2 cm) apart. Fold the other half of each piece of dough over the top, pressing down between the filling with your fingers. Use a fluted round pastry cutter to cut out the pastries and seal the edges. Bend the ends inward to create a crescent shape. • Bake for 8–10 minutes, or until lightly browned, rotating the sheets halfway through the baking. • Serve warm.

Makes 40 cookies • Prep: 40 min • Cooking: 8–10 min • Level: 2

- 3¹/₄ cups/500 g blanched and peeled almonds
- 1 cup/150 g confectioners'/icing sugar
- ¹/₄ cup/60 ml orange-flower water
- 2 tablespoons butter, melted

Dough

- 1¹/₂ cups/225 g all-purpose flour
- 2 tablespoons butter, melted
- cold water

SWEET COUSCOUS

Mesfouf

- 1¹/₂ lb/750 g couscous
- ²/₃ cup/150 g butter
- 3 tablespoons orange-flower water (optional)
- 1 cup/180 g raisins
- 1 cup/150 g hazelnuts
- 1 cup/150 g pistachios
- 1 cup/150 g walnuts
- 1 cup/150 g dates, pitted

This nutritious Tunisian dish is usually served just before sunrise during the month of Ramadan. Ours is a very rich dish, but it can also be made with just a simple mix of couscous, butter, raisins, and a little cinnamon and sugar. Serve with natural yogurt.

Prepare the couscous as explained on page 140. Place vanilla-scented water in the bottom pot of the couscoussière or two-tiered vegetable steamer and steam for 55 minutes. • If using instant couscous, follow the instructions on the package. • Spoon onto a serving plate and mix in the butter. • Drizzle with the orange-flower water, if using. Toss with the raisins, hazelnuts, pistachios, walnuts, and dates. • Serve hot or cold, with the sugar in a separate bowl.

Serves 6–8 • Prep: 15 min • Cooking: 55 min • Level: 1

Gazelle horns

STUFFED DATES

Dattes farcies

- 1³/₄lb/850 g dates
- 3 cups/300 g finely ground almonds
- 1 cup/200 g raw sugar
- 1 tablespoon orange-flower water or rose water
- ¹/₄ teaspoon green food coloring
- 1 cup/150 g confectioners'/icing sugar
- 2 tablespoons water, or more as needed
- ¹/₂ cup/100 g granulated sugar

The best dates to use are the finest Tunisian dates, called deglat en nour *(fingers of light).*

Pit the dates by cutting them lengthwise on one side only. • Stir together the almonds and raw sugar in a large bowl. • Mix the orange-flower water and food coloring in a small bowl. Stir into the almond mixture until well mixed. • Mix the confectioners' sugar with enough water to make a thick paste. • Fill the dates with the almond paste. Dip in the confectioners' sugar paste, then roll in the granulated sugar.

Serves 10–12 • Prep: 15 min • Level: 1

Mint tea

In North Africa, it is unthinkable to refuse tea if it is offered. To prepare mint tea for 2–4 people: Bring 1 quart (1 liter) of water to a boil. Place 2–3 teaspoons of green tea in a large teapot and add 2 tablespoons of sugar and a bunch of fresh mint. Pour in the boiling water and infuse for 5 minutes before pouring into glasses.

STUFFED APRICOTS

Abricots farcis

- ¹/₂ cup/100 g granulated sugar
- 2 tablespoons fresh lemon juice
- 2 cups/500 ml water
- 1 cup/100 g finely ground almonds
- ¹/₂ cup/75 g confectioners'/icing sugar
- 2 tablespoons butter, melted
- ¹/₂ teaspoon almond extract
- 2 lb/1 kg fresh apricots, halved and pitted

Preheat the oven to 350°F/180°C/gas 4. • Set out an ovenproof dish. • Bring the granulated sugar, lemon juice, and water to a boil in a large saucepan over medium heat. • Simmer for 10 minutes. Remove from the heat. • Stir together the almonds, confectioners' sugar, butter, and almond extract in a medium bowl to form a smooth paste. • Use a teaspoon to stuff each apricot with the almond mixture. • Place in the dish and pour the sugar syrup over. Cover with aluminum foil. • Bake for 25–30 minutes, or until the apricots have softened slightly. • Serve warm.

Serves 4 • Prep: 15 min • Cooking: 25–30 min • Level: 1

MAKROUD

Syrup: Dissolve the sugar in the water in a small saucepan over medium heat. Bring to a boil and cook for 3 minutes. • Mix the honey into the sugar syrup until it dissolves. Remove from the heat. • Pastry: Stir together the semolina, couscous, and salt on a clean work surface. Make a well in the center and add the oil and enough water to form a smooth dough. Set aside for 30 minutes. • Filling: Place the dates, oil, cinnamon, and cloves in a medium bowl. Shape the date mixture into three sausage shapes. Set aside. • Divide the dough into three parts. Roll out each dough part on a work surface to a rectangle that is just slightly longer than the rolls of date mixture. The dough should be about ¹/₂ inch (1 cm) thick. • Place each date mixture sausage in the center of each dough rectangle. Fold over the edges and roll up to make a sausage. Flatten slightly. • Cut into 1-inch (2.5-cm) rectangles or diamond shapes. • Brush with a little olive oil and set aside for frying. • Reheat the syrup. • Heat the oil in a deep fryer and fry the cookies in batches for 5–7 minutes, or until golden brown. Drain well on paper towels. Place in the hot syrup for 10 minutes. • Drain well and serve.

Serves 10–12 • Prep: 40 min • Cooking: 23–31 min • Level: 3

Syrup
- 2 cups/400 g granulated sugar
- 1 cup/250 ml water
- ¹/₄ cup/60 ml honey

Pastry
- 3 cups/400 g semolina
- 3 oz/90 g precooked couscous
- 2 tablespoons extra-virgin olive oil, lukewarm
- ¹/₄ cup/60 ml water, + more as needed

Filling
- 1¹/₂ cups/250 g dates, pitted and finely chopped
- 1 tablespoon extra-virgin olive oil
- 1 teaspoon ground cinnamon
- ¹/₄ teaspoon ground cloves
- olive oil, for frying
- salt

MAKING MAKROUD

1. Stir together the semolina, couscous, and salt on a clean work surface and make a well in the center. Add the oil and lukewarm water. Mix with your hands to make a smooth dough.

2. Finely chop the dates with a meat grinder or in a food processor or blender and mix with the oil, cinnamon, and capers in a medium bowl. Use your hands to form the date mixture into three long, thin sausage shapes.

3. Divide the dough into three equal portions and roll it out into rectangles the same length as the date sausages. Place one date sausage in the center of each rectangle.

4. Fold over the pastry so that the date mixture is enclosed. Flatten them slightly. Use a sharp knife to cut into small rectangles or diamond shapes about 1 inch (2.5 cm) wide.

5. Heat the frying oil to in a deep fryer to very hot. Fry the makroud in small batches for 5–7 minutes, or until golden brown. Dip in the hot sugar syrup and serve.

MIDDLE EAST

Middle Eastern cooking is based in the peasant traditions of the farmers and nomadic peoples who have inhabited the region for thousands of years. It is an ancient cuisine and many of the same dishes described in Egyptian texts and in the Bible are still eaten in the Middle East today. Its influence was spread all around the Mediterranean by Islamic warriors as they conquered North Africa, Spain, and other northern areas.

Stuffed kibbe balls
(see page 154)

Appetizers

SPINACH PIES

Fatayer bi sabanikh

Dough

- 1 oz/30 g fresh yeast or 2 (¼-oz/7-g) packages active dry yeast
- 1 teaspoon granulated sugar
- 1 cup/250 ml lukewarm water, or more if needed
- 3½ cups/525 g all-purpose/plain flour
- 1 teaspoon salt
- ¾ cup/180 ml extra-virgin olive oil or sesame oil

Filling

- 1 lb/500 g spinach, coarsely chopped
- 2 small onions, finely chopped
- salt and freshly ground black pepper
- ½ teaspoon red pepper flakes (optional)
- 3 tablespoons fresh lemon juice
- ⅓ cup/80 ml extra-virgin olive oil

Dough: Dissolve the yeast and sugar in ½ cup (125 ml) of water in a small bowl. Let stand for 10 minutes, or until foamy. • Sift the flour and salt into a large bowl and make a well in the center. Pour in the oil and mix well. • Add the yeast mixture and enough of the remaining ½ cup (125 ml) water to make a firm dough. • Transfer to a lightly floured work surface and knead, adding more water if needed, until smooth and elastic. • Shape into a ball and place in an oiled bowl. Cover with a clean cloth and let rise in a warm place for 1 hour, or until doubled in bulk. • Filling: Mix the spinach and onions in a large bowl. Season with salt. Let stand for 5 minutes. Use your hands to work the mixture until wilted and watery. • Squeeze out any excess moisture and place in a large bowl. • Season with pepper. Add the red pepper flakes, if using, lemon juice, and oil. • Divide the dough into balls the size of walnuts. Place on a clean cloth and let stand for 15 minutes. • Preheat the oven to 300°F/150°C/gas 2. • Grease two large baking sheets with oil. • Roll out each piece of dough to ¼-inch (5-mm) thick square. • Spoon a heaped teaspoon of filling into the center, leaving a border around the edges. • Fold the bottom left and right corners into the center, then bring down the top piece to form a triangle. Pinch to seal. • Place the spinach pies on the baking sheets. • Bake for 20–25 minutes, or until golden brown, rotating the sheets halfway through for even baking. • Serve hot or at room temperature.

Serves 6 • Prep: 40 min + 75 min to rest • Cooking: 20–25 min • Level: 2

These delicious *little pies freeze well. Prepare a double batch and freeze half for later use. To serve the frozen pies, just reheat in a hot oven for 10–15 minutes.*

Spinach pies

Hummus

HUMMUS
Hummus bi tahina

- 2¹/₂ cups/300 g dried garbanzo beans/ chickpeas, soaked overnight and drained
- ¹/₂ cup/125 ml tahini (sesame seed paste)
- ¹/₄ cup/60 ml fresh lemon juice
- 2 cloves garlic, finely chopped
- ¹/₂ cup/125 ml water, or more if needed
- salt
- 1 sprig parsley, to garnish
- 1 tablespoon extra-virgin olive oil

Tahini is available at Middle Eastern markets, in health food stores, and in most large supermarkets.

Cook the garbanzo beans in a large pot of boiling water for 1¹/₂–2 hours, or until very tender. • Transfer the garbanzo beans to a food processor, reserving a few whole to garnish. Add the tahini, lemon juice, and garlic and process until pureed. • Add enough water to obtain a creamy mixture. Season with salt. • Garnish with parsley and the reserved garbanzo beans. Drizzle with the oil.

Serves 6–8 • Prep: 20 min • Cooking: 1¹/₂–2 hr • Level: 1

Grape leaf treats

Grape leaves packed in brine are available wherever Middle Eastern or Greek foods are sold. Remember that the stuffed leaves take a while to assemble and cook. Make them ahead of time—they also taste better when prepared the day before.

STUFFED GRAPE LEAVES
Waraq dawaali

Soak the grape leaves in hot water for 1 hour to remove excess salt. • Drain well and pat dry with paper towels. • Place the rice in a medium bowl and cover with boiling water. Let soak for 30 minutes. • Drain well and transfer to a large bowl. • Stir in the beef, allspice, cinnamon, and 2 tablespoons of butter. Season with salt and pepper. • Place the grape leaves, shiny-side down on a work surface. Use a tablespoon to spoon the filling onto the center of the leaves. • Fold the sides of each leaf over the filling, then fold over the top and bottom. Roll until slightly flattened. • Place a layer of stuffed leaves seam-side down in a large saucepan. Top with another layer of stuffed leaves arranged perpendicularly to the first layer. Repeat until all the stuffed leaves are in the saucepan. • Pour in the boiling water and bring to a boil over medium heat. • Simmer, covered, for 55–65 minutes, or until the leaves are tender and the rice is cooked. • Use a slotted spoon to remove the stuffed leaves and place them on a serving plate. Brush with the remaining 1 tablespoon butter and drizzle with the lemon juice. • Serve hot.

Serves 6–8 • Prep: 50 min + 1 hr to soak • Cooking: 55–65 min • Level: 2

- 45 brined grape leaves
- 1¹/₄ cups/250 g short-grain rice
- 1 lb/500 g ground/ minced lamb or beef
- ¹/₂ teaspoon ground allspice
- ¹/₂ teaspoon ground cinnamon
- 3 tablespoons butter
- salt and freshly ground black pepper
- 2 tablespoons fresh lemon juice

Appetizers

STUFFED KIBBE BALLS

Akras kibbe maklieh

- 2 lb/1 kg fine-grind bulgur
- 2 lb/1 kg ground/ minced beef
- 1 large onion, finely chopped
- 1/2 teaspoon freshly grated nutmeg
- 1/2 teaspoon ground cinnamon
- salt and freshly ground black pepper

Filling
- 1/4 cup/60 ml extra-virgin olive oil
- 4 medium onions, finely chopped
- 1 lb/500 g ground/ minced lamb
- salt
- 1/2 teaspoon ground cinnamon
- 1/2 teaspoon ground allspice
- 1 cup/250 ml olive or sesame oil, for frying

Place the bulgur in a bowl and cover with cold water. Let stand for 30 minutes. • Drain well. • Mix the beef and onion in a large bowl. Stir in the bulgur, nutmeg, and cinnamon. Season with salt and pepper. • Use your hands to knead the mixture until well mixed. Shape into a ball, return to the bowl, and refrigerate for 30 minutes. • Filling: Heat the oil in a large frying pan over medium heat. • Sauté the onions for 8–10 minutes, or until lightly browned. Add the lamb and season with salt. Add the cinnamon and allspice. • Cook the mixture for 10–15 minutes, or until the meat has browned. • Remove from the heat and set aside. • Use a teaspoon to scoop out enough of the bulgur mixture to form balls the size of golf balls. • Use your index finger to make a hollow in the center, working until you have a shell of even thickness. • Spoon in the filling and close up the opening. Repeat until both mixtures are used up. • Heat the frying oil in a large frying pan to 325°F/160°C. • Fry the balls in batches for 8–10 minutes, or until browned all over. Drain on paper towels. • Serve hot.

Serves 6–8 • Prep: 25 min + 1 hr to stand + 30 min to chill Cooking: 40–50 min • Level: 2

EGGPLANT DIP

Baba ghanoush

Traditionally, the eggplants were grilled over an open fire, which added a lovely smoky taste to this dip. Try roasting them on a barbecue to recapture some of the dish's authentic flavor.

Preheat the oven to 400°F/200°C/gas 6. • Arrange the eggplants in a baking pan. • Roast for 20–30 minutes, turning often, until the skin has blackened and the insides are tender. • Remove from the oven and let cool completely. • Cut the eggplants in half and use a spoon to scoop out the flesh. • Place the eggplant flesh in a large bowl with the garlic and use a fork to mash until smooth. • Mix the tahini and lemon juice in a small bowl. Pour in the water and season with salt. • Add to the eggplant mixture. • Refrigerate for at least 1 hour. • Sprinkle with parsley and chile pepper, if using, and drizzle with the oil.

Serves 6 • Prep: 30 min + 1 hr to chill • Cooking: 20–30 min • Level: 1

- 2 large eggplants/ aubergines
- 3 cloves garlic, finely chopped
- 1/2 cup/125 ml tahini (sesame seed paste)
- juice of 2 lemons
- 1/4 cup/60 ml water
- salt
- 3 tablespoons finely chopped fresh parsley
- 1 red fresh chile pepper, finely chopped (optional)
- 2 tablespoons extra-virgin olive oil

ONIONS WITH VINEGAR

Sarkeh piaz

Place the onions in a large bowl and season with salt. • Pour in the vinegar and add the mint. • Toss well and let stand for at least 1 hour before serving.

Serves 4 • Prep: 10 min + 1 hr to stand • Level: 1

- 2 large onions, halved and thinly sliced
- coarse sea salt
- 3 tablespoons red wine vinegar
- 1 tablespoon finely chopped fresh mint

Appetizers

MEATBALL APPETIZERS

Koukla

- 1 lb/500 g ground/minced beef or lamb
- 1 clove garlic, finely chopped
- 1 small onion, very finely chopped
- 1/2 teaspoon freshly ground cumin seeds
- 6 tablespoons finely chopped fresh parsley
- salt and freshly ground black pepper

Preheat the oven to 400°F/200°C/gas 6. • Oil a baking sheet. • Stir the beef, garlic, onion, cumin, and parsley in a large bowl until well blended. Season with salt and pepper. • Shape the mixture into balls the size of large marbles. • Place on the prepared baking sheet, spacing well apart. • Bake for 10–15 minutes, or until the meat is cooked through. • Serve hot or at room temperature.

Serves 4–6 • Prep: 20 min • Cooking: 10–15 min • Level: 1

LENTILS AND LEMON JUICE

Adas bil hamod

- 1 1/2 lb/750 g red lentils
- 2 medium potatoes, peeled and coarsely chopped
- 2 tablespoons extra-virgin olive oil
- 6 cloves garlic, finely chopped
- 1/4 cup/60 g finely chopped fresh cilantro/coriander
- 2 tablespoons all-purpose/plain flour
- 2 tablespoons water
- salt
- 1/4 cup/60 ml fresh lemon juice

Cook the lentils in a large pot of salted boiling water for 15 minutes. • Add the potatoes and cook for 15–20 minutes more, or until the potatoes and lentils are tender. • Drain the lentil mixture and set aside. • Heat the oil in a large frying pan over medium heat. Sauté the garlic and cilantro for 3 minutes. • Stir in the lentil mixture. • Mix the flour and water in a small bowl. Add to the lentil mixture. • Cover and cook for 30 minutes. • Season with salt. Drizzle with the lemon juice and serve at room temperature.

Serves 6 • Prep: 15 min • Cooking: 65 min • Level: 1

GARBANZO BEANS WITH TOAST

Fattet hummus

Cook the garbanzo beans in a large pot of boiling water for 1 1/2–2 hours, or until very tender. Season with salt. Drain the beans, reserving 1 tablespoon of the cooking liquid. Reserve 2 tablespoons of the beans. • Mix the yogurt and garlic in a medium bowl. Season with pepper. • Open out the pita breads and toast until crispy and brown. Crumble onto a large serving plate. • Pour the garbanzo beans and the reserved cooking liquid over the bread, soaking well. • Pour the yogurt mixture over the garbanzo beans. Sprinkle with the mint. • Melt the butter in a small frying pan over medium heat. Sauté the pine nuts for 3–5 minutes, or until golden brown. • Sprinkle over the yogurt and decorate with the reserved garbanzo beans.

Serves 6 • Prep: 20 min • Cooking: 1 1/2–2 hr • Level: 1

- 2 cups/250 g garbanzo beans/chickpeas, soaked overnight and drained
- salt
- 2 cups/500 ml plain yogurt
- 3 cloves garlic, very finely chopped
- freshly ground white pepper
- 2 pita breads, store-bought or homemade (see page 158)
- 1 tablespoon finely chopped dried mint leaves
- 1 tablespoon butter
- 3 tablespoons pine nuts or flaked almonds

Cilantro

Cilantro (coriander) is a favorite herb in Middle Eastern cuisine. It has a delicate musty flavor and resembles flat-leaf parsley. It acts as a cooling influence against piquant ingredients, such as chiles. The seed of the plant has a sweet flavor and is available whole or ground. Although fresh cilantro is generally available year-round, it can be substituted with parsley if necessary.

Meat pies

MIDDLE EASTERN MEAT PIES

Sheefa

Dough

- 1 oz/30 g fresh yeast or 2 (¹/₄-oz/7-g) packages active dry yeast
- 1 teaspoon granulated sugar
- 1¹/₄ cups/310 ml lukewarm water, or more if needed
- 5¹/₂ cups/825 g all-purpose/plain flour
- 1 teaspoon salt
- ³/₄ cup/180 g butter, softened

Topping

- ¹/₄ cup/60 ml extra-virgin olive oil
- 2 onions, finely chopped
- 2 lb/1 kg beef, cut into very small cubes
- ¹/₄ cup/30 g pine nuts
- 1 teaspoon ground allspice
- ¹/₂ teaspoon red pepper flakes
- 1 teaspoon ground cinnamon
- salt
- 1 cup/250 ml plain yogurt

Dissolve the yeast and sugar in ¹/₂ cup (125 ml) of the water in a small bowl. Let stand for 10 minutes, or until foamy. • Sift the flour and salt into a large bowl. Use your fingertips to rub in the butter until the mixture resembles coarse crumbs. • Pour in the yeast mixture and enough of the remaining ³/₄ cup (80 ml) water to form a firm dough. • Transfer to a lightly floured work surface and knead, adding more water if needed, until smooth and elastic. • Shape into a ball and place in an oiled bowl. Cover with a clean cloth and let rise for 1 hour, or until doubled in bulk. • Topping: Heat the oil in a large frying pan over medium heat. • Sauté the onions for 8–10 minutes, or until lightly browned. • Brown the beef for 5

minutes, draining off excess liquid. • Add the pine nuts, allspice, red pepper flakes, and cinnamon. Season with salt. • Cook over low heat for 30 minutes. • Remove from the heat and stir in the yogurt. • Preheat the oven to 350°F/180°C/ gas 4. • Butter two baking sheets. • Punch down the dough and break into pieces the size of eggs. Roll into balls, cover with a clean cloth, and let rest for 15 minutes. • Place the balls on the baking sheets, pressing down to spread them to ¹/₄ inch (5 mm) thick. Spread with the topping. • Bake for 25–30 minutes, or until the pastry edges are golden brown. • Serve hot or at room temperature.

Serves 6–8 • Prep: 1 hr + 100 min to rest • Cooking: 68–75 min Level: 2

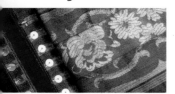

Meat skewers

FRIED KEFTA ON PITA BREAD

Kefta makli

- 1 lb/500 g ground/ minced beef or lamb
- 1 tablespoon freshly grated ginger
- 2 cloves garlic, finely chopped
- 4 green chiles, finely chopped
- 1 small onion, finely chopped
- 1 egg, lightly beaten
- 1 teaspoon ground turmeric
- $^1/_4$ cup finely chopped fresh cilantro/ coriander
- 4 leaves fresh mint, finely chopped
- 1 large potato, coarsely grated
- salt
- 1 cup/250 ml oil, for frying
- 4 pita breads, store-bought or homemade (see recipe below)

Kefta are a popular Middle Eastern fried treat. For a lighter dish, broil (grill) the kefta or bake them in a hot oven with 2 tablespoons of oil to prevent them from sticking to the pan.

Mix the beef, ginger, garlic, chiles, onion, egg, turmeric, cilantro, and mint in a large bowl until well blended. • Stir in the grated potato. Season with salt. • Shape the mixture into balls the size of golf balls. • Let rest for 30 minutes. • Heat the oil in a large deep frying pan to very hot. • Fry the kefta in batches for 8–10 minutes, or until brown all over. • Drain well and dry on paper towels. • Serve hot on the pita breads.

Serves 4 • Prep: 40 min + 30 min to rest • Cooking: 30 min • Level: 1

MEAT SKEWERS

Laham mishwi

Thread the beef, onions, bell peppers, and tomatoes alternately onto skewers. • Season with salt and pepper. Drizzle with the oil. • Turn on the broiler (grill). • Broil the skewers 4–6 inches (10–15 cm) from the heat source for 10–15 minutes, or until the meat is cooked, turning frequently. • Serve hot.

Serves 4 • Prep: 30 min • Cooking: 10–15 min • Level: 1

- 2 lb/1 kg beef or lamb, cut into small chunks
- 12 small white onions
- 2 large yellow bell peppers/capsicums, seeded and cut into squares
- 12 cherry tomatoes
- salt and freshly ground black pepper
- $^1/_4$ cup/60 ml extra-virgin olive oil

Fried kefta on pita bread

MAKING PITA BREAD

Makes 8 pita breads

1. Dissolve $^1/_2$ oz (15 g) fresh yeast or 1 ($^1/_4$-oz/7-g) package active dry yeast and 1 teaspoon sugar in $^1/_2$ cup (125 ml) warm water. Set aside for 10 minutes, until foamy.

2. Sift 3$^1/_2$ cups (500 g) flour and $^1/_2$ teaspoon salt into a large bowl.

3. Make a well in the center. Use your hands to mix in the yeast mixture and sufficient water to make a smooth dough.

4. Transfer the dough to a lightly floured work surface and knead until smooth and elastic, about 10 minutes.

5. Place the dough in an oiled bowl. Cover with a clean cloth and let rise in a warm place until doubled in bulk, about 2 hours.

6. Preheat the oven to 450°F/220°C/gas 7. Shape the dough into small balls, then stretch it a little with your hands.

7. Roll each piece of dough out into ¼-inch (5-mm) thick rounds.

8. Transfer to the baking sheets. Spray with a little water and bake for 8–10 minutes, or until puffed and golden brown. Cool on wire racks.

Salads & Vegetables

POTATO SALAD

Salatet batata

- 6 medium potatoes, well-washed
- 2 tablespoons finely chopped fresh parsley
- 2 scallions/spring onions, trimmed and finely chopped

Lemon Dressing
- 1 clove garlic, finely chopped
- juice of 1 lemon
- $^1/_2$ cup/125 ml extra-virgin olive oil

Boil the potatoes in their skins in a large pot of salted boiling water for 20–25 minutes, or until cooked. • Drain well and let cool completely. • Slip off the skins and cut into small cubes. • Mix the potatoes, parsley, and scallions in a large salad bowl. • Lemon Dressing: Mix the garlic, lemon juice, and oil in a small bowl. Pour over the potatoes and toss well. • Refrigerate for at least 1 hour before serving.

Serves 4 • Prep: 10 min + 1 hr to chill • Cooking: 20–25 min • Level: 1

TABBOULEH

Place the bulgur in a bowl and cover with cold water. Let stand for 30 minutes, or until the grains have softened. • Drain well, squeezing out excess moisture, and transfer to a large salad bowl. • Season with salt and pepper and drizzle with half the lemon juice and the oil. Let stand for 30 minutes. • Add the parsley, scallions, mint, and tomatoes to the bulgur. • Toss well with the remaining lemon juice and serve.

Serves 4–6 • Prep: 20 min + 1 hr to rest • Level: 1

- $^1/_2$ cup/125 g fine- or medium-grind bulgur
- salt and freshly ground black pepper
- juice of 1–2 lemons
- $^1/_2$ cup/125 ml extra-virgin olive oil
- 3 cups/150 g finely chopped fresh parsley
- 4 scallions/spring onions, trimmed and finely chopped
- 20 leaves fresh mint, finely chopped
- 3 tomatoes, chopped

MUSHROOM SALAD

Salatet futter

- 1 lb/500 g fresh button mushrooms, cleaned, trimmed, and thinly sliced
- 2 cloves garlic, finely chopped
- 1 small onion, thinly sliced
- 1 green bell pepper/capsicum, cut into thin strips
- $^1/_4$ cup/60 g finely chopped fresh parsley
- salt and freshly ground black pepper
- 2 tablespoons fresh lemon juice
- $^1/_4$ cup/60 ml extra-virgin olive oil

Place the mushrooms in a large salad bowl. • Add the garlic, onion, bell pepper, and parsley and toss well. • Season with salt and pepper and drizzle with the lemon juice and oil. • Toss well and serve.

Serves 4–6 • Prep: 20 min • Level: 1

FRIED EGGPLANT SALAD

Patlican soslu

Place the eggplants in a colander and sprinkle with salt. Let drain for 1 hour. • Heat the oil in a large deep frying pan to very hot. • Fry the eggplants in batches for 5–7 minutes, or until tender. • Drain on paper towels. • In the same skillet, sauté the onion for 8–10 minutes over medium heat, or until lightly browned. • Stir in the tomatoes, fried eggplants, and the pickle. Cook for 5 minutes more. • Serve hot.

Serves 4 • Prep: 5 min + 1 hour to drain eggplants • Cooking: 40 min • Level: 1

- 2 lb/1 kg eggplants/aubergines, cut into $^1/_2$-inch/1-cm thick slices
- 1 tablespoon salt
- $^1/_2$ cup/125 ml extra-virgin olive oil, for frying
- 1 large onion, finely chopped
- 1 lb/500 g tomatoes, peeled and thinly sliced
- $^1/_4$ cup/60 ml mustard-flavored cucumber pickle

Soups

WINTER SQUASH SOUP

Hamraak garaqh

- 3/4 cup/150 g short-grain rice
- 4 lb/2 kg winter squash or pumpkin, peeled, seeded, and cut into small cubes
- 2 quarts/2 liters chicken stock or broth
- 1 cup/250 ml milk
- salt and freshly ground white pepper

This delicate soup is a lovely orange color and looks especially appetizing.

Cook the rice in a large pot of salted boiling water for 15–20 minutes, or until tender. Drain. • Place the winter squash, stock, and milk in a large saucepan over medium heat. Bring to a boil and season with salt and pepper. • Simmer for 15–20 minutes, or until the squash is tender. • Remove the squash and process in a food processor until smooth. Return to the saucepan and bring to a boil. • Stir in the cooked rice and cook for 2–3 minutes before serving.

Serves 6–8 • Prep: 20 min • Cooking: 40 min • Level: 1

SPINACH AND BEEF SOUP

Shourbit sabanikh

Heat 1/4 cup (60 ml) oil in a large saucepan over medium heat. Sauté the onions, garlic, and carrot for 8–10 minutes, or until lightly browned. • Add the beef and sauté for 10 minutes. • Pour in the water and tomatoes. Lower the heat, cover, and cook over low heat for 1 1/2 hours, or until the beef is tender. • Stir in the rice and cook for 15 minutes. • Add the spinach and cinnamon. Season with salt and pepper. Cook for 10 minutes more. • Add the parsley and remaining 2 tablespoons of oil just before serving.

Serves 4 • Prep: 30 min • Cooking: 2 hr 15 min • Level: 1

- 1/3 cup/80 ml extra-virgin olive oil
- 2 onions, chopped
- 4 cloves garlic, chopped
- 1 small carrot, sliced
- 1 1/2 lb/750 g stewing beef, cut into small chunks
- 3 quarts/3 liters cold water
- 2 tomatoes, chopped
- 3/4 cup/150 g long-grain rice
- 2 lb/1 kg fresh or 1 lb/ 500 g frozen spinach
- 1 teaspoon cinnamon
- salt and freshly ground black pepper
- 6 tablespoons finely chopped fresh parsley

COOL CUCUMBER SOUP

Jalik

- 4 medium cucumbers, peeled and quartered lengthwise
- 1 tablespoon salt
- 2 cloves garlic, finely chopped
- 2 tablespoons fresh lemon juice
- 6 cups/1.5 liters plain yogurt
- 1 tablespoon finely chopped fresh dill
- 1/4 cup/60 ml extra-virgin olive oil
- 1 tablespoon finely chopped fresh mint

Use a teaspoon to remove the seeds from the cucumbers and slice very thinly. • Place the cucumber slices in a colander. Sprinkle with salt and let drain for 20 minutes. • Mix the garlic, lemon juice, yogurt, and dill in a large bowl until well blended. • Stir in the cucumbers. • Drizzle with the oil and sprinkle with the mint. • Refrigerate for at least 30 minutes before serving.

Serves 4 • Prep: 20 min + 50 min to drain and chill • Level: 1

CREAMY ALMOND SOUP

Shorba looz

Melt the butter in a large saucepan over medium heat. Sauté the onions for 5–7 minutes, or until softened. • Add the flour and stir until well blended. • Pour in the stock and cook for 5 minutes. Add the almonds and cook for 20 minutes more, stirring often. • Stir in the cream and season with salt and pepper. • Serve hot.

Serves 4 • Prep: 15 min • Cooking: 30–35 min • Level: 1

- 2 tablespoons butter
- 3 medium onions, finely chopped
- 2 tablespoons all-purpose/plain flour
- 1 quart/1 liter chicken stock or broth
- 1/2 cup/75 g finely ground almonds
- 1/2 cup/125 ml heavy/ double cream
- salt and freshly ground white pepper

Winter squash and pumpkin

Winter squash and pumpkin originally came from North America, but they have been adopted by cuisines throughout the Mediterranean region. They are key ingredients in many distinctive dishes, including the sweet pasta filling in northern Italian cuisine (see page 29) and this delicately flavored rice soup.

Soups

RED LENTIL SOUP

Shourabit adas

- 1 1/2 quarts/1.5 liters chicken stock or broth
- 3 cups/300 g red lentils
- 1 teaspoon freshly ground cumin
- 1 small onion, finely chopped
- 1/8 teaspoon cayenne pepper
- 2 tablespoons finely chopped fresh parsley

Mix the stock, lentils, cumin, onion, and cayenne pepper in a large saucepan over medium heat. • Bring to a boil and simmer, covered, for 30–40 minutes, or until the lentils have softened. • Pour the mixture into a food processor and process until smooth. • Return to the saucepan and simmer, stirring often, until heated through. • Garnish with the parsley and serve.

Serves 4–6 • Prep: 10 min • Cooking: 35–45 min • Level: 1

CHILLED TOMATO SOUP

Hasa laban ma' tomata

Mix the tomato juice, yogurt, lemon juice, oil, and cayenne pepper in a large bowl until well blended. • Season with salt and pepper. • Refrigerate for at least 2 hours. • Spoon into individual bowls. Garnish with the cilantro and serve.

Serves 4 • Prep: 10 min + 2 hr to chill • Level: 1

- 1 quart/1 liter tomato juice
- 2 cups/500 ml plain yogurt
- 1/4 cup/60 ml fresh lemon juice
- 2 tablespoons extra-virgin olive oil
- 1/4 teaspoon cayenne pepper
- salt and freshly ground black pepper
- 2 tablespoons finely chopped fresh cilantro/coriander

CUMIN BEAN SOUP

Shourabit adas mah fasoolia

- 2 cups/200 g dried garbanzo beans/chickpeas, soaked overnight and drained
- 1 cup/100 g dried lima or butter beans, soaked overnight and drained
- 1 cup/100 g dried red kidney beans, soaked overnight and drained
- 2 cups/200 g red lentils
- 2 1/2 quarts/2.5 liters water
- 1/4 cup/60 ml extra-virgin olive oil
- 1 large onion, finely chopped
- 1 cup/200 g short-grain rice
- 1 teaspoon freshly ground cumin
- salt and freshly ground black pepper

Place all the beans and lentils in a large saucepan. Pour in the water and place over high heat. • Bring to a boil and lower the heat. Cook, covered, for 1 1/2–2 hours, or until the beans are tender. • Heat the oil in a large frying pan over medium heat. Sauté the onion for 8–10 minutes, or until lightly browned. • Transfer to the bean mixture and add the rice and cumin. Season with salt and pepper. • Continue cooking for 30 minutes. • Serve hot.

Serves 4 • Prep: 15 min + overnight to soak the beans • Cooking: 2 hr 8–40 min • Level: 1

BULGUR AND LAMB SOUP

Ha-saa al-gereesh

Place the bulgur in a bowl and cover with cold water. Let stand for 30 minutes. • Drain well. • Heat the oil in a large saucepan over medium heat. Sauté the onions for 8–10 minutes, or until lightly browned. • Add the lamb and brown for 10 minutes. • Pour in the water and cook for 10 minutes more. • Stir in the tomatoes and cinnamon. Season with salt and pepper. • Add the bulgur and cook, covered, for 20 minutes. • Remove the cinnamon sticks and serve hot.

Serves 4–6 • Prep: 15 min + 30 min to stand • Cooking: 50 min • Level: 1

- 1/2 cup/125 g fine-grind or medium-grind bulgur
- 2 tablespoons extra-virgin olive oil
- 2 medium onions, finely chopped
- 12 oz/350 g lamb, cut into small chunks
- 1 1/4 quarts/1.25 liters water
- 5 medium tomatoes, peeled and finely chopped
- 4 sticks cinnamon
- salt and freshly ground black pepper

Chicken soup with garbanzo beans

CHICKEN SOUP WITH GARBANZO BEANS

Shourabit djaj mah hummus

- 1 small chicken, weighing about 2 lb/ 1 kg, cut into 8 pieces
- 1 cup/100 g dried garbanzo beans/ chickpeas, soaked overnight and drained
- 2¹/₂ quarts/2.5 liters cold water
- ¹/₂ cup/100 g long-grain rice
- 1 large onion, finely chopped
- 2 tablespoons finely chopped fresh parsley
- 2 tablespoons extra-virgin olive oil
- salt and freshly ground black pepper
- ¹/₂ teaspoon ground cinnamon

Place the chicken and garbanzo beans in a large pot with the water. Bring to a boil and lower the heat. Cover and cook for 75 minutes. • Stir in the rice and cook for 15–20 minutes, or until the rice is tender. • Heat the oil in a medium frying pan over medium heat. Sauté the onion and parsley for 8–10 minutes, or until the onion is lightly browned. • Season with salt and pepper and sprinkle with cinnamon. Stir the onion mixture into the soup. • Serve hot.

Serves 4–6 • Prep: 30 min • Cooking: 98–105 min • Level: 1

DRIED FRUIT SOUP

Abgushte miveh

This unusual recipe combining dried apricots, peaches, and citrus juices is an Iranian favorite.

Use a sharp knife to cut the beef into small chunks. • Place the beef in a large pot with the bone and water. Bring to a boil and season with salt and pepper. • Cover and cook for 1–1¹/₂ hours, or until the beef is tender. • Discard the bone. • Melt the butter in a large frying pan over medium heat. Sauté the onion for 5–7 minutes, or until softened. Add the turmeric. • Stir the onion mixture, prunes, apricots, and peaches into the soup. • Cook for 30 minutes. • Stir in the brown sugar and lime juice. • Serve hot.

Serves 4 • Prep: 30 min • Cooking: 90–120 min • Level: 2

- 1 lb/500 g stewing beef or lamb, with the bone
- 2 quarts/2 liters water
- salt and freshly ground black pepper
- 2 tablespoons clarified butter
- 1 large onion, finely chopped
- 2 teaspoons ground turmeric
- 1 cup/250 g dried prunes, pitted
- ¹/₂ cup/125 g dried apricot halves
- ¹/₂ cup/125 g coarsely chopped dried peaches
- ¹/₃ cup/70 g firmly packed dark brown sugar
- 2 tablespoons fresh lime juice

Beef, Chicken & Lamb

BEEF STEW WITH FRESH FAVA BEANS

Mefarka

- 2 tablespoons extra-virgin olive oil
- 2 lb/1 kg lean stewing beef, cut into cubes
- 2¹/₂ cups/500 g shelled fava/broad beans
- 2 cloves garlic, finely chopped
- 1 teaspoon freshly ground coriander seeds
- salt and freshly ground black pepper
- 2 quarts/2 liters water

Heat the oil in a large saucepan over medium heat. Brown the beef for 10 minutes. • Add the fava beans, garlic, and coriander. Season with salt and pepper. Pour in the water. • Bring to the boil and simmer, covered, for about 2 hours, or until very tender. • Serve hot.

Serves 4 • Prep: 15 min • Cooking: 2 hr • Level: 1

LEG OF LAMB

Koozy

Cook the rice in a large pot with the water for 15–20 minutes, or until tender. Add the oil, salt, and 1 tablespoon harissa. • Place the onion in a large deep saucepan. • Sprinkle the lamb with the remaining 2 tablespoons harissa. • Place the lamb on top of the onion, fat-side down. • Pour the rice mixture over to cover the lamb completely. • Cover and cook over low heat for 2¹/₂–3 hours. Do not remove the cover until the end of the second hour, or the steam will escape. Remove from the heat and set aside for 10 minutes. • Spoon the rice onto a large serving dish. Cover with the lamb and serve hot.

Serves 4 • Prep: 25 min • Cooking: 2 hr 30 min–3 hr • Level: 2

- 2 cups/400 g long-grain rice
- 1 quart/1 liter water
- 3 tablespoons vegetable oil
- 1 tablespoon salt
- 3 tablespoons harissa (see page 133)
- 1 large onion, thinly sliced
- 3 lb/1.5 kg boneless leg of lamb

CHICKEN BALLS

Koftit ferakh

- 2 slices white sandwich bread, crusts removed
- ¹/₄ cup/60 ml milk
- 1 lb/500 g ground/minced chicken
- 1 large egg, lightly beaten

These delicious little balls can be served as an appetizer (for four people) or with a salad and rice or potatoes as a light lunch or supper (for two people).

Soak the bread in the milk in a small bowl for 5 minutes. Drain well, squeezing out the excess. • Mix the chicken, soaked bread, and egg in a large bowl. Season with salt and pepper. • Use your hands to bind the mixture and shape into balls the size of large marbles. • Roll the balls in the flour. • Heat the oil to very hot in a large deep frying pan. • Fry the chicken balls in batches for 5–7 minutes, or until brown all over. • Drizzle with the lemon juice just before serving. Serve hot or at room temperature.

Serves 2–4 • Prep: 15 min + 5 min to soak • Cooking: 25 min • Level: 1

- salt and freshly ground black pepper
- ¹/₂ cup/75 g all-purpose/plain flour
- 1 cup/250 ml olive oil, for frying
- juice of ¹/₂ lemon

GROUND MEAT SKEWERS

Kofta Meshweya

- 2 lb/1 kg ground/ minced beef
- 1 large onion, very finely chopped
- 1 teaspoon freshly ground cumin seeds
- 1 teaspoon ground cinnamon
- 1 large egg, lightly beaten
- salt and freshly ground black pepper
- 2 tablespoons coarsely chopped pine nuts

The secret in making these delicious koftas lies in having very finely ground meat and mixing the ingredients until very smooth.

Process the beef and onion in a food processor until smooth. Add the cumin, cinnamon, and egg. Season with salt and pepper. Process briefly to mix well. • Transfer the mixture to a large bowl. • Rinse your hands in cold water and knead the mixture until very smooth. Add the pine nuts. • Shape the mixture into sausage shapes and wrap them around the skewers. • Place under the broiler (grill) or over the glowing embers of a barbecue and turn until browned all over, 15–20 minutes. • Serve hot with fresh, plain yogurt on a rice pilaf with a green or mixed salad.

Serves 4 • Prep: 25 min • Cooking 15–20 min • Level: 1

Ground meat skewers

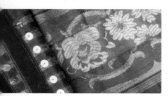

Beef, Lamb, & Turkey

GREEN BEAN AND MEAT STEW

Lubi bi laham

- 1/4 cup/60 ml extra-virgin olive oil
- 2 large onions, coarsely chopped
- 2 cloves garlic, finely chopped
- 1 lb/500 g beef or lamb, cut into small chunks
- 2 lb/1 kg fresh or frozen green beans, trimmed and cut into 2-inch/5-cm lengths
- 1 1/2 cups/375 ml water, or more if needed
- 1 2/3 cups/400 g chopped tomatoes
- 1/2 teaspoon ground cinnamon
- salt and freshly ground black pepper
- hot cooked rice, to serve

Heat the oil in a large frying pan over medium heat. • Sauté the onions and garlic for 8–10 minutes, until lightly browned. • Add the beef and brown for 10 minutes. • Add the beans and pour in the water. Bring to a boil, cover, and cook over low heat for 40–45 minutes, or until the beans are tender. Add more water if the mixture becomes too dry. • Add the tomatoes and cinnamon and season with salt and pepper. • Cook over low heat for 30 minutes more. • Serve hot on a bed of rice.

Serves 4 • Prep: 25 min • Cooking: 88–95 min • Level: 1

STUFFED TURKEY

Habash mahshi

The trussing in this recipe requires a degree of strength, but yields an authentic and impressive-looking result.

Preheat the oven to 325°F/170°C/gas 3. • Set out a large roasting pan. • Rinse the turkey and dry well. Rub inside and out with a generous seasoning of salt and pepper. Rub in the allspice. • Heat the oil in a large frying pan over medium heat. Sauté the garlic, parsley, and pine nuts for 5 minutes. • Brown the beef for 10 minutes. • Stir in the rice, nutmeg, cinnamon, cumin, and 1 cup (250 ml) water. Season with salt and pepper. • Bring to a boil and simmer, uncovered, for 15–20 minutes, or until the rice is tender. • Spoon the mixture into the turkey cavity and sew up the cavity with kitchen string. • Rub the turkey with butter and place in the pan. • Pour the remaining 1 cup (250 ml) water into the pan and cover with aluminum foil. • Roast for 1 1/2 hours. Remove the foil and roast for 30 minutes more, or until tender. • Serve hot or at room temperature.

Serves 8–10 • Prep: 30 min • Cooking: 3 hr • Level 1

- 1 turkey, weighing about 8 lb/4 kg
- salt and freshly ground black pepper
- 1 teaspoon ground allspice
- 1/4 cup/60 ml extra-virgin olive oil
- 2 cloves garlic, finely chopped
- 2 tablespoons finely chopped fresh parsley
- 1/2 cup/90 g pine nuts
- 1 lb/500 g ground/minced beef
- 2 cups/400 g long-grain rice
- 1 teaspoon freshly grated nutmeg
- 1 teaspoon ground cinnamon
- 1/2 teaspoon cumin seeds
- 2 cups/500 ml water
- 1/4 cup/60 g butter, cut up

Green bean and meat stew

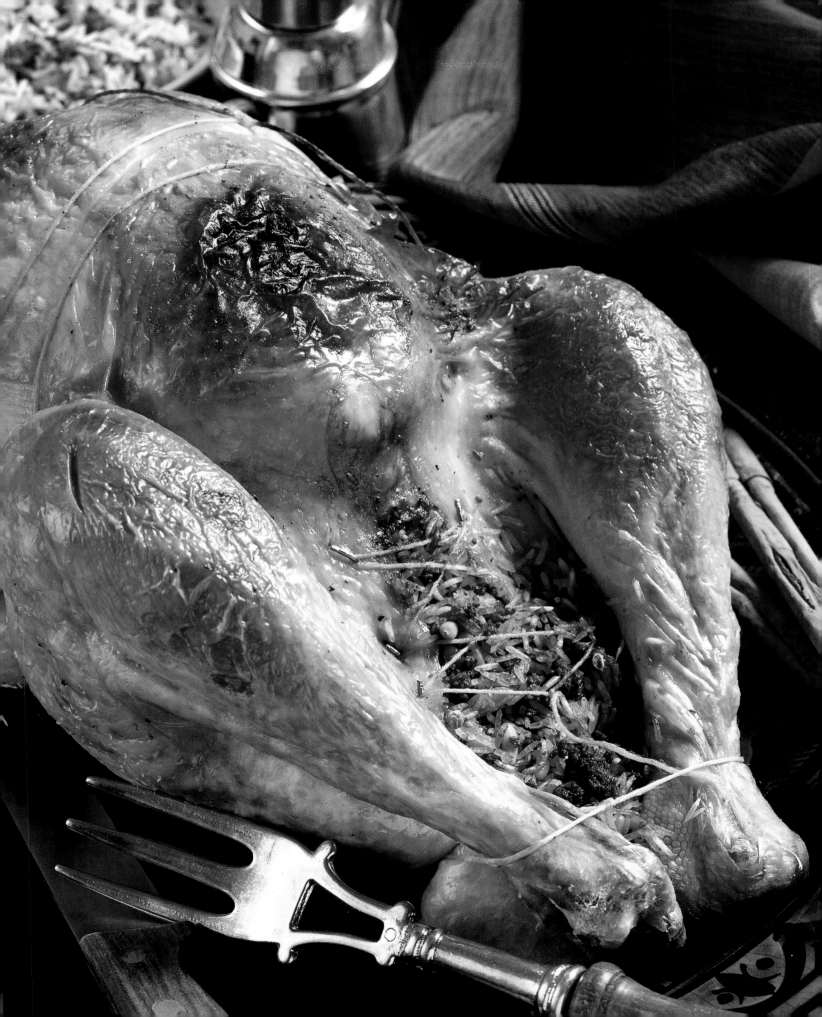

Beef & Lamb

SPINACH STEW

Sabanikh mah laham

- 1 lb/2 kg boneless lamb, cut into small cubes
- 1 small onion, whole + 1 small onion, finely chopped
- 1 quart/1 liter water
- ¼ cup/60 g butter
- 1 clove garlic, finely chopped
- 1 lb/2 kg fresh spinach, well-washed and coarsely chopped
- 1 teaspoon freshly ground coriander seeds
- salt and freshly ground black pepper
- juice of ½ lemon
- hot cooked rice, to serve

Place the lamb and whole onion in a large saucepan over high heat. Pour in the water. • Bring to a boil and lower the heat. Cover and simmer for 50–60 minutes, or until the lamb is tender. • Melt the butter in a large saucepan. Sauté the finely chopped onion for 8–10 minutes, or until lightly browned. • Add the garlic, spinach, and coriander. Season with salt and pepper. • Cook, stirring occasionally, over medium heat until the spinach has wilted. Add the meat and cooking liquid. Cover and cook for 10–15 minutes over low heat until the meat is tender. • Drizzle with the lemon juice. Serve hot on a bed of rice.

Serves 6–8 • Prep: 15 min • Cooking: 70–85 min • Level: 1

MEAT ROLLS WITH PINE NUTS

Kofta mabrouma

- 2 lb/1 kg ground/minced lamb or beef
- 2 onions, very finely chopped
- 2 eggs, lightly beaten
- salt and freshly ground black pepper
- ¼ cup/25 g pine nuts
- 3 tablespoons butter
- 3 tablespoons water
- fresh parsley, coarsely chopped
- slices of lemon, to garnish

This is a specialty of Aleppo in Syria, where it is baked and served in a round dish, with the meat rolls arranged decoratively in circles.

Preheat the oven to 400°F/200°C/gas 6. • Set out a large baking dish. • Mix the lamb, onions, and eggs in a large bowl. Season with salt and pepper. • Use your hands to knead the mixture until well mixed. • Turn out onto a work surface and flatten into six rectangles. • Place pine nuts about ½-inch (1-cm) from one of the long sides of each rectangle. Roll up into a sausage shape, starting from the edge lined with pine nuts. • Place the rolls in the baking dish. Dot with the butter and drizzle with the water. • Bake for 50–60 minutes, or until well browned. • Transfer to a preheated serving dish. Garnish with the parsley and slices of lemon. Serve hot.

Serves 4 • Prep: 15 min • Cooking: 50–60 min • Level: 2

ZUCCHINI STUFFED WITH LAMB

Ablama

Preheat the oven to 350°F/180°C/gas 4. • Set out an ovenproof baking dish. • Heat the oil in a medium frying pan over medium heat. Sauté the onion for 8–10 minutes, or until lightly browned. • Add the garlic, pine nuts, raisins, and cinnamon. Season with salt and pepper. • Cook for 5 minutes more, then add the lamb and brown for 10 minutes. • Blanch the zucchini in a large pot of salted boiling water for 5 minutes, or until almost tender. Drain well. • Cut a lid out of the top of each zucchini and use a teaspoon to hollow out the flesh. • Add the zucchini flesh to the meat mixture and cook until all the liquid has been absorbed. • Place the hollowed-out zucchini in the baking dish. Spoon enough filling into each one to fill. • Season the tomatoes with salt and pepper. Pour into the baking dish with the zucchini. • Bake for 40–50 minutes, or until tender and well cooked. • Place the zucchini on a serving dish and spoon the tomato sauce over the top.• Serve hot.

Serves 4 • Prep: 30 min • Cooking: 70–80 min • Level: 1

- ¼ cup/60 ml extra-virgin olive oil
- 1 large onion, finely chopped
- 2 cloves garlic, finely chopped
- ½ cup/90 g pine nuts
- ¼ cup/25 g raisins
- ½ teaspoon ground cinnamon
- salt and freshly ground black pepper
- 1 lb/500 g ground/minced lamb
- 6 medium round zucchini/courgettes (or 8 medium long zucchini)
- 1 lb/500 g peeled and chopped tomatoes

Spinach

Otherwise known as Persian herb, spinach is an adaptable ingredient that tastes equally good cooked or raw. In Middle Eastern cooking, it is often used in soups and stews to blend with the flavor of the meat.

Fish

BAKED FISH AND VEGETABLES
Samak bi-al-khudar

- ¹/₄ cup/60 ml extra-virgin olive oil
- 5 cloves garlic, finely chopped
- 1 teaspoon ground cumin
- ³/₄ cup/180 ml fresh lemon juice
- salt and freshly ground black pepper
- 4 medium potatoes, with skins, thinly sliced
- 4 medium carrots, thinly sliced
- 2 large tomatoes, finely chopped
- 2 lb/1 kg fresh or frozen fish fillets, thawed if frozen, such as sole or plaice
- ¹/₂ cup/90 g pine nuts
- 1 bunch parsley

Preheat the oven to 350°F/180°C/gas 4. • Pour the oil, 4 cloves garlic, cumin, ¹/₄ cup (60 ml) of lemon juice, salt, and pepper in an ovenproof baking dish. • Place a layer of potatoes, carrots, and tomatoes on top and cover with the fish fillets. Arrange the remaining vegetables over the fish. • Bake for 40–45 minutes, or until the fish and vegetables are tender. • Just before the fish comes out of the oven, process the pine nuts, parsley, remaining ¹/₂ cup (125 ml) of lemon juice, and remaining clove garlic in a food processor until smooth. • Spoon the sauce over the fish and vegetables. • Serve hot.

Serves 6 • Prep: 20 min • Cooking: 40–45 min • Level: 1

FISH WITH ONIONS AND RAISINS
Samak bil bassal

Preheat the oven to 325°F/170°C/gas 3. • Use a sharp knife to cut the fish skin diagonally in the thicker parts. • Heat 2 tablespoons of oil in a large frying pan over medium heat. • Sauté the onions for 8–10 minutes, or until lightly browned. Season with salt and pepper. • Drizzle the fish with the remaining 2 tablespoons oil. Sprinkle with the cinnamon, ginger, and nutmeg. • Transfer to a large ovenproof dish. Sprinkle with the parsley and cover with the onion mixture and raisins. Pour in the water. • Bake for 40–45 minutes, or until the raisins and onions form a golden crust.

Serves 6 • Prep: 30 min • Cooking: 50–55 min • Level: 1

- 1 sea bass, weighing about 3 lb/1.5 kg, gutted
- ¹/₄ cup/60 ml extra-virgin olive oil
- 2 large onions, finely chopped
- salt and freshly ground black pepper
- 1 teaspoon ground cinnamon
- 1 teaspoon ground ginger
- ¹/₈ teaspoon freshly grated nutmeg
- 1 tablespoon finely chopped fresh parsley
- 1²/₃ cups/240 g raisins
- ¹/₄ cup/60 ml water

FRIED FISH
Samak maqli

- 3 lb/1.5 kg red snapper or other white, firm-textured fish, gutted
- salt
- 2 cups/500 ml olive oil, for frying
- 1 cup/250 ml tahini (sesame seed paste)
- ¹/₄ cup/60 ml fresh lemon juice
- 2 cups/500 ml water
- 3 onions, finely chopped
- ¹/₄ teaspoon ground cinnamon
- freshly ground black pepper

Sprinkle the fish with salt and let stand for 1 hour. • Preheat the oven to 350°F/180°C/gas 4. • Heat the oil in a large frying pan to very hot. • Fry the fish for 5–7 minutes, or until golden brown. • Drain well and pat dry with paper towels. • Transfer to a large baking dish, reserving ¹/₂ cup (125 ml) of oil. • Mix the tahini, lemon juice, and water in a small bowl. Season with salt. • Heat the reserved oil in a large frying pan over medium heat. • Sauté the onions for 8–10 minutes, or until lightly browned. • Add the tahini mixture and bring to a boil for 1 minute. • Pour the onion mixture over the fish. Sprinkle with cinnamon and season with pepper. • Bake for 8–10 minutes, or until well cooked. Serve hot.

Serves 6 • Prep: 20 min + 1 hr to stand • Cooking: 22–28 min • Level: 1

SARDINES IN GRAPE LEAVES
Sardin bi uarak al inab

Poach the grape leaves in a large pot of boiling water for a few seconds until they change color. • Stuff the sardines with the parsley, cilantro, and garlic. Season with salt and pepper and drizzle with the oil. • Roll each sardine up in one or two grape leaves. • Turn on the broiler. • Broil the fish 3–5 inches (8–13 cm) from the heat source, turning frequently, for 10–15 minutes, or until lightly golden. • Drizzle with lemon juice. • Serve hot or at room temperature.

Serves 4 • Prep: 10 min • Cooking: 10–15 min • Level: 2

- 12 large fresh grape leaves (or 24 small ones)
- 12 large sardines, gutted and heads removed
- 2 tablespoons finely chopped fresh parsley
- 2 tablespoons finely chopped fresh cilantro/coriander
- 3 cloves garlic, finely chopped
- salt and freshly ground black pepper
- 3 tablespoons extra-virgin olive oil
- juice of 1 lemon

Vegetables

POTATO AND ZUCCHINI FRY WITH EGGS

Batates ua baid

- ¹/₄ cup/60 ml extra-virgin olive oil
- 1 onion, finely chopped
- 2 cloves garlic, chopped
- 4 medium carrots, sliced
- 1 lb/500 g fresh spinach, tough stems removed
- ¹/₄ cup/45 g pine nuts
- salt and freshly ground black pepper

Heat the oil in a large frying pan over medium heat. Sauté the onion for 8–10 minutes, or until lightly browned. • Add the garlic, carrots, spinach, and pine nuts. Season with salt and pepper. • Sauté for 8–10 minutes, or until the vegetables are tender. • Serve hot.

Serves 4 • Prep: 10 min • Cooking: 15–20 min • Level: 1

SPICED POTATOES

Batata harra

Cook the potatoes in a large pot of salted boiling water for 15–20 minutes, or until tender. • Drain well and transfer to a large frying pan. Drizzle with the oil and add the garlic and cayenne pepper. Season with salt and pepper. Cook over medium heat for 5 minutes until the garlic is pale gold. • Serve warm.

Serves 4–6 • Prep: 20 min • Cooking: 20–25 min • Level: 1

- 2 lb/1 kg small new potatoes
- ¹/₄ cup/60 ml extra-virgin olive oil
- 5 cloves garlic, chopped
- 2 teaspoons cayenne pepper
- salt and freshly ground black pepper

LEBANESE VEGETABLES

Khodra al lubnania

- ¹/₄ cup/60 ml extra-virgin olive oil
- 1 large onion, finely chopped
- 2 cloves garlic, finely chopped
- 8 oz/250 g ground/minced beef
- salt and freshly ground black pepper
- 1 teaspoon ground cinnamon
- 2 medium potatoes, peeled and cut into cubes
- 2 medium zucchini/courgettes, cut into cubes
- 4 large eggs
- 2 tablespoons finely chopped fresh parsley

Heat the oil in a large saucepan over medium heat. Sauté the onion and garlic for 8–10 minutes, or until lightly browned. • Add the beef and brown for 10 minutes. Season with salt and pepper. Sprinkle with cinnamon. • Add the potatoes and cook for 10 minutes, stirring occasionally. • Add the zucchini and cook for 10 minutes more, stirring occasionally. • When the potatoes and zucchini are almost tender, break the eggs over the mixture, stirring to break the yolks. • Cook for 5 minutes more, or until the eggs are set. • Sprinkle with parsley and serve hot.

Serves 4 • Prep: 15 min • Cooking: 35 min Level: 1

LEEKS WITH LEMON

Karrat al hamed

Heat the oil in a large frying pan over medium heat. Sauté the garlic with the sugar for 2 minutes, or until slightly caramelized. • Stir in the leeks and sauté over medium heat for 8–10 minutes, or until lightly browned. • Drizzle with the lemon juice and season with salt and pepper. • Cover and cook over very low heat for 15–20 minutes, or until tender. • Serve hot.

Serves 4 • Prep: 20 min • Cooking: 25–30 min • Level: 1

- ¹/₄ cup/60 ml extra-virgin olive oil
- 3 cloves garlic, finely chopped
- 1 tablespoon sugar
- 2 lb/1 kg leeks, white parts only, thinly sliced
- juice of 1 lemon
- salt and freshly ground black pepper

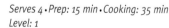
Lebanese vegetables

Vegetables

SAUTÉED SPINACH

Sabanekh bi looz

- 2 tablespoons extra-virgin olive oil
- 1 onion, finely chopped
- 2 lb/1 kg spinach, well-washed and tough stems removed
- salt and freshly ground black pepper
- 4 tomatoes, peeled and sliced
- ¹/₄ cup/40 g flaked almonds

Heat the oil in a large frying pan over medium heat. • Sauté the onion for 8–10 minutes, or until lightly browned. • Add the spinach and cook, stirring often, until it begins to wilt. • Season with salt and pepper. Stir in the tomatoes and cook until slightly softened. • Add the almonds just before serving. • Serve hot.

Serves 4 • Prep: 10 min • Cooking: 15 min • Level: 1

DEEP-FRIED CAULIFLOWER

Karnabeet makly

Cook the cauliflower florets in a large pot of salted boiling water for 10 minutes, or until just tender. • Drain well and let cool completely. • Dip the florets in the egg, and roll in the flour. • Heat the oil to very hot in a deep frying pan. • Fry the florets in batches for 5–7 minutes, or until golden brown all over. • Drain well on paper towels. • Serve with the yogurt.

Serves 4 • Prep: 15 min • Cooking: 20 min • Level: 1

- 1 cauliflower, weighing about 2 lb/1 kg, divided into small florets
- 1 large egg, lightly beaten
- ¹/₂ cup/75 g all-purpose/plain flour
- 2 cups/500 ml olive oil, for frying
- 1 cup/250 g plain yogurt

Kibbe

Kibbe is the Middle Eastern version of the Western meatball. The texture and subtlety of the flavor is achieved by grinding the meat very finely. Kibbe is often bound together with bulgur and various aromatic seasonings. In vegetarian versions, well-seasoned bulgur usually replaces the meat.

VEGETARIAN KIBBE WITH YOGURT

Kibbe nabatia maa al laban zabadi

Place the bulgur in a bowl and cover with cold water. Let stand for 30 minutes. • Drain well, squeezing out excess moisture. • Season with salt and pepper. Stir in the flour, adding water if the mixture is too dry. • Shape the dough into balls the size of walnuts. • Cook the bulgur balls in a large pot of salted simmering water for 15–20 minutes. Drain well and let cool completely. • Place the yogurt in a serving bowl and add the bulgur balls, garlic, and mint. Season with salt and pepper. • Refrigerate for 30 minutes before serving.

Serves 4 • Prep: 45 min + 60 min to stand and chill • Cooking: 15–20 min • Level: 2

- 1¹/₂ cups/150 g fine-grind bulgur
- salt and freshly ground black pepper
- ¹/₂ cup/75 g all-purpose/plain flour
- 1¹/₄ quarts/1.25 liters plain yogurt
- 2 cloves garlic, finely chopped
- 2 tablespoons finely chopped fresh mint

Vegetables

CARAMELIZED CARROTS WITH CARDAMOM

Helawat al jazr

- 1 lb/500 g carrots, finely grated
- 1 cup/200 g sugar
- 2 cups/500 ml milk
- 1/4 teaspoon ground cardamom
- 2 teaspoons grated lemon zest
- 2 tablespoons butter
- 2 tablespoons all-purpose/plain flour

Cook the carrots, sugar, milk, cardamom, and lemon zest in a large saucepan over medium heat for 10 minutes, or until the carrots are tender. • Drain, reserving the liquid. • Melt the butter in a small saucepan over medium heat. Stir in the flour until smooth and continue cooking until the mixture is fragrant, 2–3 minutes. • Pour in the carrots, coating them well. Cook for 5 minutes. • Pour in the reserved cooking liquid and mix. • Cook for 5 minutes more. • Serve hot.

Serves 6 • Prep: 15 min • Cooking: 25 min • Level: 1

FALAFEL

Process the garbanzo beans, onion, garlic, potato, and parsley in a food processor until finely chopped. • Add the coriander, cumin, oregano, and flour, and process until well blended. • Season with salt and pepper. • Let rest for 2 hours. • Stir the baking powder into the mixture and shape into flattened patties. • Heat the oil in a large frying pan to very hot. • Fry the patties in batches for 5–7 minutes, or until golden brown. • Drain well and pat dry on paper towels. • Serve warm with pita bread filled with sliced tomatoes and lettuce.

Serves 6–8 • Prep: 20 min + 2 hr to rest • Cooking: 25 min • Level: 2

- 1 lb/500 g dried garbanzo beans/ chickpeas, soaked overnight and drained
- 1 medium onion
- 3 cloves garlic, peeled
- 1 medium potato, peeled
- 1 bunch parsley
- 1 teaspoon freshly ground coriander seeds
- 1 teaspoon freshly ground cumin
- 1 teaspoon dried oregano
- 2 tablespoons all-purpose/plain flour
- salt and freshly ground white pepper
- 2 teaspoons baking powder
- 2 cups/500 ml olive oil, for frying
- pita bread, store-bought or homemade (see page 158), to serve
- sliced tomatoes and lettuce, to serve

MASHED POTATOES, LEBANESE-STYLE

Batata madooa siyemeù

- 6–8 medium potatoes, peeled and quartered
- 1/3 cup/80 ml extra-virgin olive oil
- 1/3 cup/80 ml fresh lemon juice
- 3 cloves garlic, finely chopped
- salt
- 3 tablespoons finely chopped fresh mint

Cook the potatoes in a large pot of salted boiling water for 15–20 minutes, or until tender. • Drain well, transfer to a large bowl, and mash until smooth. • Add the oil, lemon juice, garlic, and salt and stir until well blended. • Sprinkle with the mint and serve warm.

Serves 4 • Prep: 15 min • Cooking: 15–20 min • Level: 1

Serving falafel

The falafel is the Middle Eastern answer to the hamburger. It is sold on street corners, in snack bars and restaurants, and served in homes throughout the region. As snacks, falafel is usually served in pita bread, along with salad greens, sliced cucumber, yogurt, spicy sauces, and onions. Falafel can also be served on its own. It makes an especially welcome addition to any table of mezza *(appetizers).*

Desserts

ALMOND BAKLAVA

Baklava

- 14 sheets frozen phyllo dough, thawed
- 2¹/₂ cups/250 g finely ground almonds
- ²/₃ cup/140 g granulated sugar
- 2 teaspoons ground cinnamon
- 1 cup/250 g butter, melted
- 2 tablespoons almonds, coarsely chopped, to decorate

Honey Syrup
- 1 cup/250 ml honey
- ¹/₄ cup/60 ml water
- ¹/₄ cup/50 g granulated sugar
- 1¹/₂ tablespoons rose water

Preheat the oven to 325°F/170°C/gas 3. • Butter a 9-inch square baking pan. • Lay the sheets of dough out flat and cover with waxed paper and a damp kitchen towel. (This will prevent them from drying out.) • Stir together the ground almonds, sugar, and cinnamon in a large bowl. • Fit one phyllo sheet in the pan, cutting the edges to fit, and brush with butter. Fit another sheet on top and brush with butter. Sprinkle with a scant ¹/₄ cup (50 g) of the almond filling. Place another sheet on top, brush with butter, and sprinkle with filling. Repeat until all the almond mixture is used. You should have about 12 layers of filled dough. • Fold the remaining sheets and place on top. Brush with butter. • Use a long knife to cut the pastry into diamond shapes about 2 inches (5 cm) square or in rectangles about 1¹/₂ x 2¹/₂ inches (4 x 6 cm). Be sure to cut through all the layers to the bottom of the pan. • Bake for 40–50 minutes, or until golden brown. • Honey Syrup: Bring the honey, water, and sugar to a boil in a saucepan over low heat until the sugar has dissolved. Remove from the heat and add the rose water. • Drizzle the syrup over the baklava as soon as it comes out of the oven. Sprinkle with chopped almonds. • Cool completely in the pan on a rack.

Serves 6–8 • Prep: 45 min • Cooking: 40–50 min • Level: 2

ALMOND YOGURT CAKE

Basbousa

- 1 cup/250 g butter
- 4 cups/400 g coarsely chopped almonds
- 1 cup/250 ml plain yogurt
- ¹/₂ cup/100 g granulated sugar
- 1 cup/200 g semolina
- 1 teaspoon vanilla extract

Syrup
- 1 cup/200 g granulated sugar
- ¹/₃ cup/80 ml water
- juice of 1 lemon
- 1 tablespoon rose water (optional)
- 1 cup/250 ml whipped cream

Preheat the oven to 400°F/200°C/gas 6. • Oil a large baking sheet. • Melt ¹/₂ cup (125 g) butter in a large frying pan over medium heat. Sauté the almonds for 5 minutes. Transfer to a plate and set aside. • Mix the yogurt and sugar in a large bowl. • Stir in the almond mixture, semolina, and vanilla. • Pour the batter into the prepared baking sheet. • Bake for 25–30 minutes, or until lightly browned. • Syrup: Mix the sugar, water, and lemon juice in a small saucepan over medium heat. Cook, stirring constantly, until thick enough to coat a metal spoon. Add the rose water, if using. Cook for 5 minutes more. • Remove from heat and let cool slightly. • Pour the syrup over the cake as soon as it comes out of the oven. • Cut into diamond shapes and return to the oven for 5 minutes more. • Melt the remaining ¹/₂ cup (125 g) butter in a small saucepan. Pour over the cake. Spread with the whipped cream and serve.

Serves 6 • Prep: 30 min • Cooking: 45–50 min • Level: 1

DATE-CAROB LOAF

Maamul bil kharnub

Mix the dates, baking soda, carob powder, and salt in a large bowl. Add the butter and water. Let stand for 20 minutes. • Preheat the oven to 350°F/180°C/gas 4. • Butter a 8¹/₂ x 4¹/₂-inch (12 x 22-cm) loaf pan. • Beat the eggs and orange-flower water in a large bowl with an electric mixer at high speed until pale and thick. • With mixer at low speed, gradually beat in the honey and flour. • Use a large rubber spatula to fold in the date mixture. • Spoon the batter into the prepared pan. • Bake for 40–45 minutes, or until a toothpick inserted into the center comes out clean. • Cool the loaf completely in the pan.

Serves 6 • Prep: 20 min + 20 min to stand • Cooking: 40–45 min • Level: 1

- 1 cup/250 g dates, pitted and coarsely chopped
- 1 teaspoon baking soda/bicarbonate of soda
- ¹/₄ cup/30 g carob powder or unsweetened cocoa powder
- ¹/₂ teaspoon salt
- 3 tablespoons butter
- ³/₄ cup/180 ml boiling water
- 2 large eggs
- 1 teaspoon orange-flower water
- ³/₄ cup/180 ml honey, warmed
- 1¹/₄ cups/180 g whole-wheat flour

Date and almond rice

DATE AND ALMOND RICE

Roz bil haleeb

- 1 quart/1 liter milk
- 2¹/₂ cups/500 g basmati rice
- ¹/₂ cup/125 g butter, cut up
- 1 cup/150 g blanched almonds, halved
- ¹/₂ cup/90 g raisins
- ¹/₂ cup/125 g dates
- ¹/₂ cup/100 g granulated sugar

Bring 3 cups (750 ml) milk to a boil in a medium saucepan. • Add the rice and boil for 2 minutes, stirring constantly. • Lower the heat and cook, covered, for 15–20 minutes, or until the rice is tender. • Melt ¹/₄ cup (60 g) butter in a medium frying pan over medium heat. Sauté the almonds for 4–5 minutes, or until the almonds are golden. • Add the raisins, dates, and sugar. Sauté for 5 minutes more. • Stir in the remaining 1 cup (250 ml) milk and simmer for 15 minutes, or until the dates are plump and the milk has been absorbed. Season with salt. • Heat 1 tablespoon butter in a large Dutch oven or saucepan over low heat and spoon in half the rice. Cover with the date mixture and top with the remaining rice. • Dot with the remaining 3 tablespoons butter and cover with a tight-fitting lid. • Cook over very low heat for 25–30 minutes, or until the rice is fluffy.

Serves 4–6 • Prep: 15 min • Cooking: 70–80 min • Level: 1

ORANGE RICE DESSERT

Haluat aruzz bil bortokal

Mistaki can be found in Middle Eastern food stores.
Preheat the oven to 400°F/200°C/gas 6. • Butter a 13 x 9-inch (23 x 33-cm) baking dish. Sprinkle with half the bread crumbs. • Heat the milk, stirring constantly, in a large pan over low heat. Add the rice and continue cooking until the mixture thickens. • Stir in the mistaki and orange-flower water. Cook for 2 minutes, then remove from the heat. Set aside. • Pour into the prepared baking dish, spreading it evenly. Sprinkle with the remaining bread crumbs and drizzle with the melted butter. • Bake for 8–10 minutes, or until firm to the touch. Cool the cake in the pan for 10 minutes. • Syrup: Mix the sugar and water in a medium saucepan over medium heat. Cook, stirring constantly, until the sugar has dissolved and the mixture begins to boil. • Add the lemon juice and orange-flower water. • Pour the syrup evenly over the cake.

Serves 6–8 • Prep: 20 min • Cooking: 20 min • Level: 1

- 1 cup/125 g fine dry bread crumbs
- 1¹/₂ quarts/1.5 liters milk
- 1 cup/200 g short-grain rice, well-washed, soaked overnight, and drained
- 6 crystals mistaki or 1 teaspoon sugar crystals, lightly crushed
- ¹/₄ cup/60 ml orange-flower water
- 2 tablespoons butter, melted

Syrup
- 2 cups/400 g granulated sugar
- 1 cup/250 ml water
- 1 tablespoon fresh lemon juice
- 2 tablespoons orange-flower water

Desserts

SESAME AND HONEY CRISPS

Sumsum mah assal

- 1¹/₃ cups/130 g sesame seeds
- 1 tablespoon tahini (sesame seed paste)
- 1 cup/250 ml honey
- 1 tablespoon finely grated lemon zest
- ³/₄ cup/75 g coarsely chopped walnuts

Place the sesame seeds in a medium frying pan over high heat and stir until nicely toasted. Set aside. • Grease an 8-inch (20-cm) square baking pan with the tahini. • Place the honey in a medium saucepan over medium heat and bring to a boil. • Stir in the lemon zest, sesame seeds, and nuts. Boil for 1–2 minutes, or until the seeds and nuts are well coated. • Spoon the honey mixture in the pan, spreading evenly with the back of a spoon. Set aside to cool, then refrigerate until set. • Cut into small squares or bars to serve.

Serves 4–6 • Prep: 10 min + 2 hr to cool • Cooking: 1–2 min • Level: 1

NUT TARTLETS

Ma'amoul

<u>Nut Filling</u>: Mix the pistachios, sugar, and rose water in a small bowl. • <u>Pastry</u>: Preheat the oven to 325°F/170°C/gas 3. • Sift the flour into a large bowl. Use a pastry blender to cut in the butter with the rose water and milk. • Shape into balls the size of walnuts. Flatten slightly, pinching up the sides. • Place over the nut filling and press until 3 inches (8 cm) in diameter. • Place on the prepared cookie sheets. • Bake for 10–15 minutes, or until browned.

Makes 20 cookies • Prep: 10 min
Cooking: 10–15 min
Level: 1

Nut Filling
- 1¹/₂ cups/150 g coarsely chopped pistachios
- 1 tablespoon sugar
- 1 tablespoon rose water

Pastry
- 3¹/₃ cups/500 g all-purpose/plain flour
- 1 cup/250 g butter
- 2 tablespoons rose water
- ¹/₄ cup/60 ml milk
- confectioners'/icing sugar, to dust

Sesame and honey crisps

Sesame cookies

SESAME COOKIES

Barazik

- 1 cup/250 g butter, softened
- 1 cup/200 g granulated sugar
- 1 tablespoon finely grated lemon zest
- 2 cups/300 g all-purpose/plain flour
- 1 large egg white, lightly beaten
- 2 tablespoons honey
- 1¹/₃ cups/130 g sesame seeds

Preheat the oven to 400°F/200°C/gas 6. • Butter two cookie sheets. • Beat the butter, sugar, and lemon zest in a large bowl with an electric mixer at high speed until pale and creamy. • With mixer at low speed, gradually beat in the flour. • Place the egg white, honey, and sesame seeds in a small bowl and mix well. The mixture should be dense and dry. • Place 2 tablespoons of the sesame mixture on a clean surface. • Scoop out 1 heaping tablespoon of dough and shape into a ball about the size of a walnut. • Place over the sesame mixture and press down with your fingers until the cookie is 3 inches (8 cm) in diameter. Repeat until all the dough and filling are used up. • Place the cookies, sesame seed-side up, on the prepared cookie sheets. • Bake for 10–15 minutes, or until golden brown, rotating the sheets halfway through for even baking.

Makes 20 cookies • Prep: 10 min • Cooking: 10–15 min • Level: 1

STUFFED DATE TARTLETS

Ma'amoul

Ma'amoul are glorious stuffed pastries that can have many different shapes and fillings. It is always a thrill to bite into them and to find walnuts, pistachios, almonds, or dates.

Date Filling: Mix the dates and water in a small saucepan over low heat. Cook, stirring often, for 6–7 minutes, or the dates have softened. • Add the lemon juice. • Transfer to a food processor and process until smooth. Let cool completely. • Pastry: Preheat the oven to 325°F/170°C/gas 3. • Sift the flour into a large bowl. Use a pastry blender to cut in the butter. Add the rose water, followed by the milk to form a soft dough. • Shape into balls the size of walnuts. Flatten slightly, pinching up the sides to form hollow rounds. • Spoon the filling into the center of the pastry rounds. Stretch the dough over the filling to make a ball. • Arrange the pastries on a large baking sheet. Use a fork to prick all over. • Bake for 20–25 minutes, or until set. While still warm they may seem soft, but on cooling they become firm. • Roll in the confectioners' sugar.

Serves 10–12 • Prep: 25 min • Cooking: 26–31 min • Level: 2

Date Filling
- 1¹/₂ cups/150 g pitted dates, coarsely chopped
- ¹/₂ cup/125 ml water
- 1 tablespoon fresh lemon juice

Pastry
- 3¹/₃ cups/500 g all-purpose/plain flour
- 1 cup/250 g butter
- 2 tablespoons rose water
- ¹/₄ cup/60 ml milk
- confectioners'/icing sugar, to dust

Cookies

Pistachio shortbread

Ghoraibi

- 1 cup/250 g butter, softened
- 1²/₃ cups/200 g confectioners'/icing sugar
- 1²/₃ cups/250 g all-purpose/plain flour
- ³/₄ cup/75 g finely chopped pistachio nuts
- 2 tablespoons granulated sugar

Preheat the oven to 350°F/180°C/gas 4. • Butter two cookie sheets. • Beat the butter and confectioners' sugar in a large bowl with an electric mixer at high speed until creamy. • With mixer at low speed, gradually beat in the flour. • Scoop out a heaping tablespoon of dough and shape into a ball the size of a walnut. • Place on a prepared cookie sheet and use your index finger to make an indentation in the center. • Stir together the pistachios and granulated sugar in a small bowl. • Fill each cookie with ¹/₂ teaspoon of pistachio mixture. • Repeat until all the dough is on the cookie sheets and filled with the pistachio mixture. • Bake for 15–20 minutes, or until golden brown, rotating the sheets halfway through for even baking.

Makes 20–24 cookies • Prep: 15 min • Cooking: 15–20 min • Level: 1

Fried cardamom cookies

Nane goosh feel

Sift the flour into a medium bowl. • Beat the egg yolks and egg white, rose water, milk, and cardamom in a large bowl with an electric mixer at high speed until pale and creamy. • Use a large rubber spatula to fold in the flour. • Turn the dough out onto a lightly floured surface. Knead until smooth and elastic. • Cover with a clean cloth and let stand for 2 hours. • Shape into balls the size of walnuts. • Roll the balls out to ¹/₈-inch (3-mm) thick and to 3 inches (8 cm) in diameter. • Carefully fold the dough in half, using a fork to seal the edges. The folded part of the cookie should be rounded and not stuck down. • Cover with a clean cloth and let stand for 5 minutes. • Heat the oil to very hot in a large skillet frying pan. • Fry the cookies in batches for 2–3 minutes, or until lightly browned all over. • Drain well on paper towels. • Dust with confectioners' sugar and serve.

Makes 20–25 cookies • Prep: 20 min + 2 hr to stand • Cooking: 10 min • Level: 2

- 2²/₃ cups/400 g all-purpose/plain flour
- 3 large egg yolks + 1 large egg white
- ¹/₄ cup/60 ml rose water
- ¹/₂ cup/125 ml milk
- ¹/₂ teaspoon ground cardamom
- 2 cups/500 ml olive oil, for frying
- ¹/₃ cup/50 g confectioners'/icing sugar, to dust

Pistachio shortbread

Almond delights

ALMOND DELIGHTS

Orass bi loz

- 1 cup/100 g finely ground almonds
- 1 cup/150 g confectioners'/icing sugar + extra to dust
- ¹/₄ cup/60 g orange-flower water
- pistachio nuts

Mix the almonds, confectioners' sugar, and orange-flower water to form a stiff paste. • Use your hands to knead the almond mixture until smooth. Let stand for 5 minutes. • Shape into small balls the size of marbles and roll in the confectioners' sugar. Press the pistachio nuts into the centers and seal into balls. Serve in individual paper cases.

Serves 6 • Prep: 10 min • Level: 1

Sweets in Middle Eastern cuisine

Sweets are not generally served at the end of a Middle Eastern meal but are reserved for guests and special occasions. Dates, almonds, and sesame seeds are common ingredients for many desserts and are prepared in many different ways to create candies and cookies.

TURKEY

Turkey has always been a bridge between Europe and the Orient, and its culinary traditions reflect myriad influences from both directions. The roots of Turkish cuisine are based in the cooking styles of the nomadic peoples who inhabited the region in medieval times, overlaid by the rich and flamboyant styles of the great Ottoman sultans and their sophisticated royal kitchens. Preparing and enjoying good food and offering hospitality to guests are as important in Turkey today as they have always been.

Ankara-style lamb au gratin
(see page 194)

Salads

SIMPLE MIXED SALAD
Yesil salatasi

- 8 oz/250 g salad greens
- 2 scallions/spring onions, finely chopped
- 2 tomatoes, thinly sliced
- 3 radishes, thinly sliced
- 2 hard-cooked eggs, cut into 6 wedges
- 2 tablespoons finely chopped fresh dill
- 2 tablespoons finely chopped fresh parsley
- 4 black olives, chopped

Dressing
- ¹/₃ cup/80 ml olive oil
- 2 tablespoons fresh lemon juice
- salt and freshly ground black pepper

Place the salad greens in a large salad bowl. Arrange the scallions, tomatoes, and radishes on top in a decorative manner. • Add the eggs, dill, parsley, and olives. • Dressing: Mix the oil and lemon juice in a small bowl. Season with salt and pepper. Pour over the salad.

Serves 4 • Prep: 15 min • Level: 1

BULGUR SALAD
Kisir

- 2 cups/200 g fine- or medium-grind bulgur
- 2 medium tomatoes, finely chopped
- 4 scallions/spring onions, finely chopped
- 1 fresh red or green chile pepper, thinly sliced
- ¹/₄ cup/60 g finely chopped fresh parsley
- 1 tablespoon finely chopped fresh mint
- ¹/₄ cup/60 ml extra-virgin olive oil
- juice of 1 lemon
- salt and freshly ground black pepper

This is a Turkish variation on the famous Middle Eastern tabbouleh salad. The chile adds real bite to this dish. If you don't like spicy food, just leave it out. Serve as an appetizer or as a side dish with grilled meat or fish.

Place the bulgur in a bowl and cover with hot water. Let stand for 30 minutes. • Drain well. • Stir in the tomatoes, scallions, chile, parsley, and mint. • Drizzle with the oil and lemon juice and season with salt and pepper. • Serve.

Serves 6 • Prep: 10 min + 30 min to soak • Level: 1

TURKISH-STYLE ZUCCHINI SALAD
Kabak salatasi

Boil the zucchini in a large pot of salted boiling water for 10–12 minutes, or until tender. • Drain well and pat dry with paper towels. Slice thinly lengthwise. Transfer to a large serving dish. • Mix the yogurt, lemon juice, oil, and dill in a medium bowl until well blended. Season with salt and pepper. • Spoon the yogurt mixture over the zucchini. Use a fork to crush the zucchini coarsely. • Refrigerate for at least 2 hours before serving.

Serves 4 • Prep: 10 min + 2 hr to chill • Cooking: 10–12 min • Level: 1

- 2 lb/1 kg zucchini/courgettes
- ¹/₂ cup/125 ml plain yogurt
- 1¹/₂ tablespoons fresh lemon juice
- ¹/₄ cup/60 ml extra-virgin olive oil
- 1 bunch dill, finely chopped
- salt and freshly ground black pepper

SHEPHERD'S SALAD
Çoban salatasi

Place the onions in a salad bowl and season with salt. • Add the tomatoes, cucumber, bell pepper, and chile. • Mix the oil and lemon juice in a small bowl. Season with salt and pepper. Drizzle over the salad and toss well. • Garnish with the olives.

Serves 4 • Prep: 15 min • Level: 1

- 2 medium onions, thinly sliced
- salt
- 2 large firm-ripe tomatoes, coarsely chopped
- 1 cucumber, cubed
- 1 green bell pepper/capsicum, seeded and cut into cubes
- 1 fresh chile pepper, finely sliced
- ¹/₃ cup/80 ml extra-virgin olive oil
- 2 tablespoons fresh lemon juice
- freshly ground black pepper
- black olives, to garnish

Bulgur
Bulgur is a staple ingredient in Turkish and Middle Eastern cooking. It is made by steaming whole wheat berries, which are then dried and cracked into grits. Since it is precooked, it is very quick to prepare and needs to soak in water for only 30 minutes before it is tender enough to eat, although it can also be cooked. It is available in health food stores and in large supermarkets.

Yogurt soup

YOGURT SOUP

Yoğurt çorbasi

- 2 quarts/2 liters meat stock or broth
- 1 cup/200 g short-grain rice
- salt
- ²/₃ cup/150 g butter
- ³/₄ cup/125 g all-purpose/plain flour
- 2 cups/500 ml plain yogurt
- 1 tablespoon finely chopped fresh mint
- 1 tablespoon sweet paprika
- 1–2 tablespoons extra-virgin olive oil

Reserve 1 cup (250 ml) of stock and bring the rest to a boil in a large saucepan. • Add the rice and season with salt. • Melt the butter in a small saucepan over low heat. Stir in the flour until smooth and continue cooking until the mixture is lightly browned, about 5 minutes. • Pour in the reserved 1 cup stock and bring to a boil. Cook for 7–10 minutes, or until the rice is still al dente. • Stir the flour mixture into the rice mixture and cook for 8–10 minutes more, or until the rice is tender. • Beat the yogurt and mint in a medium serving bowl until well blended. Pour in the soup and mix well. • Mix the oil and paprika and drizzle over the soup. Serve hot.

Serves 6–8 • Prep: 15 min • Cooking: 25–30 min • Level: 1

TURKISH CARROT SOUP

Havuç çorbasi

Melt 2 tablespoons butter in a large frying pan over medium heat. Sauté the carrots for 8–10 minutes, or until lightly browned. • Pour in the water and season with salt and pepper. Sprinkle with the sugar. • Bring to a boil, lower the heat, cover, and cook for 15–20 minutes, or until the carrots are very soft. • Drain well. • Use a fork to mash the carrots until smooth. • Mix the carrots and chicken stock in a large saucepan. • Bring to a boil and cook over low heat for 5–10 minutes, or until the carrots have almost dissolved into the stock. • Melt the remaining 2 tablespoons butter in a small saucepan over low heat. Stir in the flour until smooth and continue cooking until the mixture is lightly browned, about 5 minutes. • Pour in the milk, all at once, stirring constantly. Cook for 5–7 minutes, or until the mixture thickens. • Remove from the heat. Stir in the egg yolks, one at a time, until just blended after each addition. • Pour the egg mixture into the stock and cook for 5 minutes. • Serve hot.

Serves 4–6 • Prep: 20 min • Cooking: 40–50 min • Level: 2

- ¹/₄ cup/60 g butter
- 1¹/₂ lb/750 g carrots, thinly sliced
- 2 cups/500 ml water
- salt and freshly ground black pepper
- 1 teaspoon sugar
- 2 quarts/2 liters chicken stock or broth
- 2 tablespoons all-purpose/plain flour
- ²/₃ cup/150 ml milk
- 3 large egg yolks

TURKISH RED LENTIL SOUP

Mercimek çorbasi

- 2 tablespoons butter
- 2 medium onions, finely chopped
- 2 cups/200 g red lentils, well-washed
- 1 quart/1 liter meat stock or broth
- 1 tablespoon tomato paste
- salt
- 1 tablespoon finely chopped fresh parsley
- croutons, to serve

Melt the butter in a large saucepan over medium heat. Sauté the onions for 8–10 minutes, or until lightly browned. • Stir in the lentils, stock, and tomato paste. Season with salt. • Cook for 25–30 minutes, or until the lentils are tender. • Remove from the heat and process in a food processor until smooth. • Sprinkle with the parsley and serve with croutons on the side. Serve warm.

Serves 4 • Prep: 10 min • Cooking: 35–40 min • Level: 1

TOMATO VERMICELLI SOUP

Sehriye çorbasi

Melt the butter in a large saucepan over medium heat. Sauté the tomatoes for 5 minutes, or until they begin to break down. • Pour in the stock and bring to a boil. Lower the heat and add the spaghetti. Cook for 10 minutes. Season with salt and pepper. • Serve hot.

Serves 4 • Prep: 20 min • Cooking: 20 min • Level: 1

- 1 tablespoon butter
- 3 tomatoes, peeled, seeded, and chopped
- 1 liter/1 quart chicken stock or broth
- 3 oz/90 g spaghetti or vermicelli, broken up into short lengths
- salt and freshly ground black pepper

Turkish red lentil soup

Lamb & Beef

DUMPLINGS WITH MEAT FILLING
Manti

Dough
- 2¹/₃ cups/350 g all-purpose flour
- 1 large egg and 1 large egg yolk, lightly beaten with 6 tablespoons water

- 2 tablespoons extra-virgin olive oil
- 2 medium onions, finely chopped
- 10 oz/300 g ground/minced lamb or beef
- salt and freshly ground white pepper
- 2 cups/500 ml beef stock or broth

Sauce
- 1²/₃ cups/400 ml plain yogurt
- salt
- 3 cloves garlic, finely chopped
- ¹/₃ cup/80 g butter, melted

Dough: Sift the flour onto a clean work surface and make a well in the center. • Pour in the egg mixture and stir until it has been absorbed. Knead the dough for 15–20 minutes, or until smooth and elastic. • Shape into a ball, wrap with plastic wrap, and set aside for 30 minutes. • Preheat the oven to 350°F/180°C/gas 4. • Butter a large baking dish. • Heat the oil in a large skillet over medium heat. Sauté the onion for 8–10 minutes, or until lightly browned. • Add the lamb and brown over high heat for 5 minutes. Season with salt and pepper. • Remove from the heat and set aside. • Divide the dough in half. Roll half the dough out very thinly and cut into 2-inch (5-cm) squares. • Spoon heaping teaspoonfuls of the filling into the center of each square. • Fold the dough up, bringing the corners together over the filling to make ravioli-type packages. Seal well with a little water. • Repeat with the remaining dough. • Arrange the dumplings in the prepared baking pan. • Bake for 15–20 minutes, or until lightly browned. • Remove from the oven and pour in the meat stock. • Return to the oven and cook for 15–20 minutes, or until the stock has reduced completely. • Sauce: Beat the yogurt, salt, and garlic in a medium bowl. • Arrange the dumplings on a large serving plate. Drizzle with half the butter, spoon the yogurt sauce over the top, and drizzle with the remaining butter. Serve hot.

Serves 10 • Prep: 50 min + 30 min to rest • Cooking: 45–55 min • Level: 3

BULGUR PILAF WITH LAMB
Bulgur pilavi

Melt the butter in a large frying pan over medium heat. Sauté the scallion for 8–10 minutes, or until lightly browned. • Add the lamb and brown over high heat for 10 minutes. • Stir in the tomatoes and cumin. Season with salt and pepper. • Lower the heat and simmer for 25–30 minutes, adding a little water if the mixture begins to dry. • Stir in the bulgur and cook for 5 minutes. • Pour in the 3 cups (750 ml) water. • Cover and cook over high heat for 5 minutes. • Lower the heat and cook for 10–15 minutes more. • Serve hot.

Serves 6 • Prep: 10 min • Cooking: 65–75 min • Level: 1

- ¹/₄ cup/60 g butter
- 1 medium scallion/spring onion, finely chopped
- 1 lb/500 g boneless lamb, cut into small cubes
- 1 cup/250 ml peeled and chopped tomatoes
- 1 teaspoon ground cumin
- salt and freshly ground black pepper
- 3 cups/750 ml hot water + more as needed
- 2¹/₂ cups/500 g fine-grind bulgur

TURKISH STUFFED EGGPLANTS
Karni yarik

Make several deep cuts in the sliced sides of the eggplants. Place the eggplants in a colander. Sprinkle with salt and let drain for 1 hour. • Heat ¹/₂ cup (125 ml) oil in a large skillet over medium heat. • Fry the eggplants for 10–15 minutes, or until the flesh has softened. • Drain well on paper towels. • Heat the remaining 3 tablespoons of oil in a large frying pan over medium heat. Sauté the onion for 8–10 minutes, or until lightly browned. • Add the beef and brown over high heat for 5 minutes. Add the cubed tomatoes and season with salt and pepper. • Lower the heat, cover, and cook for 30 minutes over low heat. • Preheat the oven to 400°F/ 200°C/gas 6. • Arrange the eggplants in a large baking dish. • Spoon the meat sauce into the cuts in the eggplants. Cover with the tomato slices. • Pour the water into the pan. • Bake for 15–20 minutes, or until tender. • Sprinkle with the parsley and serve hot.

Serves 3–4 • Prep: 25 min + 1 hr to drain • Cooking: 70–80 min • Level: 1

- 3 medium eggplants/aubergines, each weighing about 1¹/₂ lb/750 g, halved lengthwise
- salt
- ¹/₂ cup/125 ml + 3 tablespoons extra-virgin olive oil
- 3 medium onions, finely chopped
- 1 lb/500 g ground/minced beef
- 4 tomatoes, cut into cubes, and 2 tomatoes, thinly sliced
- freshly ground black pepper
- 1 cup/250 ml water
- 1 tablespoon finely chopped fresh parsley

ZUCCHINI MOUSSAKA

Kabak musakka

- ¹/₄ cup/60 ml extra-virgin olive oil
- 2 medium onions, finely chopped
- 1¹/₂ lb/750 g ground/minced beef
- salt and freshly ground black pepper
- 2 lb/1 kg firm-ripe tomatoes, peeled and cut into cubes
- 1 tablespoon finely chopped fresh parsley
- ¹/₂ teaspoon freshly ground cumin
- ¹/₄ teaspoon freshly grated nutmeg
- water (optional)
- 2 lb/1 kg zucchini/courgettes, cut lengthwise into ¹/₂-inch/1-cm slices

Heat 2 tablespoons of oil in a large frying pan over medium heat. Sauté the onion for 8–10 minutes, or until lightly browned. • Add the beef and brown over high heat for 5 minutes. • Season with salt and pepper. Add the tomatoes and sprinkle with the parsley, cumin, and nutmeg. • Cook for 45 minutes over low heat, adding a little water if the mixture begins to dry. • Heat the remaining 2 tablespoons oil in a large frying pan over high heat. Sauté the zucchini for 5–7 minutes, or until lightly browned. • Season with salt. Cook for 10 minutes over medium heat. • Stir the zucchini into the meat sauce. • Serve hot.

Serves 8 • Prep: 15 min • Cooking: 75 min • Level: 1

CHICKEN WITH RICE

Pirinçli piliç

- 1¹/₄ cups/250 g short-grain rice
- ¹/₄ cup/60 g extra-virgin olive oil
- 1 chicken, weighing about 2 lb/1 kg, cut into 6–8 pieces
- 1 medium onion, finely chopped
- 1 chicken liver, trimmed and coarsely chopped
- 1 tomato, peeled and coarsely chopped
- 2 tablespoons dried currants
- salt
- 2¹/₂ cups/625 ml chicken stock or broth, + more as needed
- 2 tablespoons pine nuts
- 1 small bunch fresh dill, finely chopped

Cook the rice in a large pot of salted boiling water for 15–20 minutes, or until tender. Drain well. • Heat 3 tablespoons oil in a large frying pan over high heat. Brown the chicken for 5 minutes. Add the onion, chicken liver, tomato, and currants. Season with salt and pour in the stock. • Lower the heat, cover, and cook for 15 minutes. • Melt the remaining 1 tablespoon oil in a large frying pan over medium-high heat. Add the rice and toast it until opaque, about 2 minutes. Stir in the pine nuts. • Transfer to the pan with the chicken, adding more stock if the mixture begins to dry. • Cover and cook over low heat for 15–20 minutes. • Garnish with the dill and serve hot.

Serves 4 • Prep: 20–25 min • Cooking: 35–40 min • Level: 1

STUFFED MUSSELS

Midye dolmasi

Heat the oil in a large frying pan over medium heat. Sauté the onions for 8–10 minutes, or until lightly browned. • Stir in the rice and toast over high heat for 2 minutes. Add the tomato sauce and water. • Bring to a boil and season with salt and pepper. Add the currants and pine nuts. • Cover and cook over medium heat for 15–20 minutes, or until the rice is tender. • Use a knife to open up the mussels. Spoon the stuffing into the center of each mussel. Close the two halves of the mussels securely. • Place the mussels in a large skillet, adding enough water to cover. Cover and cook for 15–20 minutes. • Serve hot.

Serves 4–6 • Prep: 30 min • Cooking: 30–40 min • Level: 2

- ¹/₂ cup/125 ml extra-virgin olive oil
- 2 medium onions, finely chopped
- ³/₄ cup/150 g short-grain rice
- 3 tablespoons tomato sauce
- 1 cup/250 ml boiling water
- salt and freshly ground black pepper
- 3 tablespoons dried currants
- 3 tablespoons pine nuts
- 3 lb/1.5 kg mussels, in shell

ANKARA-STYLE LAMB AU GRATIN

Kuzu Ankara tavasi

Heat 2 tablespoons oil in a large saucepan over high heat. Brown the lamb for 5 minutes. • Pour in the water and cook for 25–30 minutes, or until the lamb is tender. • Heat the remaining 2 tablespoons oil in a large frying pan over medium heat. Sauté the onion and carrot for 8–10 minutes, or until lightly browned. • Add to the lamb and cook for 15–20 minutes, or until the lamb and vegetables are cooked, adding more water if it begins to dry. • There should be about 2 tablespoons of liquid for the sauce. • Preheat the oven to 350°F/180°C/gas 4. • Yogurt Sauce: Mix the flour and yogurt in a small saucepan. Stir in the 2 tablespoons of cooking liquid from the lamb. • Bring to a boil and cook for 5–7 minutes. • Remove from the heat and stir in the egg yolks. Season with salt and pepper. • Transfer the lamb to a roasting pan and cover with the yogurt sauce. • Bake for 15–20 minutes. • Serve hot.

Serves 4–6 • Prep: 30 min • Cooking: 75–85 min. • Level: 2

- ¹/₄ cup/60 ml extra-virgin olive oil
- 1¹/₂ lb/750 g lean lamb, cut into pieces, with the bone
- 2 cups/500 ml water, or more if needed
- 1 medium onion, finely chopped
- 1 carrot, finely chopped

Yogurt Sauce
- 2 tablespoons all-purpose/plain flour
- 2 cups/500 ml plain yogurt
- 2 large egg yolks
- salt and freshly ground white pepper

Grilled lamb patties

GRILLED LAMB PATTIES

Koftesi

- 1¹/₂ lb/750 g ground/ minced lamb
- 2 medium onions, very finely chopped + 1 medium onion, cut into rings
- 1 large egg, lightly beaten
- 1 teaspoon freshly ground cumin
- 1 teaspoon sweet paprika
- salt and freshly ground black pepper
- 2 tablespoons extra-virgin olive oil
- 1–2 green chile peppers

Place the lamb in a large bowl. • Mix in the chopped onions, egg, cumin, and paprika. Season with salt and pepper. • Shape the mixture into 12 patties. Brush with the oil. • Refrigerate for 15 minutes. • Cook the meat on a very hot grill for 4–5 minutes on each side, or until browned. • Arrange the patties on a serving plate and place the onion rings in the center. Broil (grill) the chilies and use them as garnish.

Makes 10 patties • Prep: 10 min + 15 min to chill • Cooking: 8–10 min • Level: 1

BEEF AND RICE KOFTE

Kandinbudu koftesi

Melt the butter in a large frying pan over medium heat. Sauté the onions for 8–10 minutes, or until lightly browned. • Stir in the rice. Season with salt and pour in the water. • Cover and cook for 10–15 minutes, or until the liquid has all been absorbed. • Mix the beef, rice, dill, cumin, and 2 whole eggs in a large bowl. Season with salt and pepper. • Shape the mixture into balls the size of golf balls. Flatten slightly. • Dip the meatballs in the beaten yolks. • Heat the oil in a large frying pan until very hot. • Fry the meatballs in batches for 5–7 minutes, or until golden brown all over. Drain on paper towels and serve hot.

Serves 6 • Prep: 20 min • Cooking: 50–55 min • Level: 1

- 1 cup/200 g short-grain rice
- 2 tablespoons butter
- 2 red onions, finely chopped
- ³/₄ cup/180 ml water
- 1¹/₂ lb/750 g ground/ minced beef
- 1 teaspoon finely chopped fresh dill
- ¹/₂ teaspoon ground cumin seeds
- 2 large eggs, + 2 large egg yolks, lightly beaten
- salt and freshly ground black pepper
- ¹/₂ cup/125 ml olive oil, for frying

Lamb & Fish

SULTAN'S DELIGHT

Hünkâr beğendi

- 3 tablespoons butter
- 3 red onions, finely chopped
- 2 lb/1 kg boneless lean lamb, cut into small chunks
- 2 tomatoes, peeled and finely chopped
- salt and freshly ground black pepper
- 1¹/₂ cups/375 ml hot water, or more as needed

Eggplant Puree

- 3 small eggplants/ aubergines, about 1 lb/500 g
- 1 tablespoon fresh lemon juice
- 2 tablespoons butter
- 2 tablespoons all-purpose/plain flour
- 1 cup/250 ml milk
- ¹/₂ cup/60 g freshly grated Kasseri or Parmesan cheese
- ¹/₂ teaspoon salt
- finely chopped fresh parsley, to garnish

Melt the butter in a large frying pan over medium heat. Sauté the onions for 8–10 minutes, or until lightly browned. • Brown the lamb for 5 minutes. • Add the tomatoes and season with salt and pepper. Pour in the water, cover, and cook over low heat for 90 minutes, adding more water if the mixture begins to dry. • Eggplant Puree: Preheat the oven to 400°F/200°C/gas 6. • Arrange the eggplants in a baking pan. • Roast for 20–30 minutes, turning often, until the skins have blackened and the insides are tender. • Remove from the oven and peel while still warm. • Drizzle with the lemon juice and use a fork to mash. • Melt the butter in a large saucepan over low heat. Stir in the flour until smooth and continue cooking until the mixture is lightly browned, about 5 minutes. Stir in the milk, eggplants, and cheese. Season with salt and cook, stirring constantly for 8–10 minutes. • Arrange the meat on a serving plate and spoon the eggplant puree over the top. • Sprinkle with the parsley and serve hot.

Serves 6 • Prep: 20 min • Cooking: 2 hr • Level: 1

KEBAB WITH YOGURT

Yoğurtlu kebabs

You will need five metal skewers to create this dish.

Marinate the lamb in a large bowl with the onion and oil for 12 hours. Season with salt and pepper. • Carefully thread the meat onto five skewers. • Cook on a very hot grill for 15–20 minutes, turning often. • Melt the butter in a large frying pan. Stir in the tomatoes and season with salt and pepper. Cook, stirring often, for 5 minutes. • Place the toast on a serving dish. Lay the skewers of cooked meat on the toast, spoon the tomato mixture over the top, and cover with the yogurt.

Serves 5 • Prep: 15 min. + 12 hr to marinate • Cooking: 20–25 min • Level: 1

- 1 lb/500 g boneless lamb or mutton, cut into small cubes
- 1 onion, finely chopped
- 3 tablespoons extra-virgin olive oil
- salt and freshly ground white pepper
- ¹/₄ cup/60 g butter
- 4 tomatoes, chopped
- 5 slices firm-textured bread, toasted
- 2 cups/500 ml plain yogurt

SWORDFISH SKEWERS

Kilic sis

Mix the oil, lemon juice, salt, paprika, and bay leaves in a large bowl. Season with pepper. • Place the swordfish in the oil mixture. Cover tightly with aluminum foil and refrigerate for at least 6 hours. • Turn on the broiler (grill). • Thread the fish, onion, and bell pepper pieces alternately onto metal skewers. • Broil 4–6 inches (10–15 cm) from the heat source for about 10 minutes, or until the fish is cooked, turning often and brushing frequently with the marinade. • Serve hot.

Serves 4 • Prep: 15 min + 6 hr to marinate • Cooking: 10 min • Level: 1

- 1 tablespoon extra-virgin olive oil
- 1 tablespoon fresh lemon juice
- 1 teaspoon salt
- 1 teaspoon paprika
- 6 bay leaves
- freshly ground black pepper
- 1 lb/500 g swordfish, washed and cut into chunks
- 1 red onion, cut into chunks
- 1 green bell pepper/ capsicum, cut into chunks

Vegetables

EGGPLANT PILAF

Patlicanli pilav

- 3 small eggplants, each weighing about 1 lb/500 g, peeled and cut into small cubes
- ²/₃ cup/150 ml extra-virgin olive oil
- 3 medium onions, finely chopped
- 1 cup/200 g long-grain rice
- 1 tablespoon pine nuts
- 2 tomatoes, peeled and finely chopped
- 1 tablespoon dried currants
- 1 tablespoon sugar
- 1 teaspoon ground cinnamon
- 1 teaspoon paprika
- salt and freshly ground black pepper
- 2 cups/500 ml meat stock or broth

Serve cold as an appetizer or for a buffet.

Place the eggplants in a colander. Sprinkle with salt and let drain for 1 hour. • Heat 6 tablespoons of oil in a large frying pan over medium heat. • Fry the eggplants for 5–7 minutes, or until softened. Drain well and dry on paper towels. • Heat the remaining oil in a large frying pan. Sauté the onions for 8–10 minutes, or until lightly browned. • Add the rice, pine nuts, tomatoes, currants, eggplants, sugar, cinnamon, and paprika. Season with salt and pepper. Pour in the stock. • Cover and cook over high heat for 5 minutes. Lower the heat and cook for 10–15 minutes, or until all the liquid has been absorbed. • Remove from the heat and cover with a clean cloth. Let stand for 15 minutes. Mix and serve.

Serves 8 • Prep: 15 min + 1 hr to drain + 15 min to stand • Cooking: 28–37 min • Level: 1

POTATO MOUSSAKA

Patata musakka

Heat 2 tablespoons of oil in a large frying pan over medium heat. Sauté the onions for 8–10 minutes, or until lightly browned. • Add the beef and brown over high heat for 5 minutes. • Season with salt and pepper. Sprinkle with the parsley and nutmeg. Cook for 45 minutes, adding a little water if the mixture begins to dry. • Preheat the oven to 350°F/180°C/gas 4. • Heat the remaining oil in a large deep frying pan to very hot. • Fry the potato slices, a few at a time, for 5–7 minutes, or until softened but not completely cooked. • Arrange a layer of potatoes in a baking pan, and cover with a layer of meat and tomatoes. Top with another layer of potatoes. Repeat until all the ingredients are used up, finishing with a layer of potatoes. • Pour in the water and cover with aluminum foil. • Bake for 45 minutes. • Remove the aluminum foil and bake for 15–20 minutes more, or until golden brown and crispy on top.

Serves 6–8 • Prep: 1 hr • Cooking: 2 hr–2 hr 10 min • Level: 2

- 1 cup/250 ml extra-virgin olive oil
- 2 medium onions, finely chopped
- 1¹/₂ lb/750 g ground/minced beef
- salt and freshly ground black pepper
- 1 tablespoon finely chopped fresh parsley
- ¹/₈ teaspoon freshly grated nutmeg
- 1 cup/250 ml water, or more if needed
- 3 lb/1.5 kg potatoes, peeled, and cut into ¹/₂-inch/1-cm slices
- 2 lb/1 kg firm-ripe tomatoes, peeled and cut into cubes

Potato moussaka

STUFFED GREEN BELL PEPPERS

Zeytinyağli biber dolmasi

Filling
- ³/₄ cup/150 g rice
- ²/₃ cup/150 ml extra-virgin olive oil
- 6 onions, finely chopped
- salt
- 2 tablespoons pine nuts
- 2 tablespoons currants
- 1 tomato, finely chopped
- 2 tablespoons sugar
- 1 teaspoon cinnamon
- 1 teaspoon paprika
- ²/₃ cup/150 ml hot water
- freshly ground black pepper
- 1 tablespoon finely chopped fresh mint
- 2 tablespoons finely chopped fresh dill
- 8 green bell peppers/capsicum, tops removed, and seeded
- ¹/₃ cup/80 ml extra-virgin olive oil
- 2 cups/500 ml water

<u>Filling</u>: Cook the rice in a large pot of salted boiling water for 15–20 minutes, or until tender. Drain well. • Heat the oil in a large frying pan over medium heat. Sauté the onions for 8–10 minutes, or until lightly browned. Season with salt. • Add the pine nuts and rice. • Cook over medium heat, stirring often, for 10 minutes. • Add the currants, tomato, sugar, cinnamon, and paprika. Pour in the water and bring to a boil. • Cover and simmer for 10–15 minutes, or until the water has been completely absorbed. • Season with pepper. Remove from the heat and add the mint and dill. Cover and let stand for 10 minutes. • Fill the bell peppers with the filling and cover with the reserved tops. • Arrange the bell peppers in a casserole into which they fit snugly. • Drizzle with the oil and enough water to cover the bottom of the pan. • Cook, covered, for 45–50 minutes, adding more water if the mixture begins to dry. • Serve hot.

Serves 4 • Prep: 10 min • Cooking: 90–115 min • Level: 1

SWOONING IMAM

Imam bayildi

- 4 eggplants/aubergines, each weighing about 1 lb/500 g, halved lengthwise
- salt
- 1 cup/250 ml extra-virgin olive oil
- 4 cloves garlic, finely chopped
- 4 onions, thinly sliced
- 2 large firm-ripe tomatoes, finely chopped
- 1 tablespoon finely chopped fresh parsley

Make several deep cuts in the cut sides of the eggplants. Place in a colander and sprinkle with salt. Let drain for 1 hour. • Preheat the oven to 350°F/180°C/gas 4. • Heat 2 tablespoons of oil in a frying pan over medium heat. Sauté the garlic and onions for 8–10 minutes, or until browned. • Season with salt, add the tomatoes, and cook for 15 minutes. • Heat the remaining oil in a large frying pan to very hot. • Fry the eggplants in batches, turning often, for 10–15 minutes, or until softened. • Place the eggplants in a baking dish and fill with the onion mixture. • Bake for 25–30 minutes, or until cooked. • Sprinkle with the parsley and serve hot.

Serves 4 • Prep: 20 min + 1 hr to drain • Cooking: 58–70 min • Level: 1

RICE PUDDING

Sütlaç

- 1¹/₄ cups/250 g short-grain rice
- 5 cups/1.25 liters milk
- ¹/₈ teaspoon salt
- 2 tablespoons rice flour
- 1 tablespoon cornstarch/cornflour
- ³/₄ cup/150 g granulated sugar
- ¹/₈ teaspoon ground cinnamon

Cook the rice in 1 cup (250) ml of milk in a large saucepan over medium heat for 6–8 minutes, or until almost all the liquid has been absorbed. • Bring the remaining 4 cups (1 liter) milk and salt to a boil in a large saucepan. Add the rice mixture. • Stir together the rice flour and cornstarch in a large bowl. Add ¹/₄ cup (60 ml) of the boiling milk mixture and stir until well blended. Pour into the rice mixture. • Cook for 10 minutes, stirring constantly. • Add the sugar and continue cooking for 15–20 minutes, stirring constantly, until the mixture is thick. • Pour into a serving dish and let cool completely. • Dust with the cinnamon and serve.

Serves 6 • Prep: 15 min • Cooking: 25–30 min • Level: 1

YOGURT BEVERAGE

Ayran

Use a wire whisk to beat the yogurt in a pitcher. Add the water, a little at a time, while beating the mixture. • Season with salt. • Refrigerate for at least 2 hours before serving.

Serves 2–4 • Prep: 5 min + 2 hr to chill • Level: 1

- 1 cup/250 ml plain yogurt
- 3 cups/750 ml cold water
- salt

Rice pudding

SEMOLINA PUDDING

Irmik helvasi

- 1 cup/250 g butter
- ²/₃ cup/120 g pine nuts + 2 tablespoons, to decorate
- 2²/₃ cups/400 g semolina
- 2 cups/500 ml milk
- 2¹/₂ cups/500 g granulated sugar
- ¹/₈ teaspoon salt

Melt 2 tablespoons of the butter in a large saucepan over medium heat. Toast ²/₃ cup of pine nuts for 3–5 minutes, or until lightly browned. • Add the remaining 14 tablespoons of butter. Stir in the semolina and cook, stirring constantly, until smooth. • Lower the heat and add the milk, sugar, and salt. • Continue cooking, stirring constantly, until the mixture thickens. Remove from the heat, cover with a clean cloth, and set aside for 15 minutes. • Use your hands to shape the mixture into balls the size of walnuts. • Sprinkle with the remaining 2 tablespoons of pine nuts and serve.

Serves 8 • Prep: 20 min + 15 min to rest • Cooking: 15 min • Level: 1

TURKISH WALNUT BAKLAVA

Baklava

Preheat the oven to 350°F/180°C/gas 4. • Butter a 10-inch (25-cm) springform baking pan. • Cut the sheets of phyllo to the size of the baking pan. • Brush one sheet of phyllo with some butter and place in the prepared baking pan. Brush with more butter. Repeat with 3 more sheets of phyllo and butter. • Do not butter the top of the last sheet of phyllo. • Sprinkle with the walnuts. • Cover with a sheet of phyllo and brush with butter. • Brush more butter on both sides of 3 more sheets of phyllo, and place them on top. • Use a sharp knife to cut the cake diagonally into 2-inch (5-cm) squares or triangles, making sure that all the layers of dough have been cut through. • Bake for 50–60 minutes, or until crisp and golden brown. • Syrup: Bring the water, sugar, and lemon juice to a boil. Boil for 20 minutes. Remove from the heat. • Pour the syrup over the baklava. • Cool completely in the pan.

Serves 8 • Prep: 20 min. • Cooking: 70–80 min. • Level: 2

- 8 sheets frozen phyllo dough, thawed
- 1 cup/250 g butter, melted
- 2³/₄ cups/280 g coarsely chopped walnuts

Syrup
- 2¹/₂ cups/600 ml water
- 3 cups/600 g granulated sugar
- 2 tablespoons fresh lemon juice

USING PHYLLO DOUGH

1. Cut the sheets of phyllo dough to the dimensions of the pan that you are using. Cover the sheets of dough with a damp cloth to prevent them from drying out.

2. Brush each sheet of dough with melted butter.

3. Place the dough sheet in the pan and brush all over with melted butter.

GREECE

Based on olive oil, sheep and goat's cheeses, grilled meats, and fresh fruit and vegetables, Greek food is the essence of Mediterranean cuisine. The geography of Greece, from the northern regions in mainland Europe to the far-flung islands of the Ionian and Aegean seas, has created a cuisine of spectacular regional variety.

Small cheese pastries
(see page 206)

Spinach pie

SPINACH PIE

Spanakopita

- $^1/_3$ cup/80 ml extra-virgin olive oil
- 4 small onions, finely chopped
- $1^1/_4$ lb/625 g spinach, boiled, squeezed dry, and finely chopped
- 1 tablespoon finely chopped fresh parsley
- 1 tablespoon finely chopped fresh dill
- 3 eggs, lightly beaten
- 1 cup/250 g crumbled Feta cheese
- salt and freshly ground white pepper
- 10 sheets frozen phyllo dough, thawed

Preheat the oven to 350°F/180°C/gas 4. • Set out a 12-inch (30-cm) round baking pan. • Heat 3 tablespoons oil in a large frying pan over medium heat. Sauté the onions for 8–10 minutes, or until lightly browned. • Add the spinach and cook for 5 minutes. Transfer to a large bowl and let cool completely • Stir in the parsley, dill, eggs, and Feta. Season with salt and pepper. • Brush the phyllo sheets on both sides evenly with the remaining 3 tablespoons oil. Arrange five sheets of phyllo dough in the pan, trimming to fit. • Spoon in the spinach filling, spreading it evenly. Cover with five more dough sheets. • Use a sharp knife to make diamond-shaped cuts in the top five sheets of phyllo dough. • Bake for 25–30 minutes, or until golden brown and crispy. Serve hot or at room temperature.

Serves 6 • Prep: 25 min • Cooking: 38–45 min • Level: 2

TOMATOES STUFFED WITH RICE

Gemista me rizi

Cut the tops off the tomatoes and use a spoon to scoop out the flesh. Reserve the flesh. • Salt the interior of the tomatoes and place them upside-down for 30 minutes in a colander. • Preheat the oven to 375°F/190°C/gas 5. • Set out a large baking dish. • Heat $^1/_4$ cup (60 ml) oil in a large frying pan over medium heat. Sauté the onion for 8–10 minutes, or until lightly browned. Add the garlic and stir in the reserved tomato flesh. • Cook for 15–20 minutes, or until the sauce has reduced. • Season with salt and pepper. • Cook the rice in a large pot of salted boiling water for 8–10 minutes, or until the rice is almost tender. • Drain well and add the rice to the sauce. Cook for 5 minutes more. Remove from the heat and let cool to warm. • Mix in the mint, parsley, and 1 tablespoon of oil. • Stuff the tomatoes, replace the tops, and arrange in the dish. Drizzle with the remaining 1 tablespoon oil. • Bake for 35–40 minutes, or until well cooked. • Serve warm.

Serves 8 • Prep: 20 min + 30 min to drain • Cooking: 50–60 min • Level: 2

- 8 large tomatoes
- salt
- 6 tablespoons extra-virgin olive oil
- 1 medium onion, finely chopped
- 1 clove garlic, finely chopped
- freshly ground black pepper
- 1 cup/200 g short-grain rice
- 3 tablespoons finely chopped fresh mint
- 1 tablespoon finely chopped fresh parsley

Tomatoes stuffed with rice

Appetizers

SMALL CHEESE PASTRIES

Tiropita

Filling
- 1 cup/250 g crumbled Feta cheese
- 1/4 cup freshly grated Kefalotiri or Parmesan cheese
- 2 large eggs, lightly beaten
- 1 tablespoon finely chopped fresh dill
- 1 tablespoon finely chopped fresh mint
- salt

Yogurt Pastry
- 1²/3 cups/250 g all-purpose/plain flour
- 1/2 cup/125 ml plain yogurt
- 1/2 teaspoon salt
- 1 large egg, lightly beaten

Preheat the oven to 350°F/180°C/gas 4. • Set out a large baking sheet. • <u>Filling</u>: Mix the Feta, Kefalotiri, eggs, dill, and mint in a large bowl. Season with salt. • <u>Yogurt Pastry</u>: Mix the flour, yogurt, and salt in a large bowl to form a smooth dough. • Roll out the dough on a lightly floured work surface to about 1/8 inch (3-mm) thick. Cut into 3-inch (8-cm) disks. • Use a teaspoon to place the filling in the center of each disk. Fold in half and use a fork to seal the edges. • Arrange on the baking sheet and brush with the beaten egg. • Bake for 25–30 minutes, or until golden brown. • Serve hot or at room temperature.

Makes 8 pastries • Prep: 30 min • Cooking: 25–30 min • Level: 2

GRAPE LEAVES STUFFED WITH RICE

Dolmadakia yalantzi

Place the rice in a medium bowl and cover with boiling water. Let soak for 30 minutes. • Drain and set aside. If using fresh leaves, blanch them in a large pot of salted boiling water for 3 minutes. • Drain well and dry on a clean cloth. • Heat 1/4 cup (60 ml) oil in a large frying pan over medium heat. Sauté the onion for 8–10 minutes, or until lightly browned. Stir in the rice. Lower the heat, cover, and cook for 5 minutes. • Add the mint and dill. Season with salt and pepper. Cover and cook for 5 more minutes over very low heat, making sure that the mixture does not stick to the pan. • Stuff the grape leaves following the method on page 153. • Place a layer of stuffed leaves seam-side down in a large saucepan. • Pour in the remaining 1/4 cup oil, water, and the lemon juice. Cover with a plate to hold the leaves firmly in position. • Cook for 50–60 minutes over medium heat, or until the sauce is reduced by half. • Serve hot or warm.

Serves 4 • Prep: 25 min + 30 min to soak • Cooking: 50–60 min • Level: 2

- 1 cup/200 g short-grain rice
- 20 fresh or preserved grape leaves
- 1/2 cup/125 ml extra-virgin olive oil
- 2 large onions, finely chopped
- 3 tablespoons finely chopped fresh mint
- 1 tablespoon finely chopped fresh dill
- salt and freshly ground black pepper
- 1 cup/250 ml water
- 1¹/2 tablespoons fresh lemon juice

BOILED OCTOPUS

Htapothi vrasto

- 1 octopus, weighing about 3 lb/1.5 kg, cleaned
- 3 cloves garlic, finely chopped
- 1/2 cup/125 ml extra-virgin olive oil
- 2 tablespoons white wine vinegar
- 1 tablespoon finely chopped fresh parsley

Octopus is usually found frozen and already cleaned. If you can't find octopus, substitute squid.

Place the octopus in a large saucepan of cold water. Bring to a boil and simmer for 60–70 minutes, or until tender. If you have time, let cool in the water as this will make it more tender. • Drain and cut the octopus into small pieces. • Mix the garlic, oil, vinegar, and parsley in a small bowl. Pour the dressing over the octopus.

Serves 4 • Prep: 20 min + time to cool • Cooking: 60–70 min • Level: 1

FRIED CHEESE WITH BELL PEPPERS

Halloumi me piperi prasino

Preheat the oven to 425°F/220°C/gas 7. • Arrange the bell peppers on a large baking sheet. • Bake for 15–20 minutes, or until the skins are blackened. Peel the skins off and place the bell peppers in a large bowl. • Pour in 1/3 cup (80 ml) of oil and the vinegar. Season with salt and pepper. • Toss well and let cool completely. • Heat the remaining 10 tablespoons oil in a large frying pan to very hot. • Fry the cheese for 5–7 minutes, or until golden brown on both sides. • Drain well on paper towels. Serve hot, with the bell peppers on the side.

Serves 4 • Prep: 15 min • Cooking: 30 min • Level: 1

- 4 bell peppers/capsicums, mixed colors, seeded and quartered
- 1 cup/250 ml extra-virgin olive oil
- 2 tablespoons red wine vinegar
- salt and freshly ground black pepper
- 12 oz/350 g Halloumi or Emmental cheese, thickly sliced

Appetizers

COD AND POTATO CROQUETTES

Bakaliaros kroketakia

- 1 lb/500 g salt cod
- 2 lb/1 kg potatoes, peeled and coarsely chopped
- $^1/_2$ cup/125 ml milk
- 1 tablespoon butter
- $^1/_8$ teaspoon freshly grated nutmeg
- 2 tablespoons finely chopped fresh parsley
- 2 eggs + 1 egg, separated
- 1 cup/125 g freshly grated Kefalotiri or Parmesan cheese
- 1 cup/125 g fine dry bread crumbs
- 2 cups/500 ml olive oil, for frying

Soak the salt cod in a large bowl of cold water for 2–3 days, changing the water every few hours. This will remove the excess salt. • Drain well, crumble, and set aside. • Boil the potatoes in salted water until tender, 15–20 minutes. Drain well. • Cook the cod, potatoes, milk, butter, and nutmeg in a large saucepan over low heat, stirring often, for about 5 minutes. • Remove from the heat and let cool completely. • Stir in the parsley, 1 whole egg + 1 egg yolk, and cheese. • Use your hands to shape the cod mixture into oval croquettes. • Use a fork to beat the remaining egg and egg white together in a small bowl. Place the bread crumbs in a small bowl. • Dip the croquettes in the egg, then roll them in the bread crumbs. • Heat the oil to very hot in a deep fryer. Fry the croquettes in batches for 5–7 minutes, or until golden brown. Drain well on paper towels. • Serve hot.

Serves 6 • Prep: 20 min + 2–3 days to soak • Cooking: 40–60 min • Level: 2

Cod and potato croquettes

Cucumber and yogurt dip

FISH ROE DIP

Taramosalata

- 2 medium white potatoes, peeled and coarsely chopped
- $^2/_3$ cup/150 g cod roe
- 1 onion, chopped
- $^3/_4$ cup/180 ml extra-virgin olive oil, or more as needed
- juice of 1 lemon
- olives, parsley, and capers, to garnish

Greek markets often carry jars of tarama, *a pink-colored cod roe. If you can't find tarama, substitute bottarga roe or smoked cod roe.*

Boil the potatoes in salted water to cover until tender, 15–20 minutes. Drain well. • Mash the potatoes in a large bowl. • Add the roe, onion, oil, and lemon juice and process in a food processor until smooth, adding more oil if needed. • Cover with plastic wrap and refrigerate for at least 2 hours. • Serve cold, garnished with olives, parsley, and capers.

Serves 4 • Prep: 15 min + 2 hr to chill • Cooking: 15–20 min • Level: 1

CUCUMBER AND YOGURT DIP

Tzatziki

If you can't find Greek yogurt, place 3 cups (750 ml) plain yogurt in a cheesecloth-lined colander set over a bowl and drain overnight in the refrigerator.

Place the grated cucumber in a colander. Season with salt and let drain for 30 minutes. • Beat the yogurt in a medium bowl until smooth. • Use a large rubber spatula to fold in the garlic, oil, vinegar, and cucumber. Season with salt and pepper. • Refrigerate for at least 2 hours before serving. • Serve garnished with olives.

Serves 6 • Prep: 15 min + 30 min to drain + 2 hr to chill • Level: 1

- 2 cucumbers, peeled seeded, and coarsely grated
- salt
- 2 cups/500 ml Greek yogurt (with 10% fat)
- 2 cloves garlic, finely chopped
- $^1/_4$ cup/60 ml extra-virgin olive oil
- 1 tablespoon white wine vinegar
- freshly ground pepper
- olives, to garnish

Mezethes

Taramosalata, tzatziki, dolmades—Greek mezethes, *or appetizers, are always tantalizing. For an informal meal or party, try serving six to eight dishes together. Choose a variety of different dishes, including one or two dips, a seafood salad, a fried dish, stuffed grape leaves, a salad or two, and some good olives. Serve with traditional Greek drinks, such as Retsina or Ouzo.*

Dips & Salads

EGGPLANT SALAD

Melinzanosalata

- 2 medium eggplants/ aubergines
- 1 tablespoon extra-virgin olive oil
- 1 tablespoon red wine vinegar or fresh lemon juice
- small bunch of parsley
- 2 cloves garlic, peeled
- salt and freshly ground black pepper
- $^1/_2$ cup/125 ml plain yogurt

Rinse the eggplants and pierce well with the tines of a fork. Roast the eggplants under a preheated broiler (grill) about 8 inches (20 cm) from the heat source, turning often until the skins are charred and the interiors very soft. • Cool enough to handle, then peel. • Place in a food processor with the oil, vinegar, parsley, and garlic and process until smooth. Season with salt and pepper. • Fold in the yogurt until well blended. • Rest for at least 2 hours before serving.

Serves 6 • Prep: 15 min + 2 hr to rest • Cooking: 30 min • Level: 1

CUCUMBER WITH FETA CHEESE AND MINT

Aggouraki me feta kai diosmo

- 1 large cucumber, very thinly sliced
- 4 oz/125 g Feta cheese, crumbled
- 1 tablespoon coarsely chopped fresh mint

Dressing
- $^1/_3$ cup/80 ml extra-virgin olive oil
- $^1/_4$ cup/60 ml fresh lemon juice
- salt and freshly ground black pepper

Place the cucumber in a salad bowl. Sprinkle with the Feta and mint. • Dressing: Mix the oil and lemon juice in a small bowl. Season with salt and pepper. • Pour over the salad and toss well.

Serves 4 • Prep: 10 min • Level: 1

CABBAGE AND CARROT SALAD

Salata me lahano kai karota

- 1 small cabbage, finely shredded
- 4 small carrots, finely shredded

Dressing
- 1 clove garlic, chopped
- $^1/_2$ cup/125 ml extra-virgin olive oil
- $1^1/_2$ tablespoons fresh lemon juice

Toss the cabbage and carrots together in a large bowl. • Dressing: Mix the garlic, oil, and lemon juice in a small bowl. • Pour over the carrot and cabbage mixture and toss well. Serve.

Serves 8 • Prep: 15 min • Level: 1

ROASTED EGGPLANT SALAD WITH CAPERS

Melitzanosalata me kapari

Rinse the eggplants and pierce well with the tines of a fork. Roast the eggplants under a preheated broiler (grill) about 8 inches (20 cm) from the heat source, turning often until the skins are charred and the interiors very soft. • Cool enough to handle, then cut in half. • Scoop out and discard as many seeds as possible. Scoop out the pulp and place in a bowl. Cut the pulp into chunks. Add the tomatoes, onion, garlic, capers, parsley, mint, oil, and vinegar. Season with salt, and pepper. • Toss well and let rest for 1–2 hours before serving.

Serves 4 • Prep: 20 min + 1–2 hr to rest • Cooking: 30 min • Level: 1

- 2 large eggplants
- 2 firm-ripe tomatoes, peeled and chopped
- 1 medium red onion, finely chopped
- 2 cloves garlic, finely chopped
- 2 tablespoons salted capers, rinsed and dried
- 2 tablespoons finely chopped fresh parsley
- 1 tablespoon finely chopped fresh mint
- $^1/_4$ cup/60 ml extra-virgin olive oil
- 2 tablespoons red wine vinegar
- salt and freshly ground black pepper

GREEK SALAD

Horiatiki

Place the lettuce in a large salad bowl. Add the Feta, tomatoes, onion, olives, mint, basil, lemon zest, garlic, and cucumber. Season with salt and pepper. • Drizzle with the lemon juice and oil. • Toss and serve.

Serves 4–6 • Prep: 15 min • Level: 1

- 2 heads Romaine or Cos lettuce, torn
- 8 oz/200 g Feta cheese, crumbled
- 6 tomatoes, thinly sliced
- 1 red onion, chopped
- $1^1/_2$ cups/150 g black olives
- 10 leaves fresh mint, torn
- 10 leaves fresh basil, torn
- 1 tablespoon finely chopped lemon zest
- 2 cloves garlic, chopped
- 1 cucumber, thinly sliced
- salt and freshly ground black pepper
- $^1/_4$ cup/60 ml fresh lemon juice
- $^1/_3$ cup/80 ml extra-virgin olive oil

Salads

Beet and potato salad

BEET AND POTATO SALAD

Pantzaria me skordalia

- 2 lb/1 kg beets/beetroot
- 1 lb/400 g potatoes, boiled and peeled
- 4 cloves garlic, finely chopped
- 1 tablespoon extra-virgin olive oil
- ¼ cup/60 ml fresh lemon juice or white wine vinegar
- salt and freshly ground black pepper

Boil the beets in their skins in a large pot of salted boiling water until tender, 30–60 minutes, depending on their size. Drain well, let cool enough to handle, then slip off the skins, and thinly slice. • Boil the potatoes in their skins in a large pot of salted boiling water for 20–25 minutes. Drain well, let cool enough to handle, then slip off the skins. • Place the potatoes in a large bowl and mash until smooth. Mix in the garlic, oil, and lemon juice. Season with salt and pepper. • Arrange the beets, overlapping them in a decorative manner, on a serving plate. • Spoon the potatoes into the center. • Refrigerate for 30 minutes before serving.

Serves 6 • Prep: 15 min + 30 min to chill • Cooking: 50–85 min • Level: 1

POTATO SALAD WITH MINT

Patatosalata me diosmo

Boil the potatoes in their skins in a large pot of salted, boiling water for 20–25 minutes, or until tender. • Drain well, let cool enough to handle, then slip off the skins. • Chop into bite-sized chunks and transfer to a large salad bowl. • Add the mint and garlic. Toss well. • Mix the oil and vinegar in a small bowl. Pour over the potatoes. Season with salt and pepper. • Serve at room temperature.

Serves 4 • Prep: 15 min • Cooking: 20–25 min • Level: 1

- 8 medium potatoes
- 1 tablespoon finely chopped fresh mint
- 2 cloves garlic, finely chopped
- 4–6 tablespoons extra-virgin olive oil
- 2 tablespoons white wine vinegar
- salt and freshly ground black pepper

SPINACH AND FETA SALAD

Salata me spanaki kai feta

- 1 lb/500 g fresh young spinach leaves
- ¹/₂ cucumber, thinly sliced
- 2 scallions/spring onions, finely chopped
- 10 cherry tomatoes, washed and halved
- 1 cup/125 g crumbled Feta cheese
- salt and freshly ground black pepper
- ¹/₃ cup/80 ml extra-virgin olive oil
- 1 tablespoon white wine vinegar

Place the spinach leaves in a large salad bowl. • Add the cucumber, scallions, and tomatoes and toss well. Sprinkle with the Feta and season with salt and pepper. • Mix the oil and vinegar in a small bowl. Drizzle over the salad and toss well.

Serves 4 • Prep: 10 min • Level: 1

SPICY EGGPLANT SALAD

Melinzanosalata me baharika

Place the eggplant in a colander. • Sprinkle with salt and let drain for 1 hour. • Heat the oil in a large frying pan over medium heat. • Fry the eggplants in batches for 5–7 minutes, or until tender. Drain on paper towels. • Place the eggplant in a large salad bowl. • Add the bell pepper, radishes, scallions, tomato, garlic, parsley, cumin, red pepper flakes, salt, lemon juice, and oil. • Toss well and serve.

Serves 4 • Prep: 15 min + 1 hr to drain • Cooking: 20 min • Level: 1

- 1 large eggplant/ aubergine, cut into 1-inch/2.5-cm cubes
- 1 cup/250 ml olive oil, for frying
- 1 green bell pepper/ capsicum, seeded and finely chopped
- 6 radishes, finely chopped
- 4 scallions/spring onions, finely chopped
- 1 firm-ripe tomato, finely chopped
- 2 cloves garlic, finely chopped
- 3 tablespoons finely chopped fresh parsley
- 1 teaspoon cumin seeds
- 1 teaspoon red pepper flakes
- ¹/₂ teaspoon salt
- 1 tablespoon fresh lemon juice
- ¹/₄ cup/60 ml extra-virgin olive oil

Spinach and Feta salad

EGG AND LEMON SOUP

Avgolemono

- 2 quarts/2 liters chicken stock or broth
- 1/2 cup/100 g short-grain rice
- 2 large eggs + 2 large egg yolks
- 1/2 cup/125 ml fresh lemon juice
- salt and freshly ground white pepper

Bring the stock (reserving 1 cup/250 ml cold stock) to a boil in a large saucepan. • Add the rice. Partially cover and cook for 15–20 minutes, or until the rice is tender. • Beat the eggs, egg yolks, and lemon juice in a medium bowl until frothy. Season with salt and pepper. • Mix in 1 cup (250 ml) of the hot stock mixture. Gradually stir the egg mixture into the soup. Remove from the heat and beat until the eggs have thickened but are not scrambled. • Serve immediately.

Serves 8 • Prep: 15 min • Cooking: 15–20 min • Level: 1

GREEK FISH SOUP

Kakavia

Heat the oil in a large saucepan over low heat. Sauté the onions, carrots, and celery for 15 minutes. • Add the parsley, peppercorns, bay leaf, and garlic. • Stir in the tomatoes and cook for 8–10 minutes, or until they have broken down. • Pour in the water and bring to a boil. Add the ocean perch. • Partially cover and cook over low heat for 1 hour. • Soak the mussels in cold water for 1 hour to purge them of sand. • Drain well and cook with the soaking water until they open up, 10 minutes. Discard any that haven't opened. • Strain the soup and return to the pan. Bring to a boil and add the whole fish and lobster. • Cook over low heat for 20 minutes. Add the shrimp and cook for 5 minutes. Add the mussels. • Remove from the heat and remove the fish and the lobster. Season with salt. • Skin and fillet the fish. Shell the lobster and cut the meat into thick slices. • Serve the broth as a first course and the fish, lobster, shrimp, and mussels as a second.

Serves 8 • Prep: 15 min + 1 hr to soak • Cooking: 130 min • Level: 2

- 1/4 cup/60 ml extra-virgin olive oil
- 2 red onions, finely chopped
- 2 carrots, finely chopped
- 2 stalks celery, finely chopped
- 2 tablespoons finely chopped fresh parsley
- 1 teaspoon black peppercorns
- 1 bay leaf
- 2 cloves garlic, finely chopped
- 1 lb/500 g tomatoes, peeled and chopped
- 2 quarts/2 liters water
- 2 lb/1 kg ocean perch or rockfish, cleaned and gutted
- 2 lb/1 kg mussels, in shell
- 1 whole fish, weighing about 2 lb/1 kg (sea bass or bream), cleaned and gutted
- 1 lobster, weighing about 2 lb/1 kg
- 1 lb/500 g shrimp, peeled and well-washed
- salt

Egg and lemon soup

CORFU FISH SOUP

Borthéto

- ¹/₄ cup/60 ml extra-virgin olive oil
- 2 medium onions, coarsely chopped
- 4 cloves garlic, finely chopped
- 2 tablespoons finely chopped fresh parsley
- 2 lb/1 kg potatoes, scrubbed and cubed
- 1 (15-oz/400 g) can diced tomatoes
- 2 lb/1 kg dogfish or white firm-fleshed fish, cleaned and gutted
- water
- salt and freshly ground white pepper

Heat 3 tablespoons of oil in a large saucepan over medium heat. • Add the onions, 3 cloves of garlic, and the parsley and sauté for 8–10 minutes until the garlic is pale gold. • Add the potatoes and sauté for 5 more minutes. • Add the tomatoes and bring to a boil • Add the fish and enough water to cover. Partially cover the pan and cook for 20–30 minutes, or until the fish is very tender. • Season with salt and pepper. Stir in the remaining 1 tablespoon oil and 1 garlic clove and let stand for 5 minutes before serving.

Serves 4 • Prep: 10 min • Cooking: 40 min • Level: 2

BEAN SOUP

Fasolada

Place the beans in a large pot with the water. Bring to a boil. Drain well, reserving the water, and set aside. • In the same pot, heat ¹/₃ cup (80 ml) of oil over medium heat. Sauté the onions for 8–10 minutes, or until lightly browned. • Stir in the beans and reserved water. Bring to a boil, lower the heat, and cook for 45 minutes. • Add the chervil and tomatoes. Continue cooking for 35–40 minutes, or until the beans are tender. • Season with salt and pepper. Drizzle with the remaining 2 tablespoons of oil and lemon juice. Serve hot.

Serves 6 • Prep: 20 min + overnight to soak beans • Cooking: 105–110 min • Level: 2

- 2¹/₂ cups/250 g dried cranberry or borlotti beans, soaked overnight and drained
- 1¹/₂ quarts/1.5 liters cold water
- ¹/₂ cup/125 ml extra-virgin olive oil
- 2 medium red onions, finely chopped
- 2 cups/200 g finely chopped fresh chervil or spinach
- 4 firm-ripe tomatoes, peeled, seeded, and finely chopped
- salt and freshly ground black pepper
- 1 tablespoon fresh lemon juice

LENTIL SOUP

Soupa me fakes

- 1¹/₂ quarts/1.5 liters water
- 1¹/₄ cups/125 g red lentils, well-washed
- 10 cloves garlic, peeled and left whole
- 2 bay leaves
- 15 peppercorns
- 2 medium onions, finely chopped
- ¹/₂ cup/125 ml extra-virgin olive oil
- 2 firm-ripe tomatoes, peeled and finely chopped
- 1 teaspoon salt
- 1 teaspoon dried oregano
- ¹/₃ cup/80 ml balsamic vinegar

Bring the water to a boil with the lentils, garlic, bay leaves, peppercorns, onions, and oil in a large saucepan. Simmer, covered, for 40–45 minutes, or until the lentils are tender. • Stir in the tomatoes and salt. • Continue cooking for 10 minutes. Remove from the heat and add the oregano and balsamic vinegar. • Serve hot.

Serves 4 • Prep: 15 min • Cooking: 50–55 min • Level: 1

SOFT CABBAGE POLENTA

Lahanosoupa

Blanch the cabbage in a large pot of salted boiling water for 3 minutes. • Drain well and set aside. • Heat the oil in a large saucepan over medium heat. Sauté the onions for 8–10 minutes, or until lightly browned. • Stir in the cabbage and cook, stirring often, for 8 minutes. • Bring the stock to a boil in a large saucepan. Gradually add the cornmeal, stirring constantly to prevent lumps from forming. • Lower the heat and continue cooking for 10–15 minutes, or until thick and smooth. • Add the cabbage mixture and cook for 10 minutes more. • Season with salt and pepper. • Serve hot.

Serves 8 • Prep: 20 min • Cooking: 40–45 min • Level: 2

- 14 oz/400 g green cabbage, finely shredded
- ¹/₂ cup/125 ml extra-virgin olive oil
- 2 large red onions, finely chopped
- 1¹/₂ quarts/1.5 liters chicken stock or broth
- ³/₄ cup/125 g finely ground yellow cornmeal
- salt and freshly ground black pepper

Fish & Seafood

FRIED CRAYFISH

Karavides tiganites

- 1¹/₃ cups/200 g all-purpose/plain flour
- ¹/₃ cup/80 ml water
- 1 large egg, lightly beaten
- 3 lb/1.5 kg frozen pre-cooked crayfish, thawed
- 1 cup/250 ml olive oil, for frying
- 2 firm-ripe tomatoes
- 1 cup/250 ml red wine vinegar
- 1 bay leaf
- 1 tablespoon finely chopped fresh rosemary
- salt and freshly ground black pepper

Sift 1 cup (150 g) of flour into a large bowl. Make a well in the center and stir in the water and egg until well blended. • Peel the crayfish carefully and twist off and discard the heads. • Dip in the batter. • Heat the oil in a large frying pan to very hot. • Fry the crayfish in batches for 8–10 minutes, or until golden brown. • Drain on paper towels. Transfer to a large serving plate and set aside in a warm place • Stir the remaining ¹/₃ cup (50 g) flour into the oil. Add the tomatoes, vinegar, bay leaf, and rosemary. Season with salt and pepper. Spoon the sauce over the crayfish. • Serve hot.

Serves 4 • Prep: 15 min • Cooking: 20–30 min • Level: 2

FRIED WHITEBAIT

Marides

Sift the flour, paprika, cayenne pepper, and salt into a large bowl. • Dip the whitebait into the flour mixture, making sure they are well coated. • Heat the oil to very hot in a large frying pan. • Fry the whitebait in batches for 5–7 minutes, or until golden brown and crispy. • Drain well on paper towels. • Serve hot, garnished with the lemon.

Serves 6 • Prep: 10 min • Cooking: 15–20 min • Level: 1

- ²/₃ cup/100 g all-purpose/plain flour
- ¹/₂ teaspoon paprika
- ¹/₂ teaspoon cayenne pepper
- ¹/₈ teaspoon salt
- 2 lb/1 kg whitebait or smelts
- 2 cups/500 ml olive oil, for frying
- lemon quarters, to garnish

OCTOPUS WITH PASTA

Htapothi me makaronaki

- 2 lb/1 kg octopus or squid, cleaned
- ¹/₂ onion + 1 onion, finely chopped
- ¹/₂ carrot
- ¹/₂ stalk celery
- 1 bunch parsley
- 2 tablespoons white wine vinegar
- ¹/₄ cup/60 ml extra-virgin olive oil
- 2 cloves garlic, finely chopped
- 1 lb/500 g tomatoes, peeled and chopped
- salt and freshly ground black pepper
- 1 lb/500 g small tube pasta, such as ditalini

Place the octopus in a large pot of cold water with ¹/₂ onion, carrot, celery, parsley, and vinegar. Bring to a boil and lower the heat. Simmer for 30 minutes. • Drain well and cut into bite-sized pieces. • Strain, reserving 1 quart (1 liter) of the cooking liquid. • Heat the oil in a large saucepan over medium heat. Sauté the finely chopped onion for 8–10 minutes, or until lightly browned. Add the garlic and tomatoes. • Bring to a boil and add the octopus. Season with salt and pepper. • Lower the heat and cook, covered, for 20 minutes over very low heat. • Bring the reserved cooking stock to a boil in a medium saucepan. Season with salt and add to the octopus, along with the pasta. • Cook over high heat for 15–20 minutes, or until the pasta is al dente. • Serve hot.

Serves 4 • Prep: 20 min • Cooking: 75–80 min • Level: 1

Beef, Chicken & Lamb

SAUSAGES WITH BELL PEPPERS

Loukanika me piperies

- 12 fresh loukanika or garlic-flavored sausages, weighing about 1¼ lb/1.25 kg
- 3 tablespoons extra-virgin olive oil
- 2 red onions, thinly chopped
- 2 cloves garlic, finely chopped
- 2 red bell peppers/capsicums, seeded and thickly sliced
- 2 green bell peppers/capsicums, seeded and thickly sliced
- salt and freshly ground black pepper

For authentic flavor, look for loukanika sausage wherever Greek foods are sold. Made from both lamb and pork, it is seasoned with orange zest.

Prick the sausages all over with a fork. • Blanch the sausages in a large pot of salted boiling water for 3 minutes. Drain well. • Heat the oil in a large frying pan over medium heat. Sauté the onions for 8–10 minutes, or until lightly browned. • Stir in the garlic and bell peppers. Sauté over high heat for 5 minutes. • Cut the sausages into bite-sized pieces and add to the bell pepper mixture. • Cook over low heat for 15–20 minutes, or until tender. Season with salt and pepper. • Serve hot.

Serves 6 • Prep: 10 min • Cooking: 35–40 min • Level: 1

CHICKEN WITH PASTA

Kotopoulo me hilopittes

Heat the oil in a large saucepan over medium heat. Sauté the onions for 8–10 minutes, or until lightly browned. • Stir in the garlic, cinnamon, and cloves. Add the chicken and brown over high heat. • Add the tomatoes and season with salt and pepper. Lower the heat and cook for 25–30 minutes, or until the chicken is tender. • Add the boiling water to the chicken. • Add the tagliatelle and cook for 10–15 minutes, or until the pasta is al dente. Remove the cloves and cinnamon stick before serving.

Serves 4 • Prep: 10 min • Cooking: 45–55 min • Level: 1

- ¼ cup/60 ml extra-virgin olive oil
- 2 onions, finely chopped
- 2 cloves garlic, finely chopped
- 1 stick cinnamon
- 2 cloves
- 1 chicken, weighing about 1¼ lb/ 625 g, cut into 8 pieces
- 3 firm-ripe tomatoes, coarsely chopped
- salt and freshly ground black pepper
- 2 cups/500 ml boiling water
- 1 lb/500 g fresh egg tagliatelle or fettuccine, broken up

Sausages with bell peppers

Beef with prunes

BEEF WITH PRUNES

Moschari me damaskina

- ¹/₄ cup/60 ml extra-virgin olive oil
- 2 lb/1 kg lean beef, cut into cubes
- 2 red onions, finely chopped
- 2 bay leaves
- ¹/₂ cup/125 ml dry red wine
- salt and freshly ground black pepper
- 1 lb/450 g peeled and chopped tomatoes
- 1 teaspoon ground cinnamon
- 1 teaspoon granulated sugar
- water (optional)
- 1¹/₂ lb/750 g pitted prunes

Serve with steamed rice or rice pilaf.

Heat the oil in a large frying pan over high heat. Brown the beef for 5 minutes. • Add the onions and bay leaves and sauté until lightly browned, 8–10 minutes. • Pour in the wine and cook until evaporated. Season with salt and pepper. • Stir in the tomatoes, cinnamon, and sugar. • Cook for 55–65 minutes, or until the beef is tender, adding water if the sauce begins to dry. • Remove the beef from the saucepan and add the prunes. Cover with the meat. • Cook over low heat for 15 minutes more. • Arrange the beef and prunes on a serving plate. Serve hot.

Serves 8 • Prep: 15 min • Cooking: 88–100 min • Level: 1

LAMB STEW WITH PASTA

Arni youvetsi

Preheat the oven to 400°F/200°C/gas 6. • Arrange the lamb in a large Dutch oven or saucepan. Dot with 4 tablespoons butter and season with salt and pepper. Drizzle with the lemon juice. • Bake for 20 minutes. If the lamb becomes too dark, lower the oven temperature. • Melt the remaining 2 tablespoons butter in a large frying pan over low heat. Sauté the onion for 8–10 minutes, or until lightly browned. Add the tomatoes and season with salt and pepper. Stir in the sugar. • Cook for 10 minutes over high heat. Add the sauce to the lamb and continue cooking over low heat until the sauce has reduced slightly. • Pour the boiling water over the lamb. Add the pasta and cover the pan. Cook for 15–20 minutes, or until the pasta is al dente. • Sprinkle with the cheese and serve hot.

Serves 4 • Prep: 15 min • Cooking: 63–70 min • Level: 1

- 1 boneless leg of lamb, weighing about 2 lb/ 1 kg, cut into 8 pieces
- ¹/₃ cup/80 g butter
- salt and freshly ground black pepper
- juice of 1 lemon
- 1 onion, finely chopped
- 1 lb/500 g firm-ripe tomatoes, peeled and chopped
- ¹/₄ teaspoon granulated sugar
- 1¹/₂ quarts/1.5 liters boiling water
- 1 lb/500 g orzo/rice-shaped soup pasta
- ¹/₄ cup freshly grated Kefalotiri or Parmesan cheese

Eggplant moussaka

Baked Dishes

EGGPLANT STUFFED WITH BEEF

Melitzanes papoutsakia

- 3 medium eggplants/aubergines, each weighing about 1¹/₂ lb/750 g, halved
- salt and freshly ground black pepper
- ¹/₃ cup/80 ml extra-virgin olive oil
- 1 onion, finely chopped
- 1 clove garlic, finely chopped
- 1 teaspoon ground cinnamon
- 1 lb/500 g ground/minced beef
- ¹/₂ cup/125 ml dry red wine
- 1 cup/250 ml canned tomatoes
- 1 tablespoon finely chopped fresh parsley
- 2 firm-ripe tomatoes, coarsely chopped

Topping
- 2 tablespoons butter
- 2¹/₂ tablespoons all-purpose/plain flour
- 1 cup/250 ml hot milk
- salt and freshly ground black pepper
- 2 tablespoons freshly grated Kefalotiri or Parmesan cheese

Make long, deep lengthwise cuts in the eggplants. Sprinkle with salt and let drain for 1 hour. • Heat ¹/₄ cup (60 ml) of oil in a large frying pan over medium heat. Fry the eggplants for 10–15 minutes, or until tender. Drain well on paper towels. • Use a spoon to scoop out the flesh. Finely chop and set aside. • Heat the remaining 2 tablespoons oil in a large frying pan over medium heat. Sauté the onion for 8–10 minutes, or until lightly browned. • Add the garlic, cinnamon, and beef and sauté over high heat until the beef is browned. • Pour in the wine and cook until evaporated. Add the canned tomatoes and parsley. Bring to a boil and season with salt and pepper. • Cover and cook over low heat for 40 minutes. • Preheat the oven to 400°F/200°C/gas 6. • Mix the meat sauce and the reserved eggplant flesh in a large bowl. • Spoon the meat mixture into the hollow eggplants. • Place in a baking pan. Top with the tomato cubes. • <u>Topping</u>: Melt the butter in a small saucepan over medium heat. Stir in the flour to make a smooth paste. Add the milk, a little at a time, stirring constantly, and continue cooking for 5 minutes, or until thick and smooth. Season with salt and pepper. Spoon over the eggplants. Sprinkle with the cheese. • Bake for 15–20 minutes, or until the cheese is golden brown. • Serve hot.

Serves 3 • Prep: 30 min + 1 hr to drain the eggplants • Cooking: 93–105 min • Level: 2

EGGPLANT MOUSSAKA

Moussaka

There are many variations on this classic dish. It is very filling and, served with a salad, makes a hearty meal. Moussaka is one of the best-known Greek dishes and is believed to have originated in Greece. However, its name is of Arabic origin, and it is served throughout the Middle East and Turkey.

Place the eggplant in a colander. Sprinkle with salt and let drain for 1 hour. • Heat 2 tablespoons of oil in a large saucepan over medium heat. Sauté the onions for 8–10 minutes, or until lightly browned. • Add the beef and sauté over high heat until well browned. • Pour in the wine and cook until evaporated. Season with salt and pepper. • Stir in the tomatoes, parsley, nutmeg, and cinnamon. Cook for 45 minutes, adding a little water if the sauce begins to dry. • Preheat the oven to 400°F/200°C/gas 6. • Melt the butter in a saucepan over medium heat. Stir in ¹/₃ cup (50 g) flour to make a smooth paste. Slowly pour in the milk, stirring constantly, until it comes to a boil. • Lower the heat to very low, cover, and cook for 10 minutes, stirring often. Remove from the heat and let cool to warm. Stir in the cheese and egg yolks. Season with salt and pepper. • Sprinkle the eggplants with the remaining 1 tablespoon flour. • Heat the remaining ²/₃ cup (150 ml) oil in a large frying pan. • Fry the eggplant in batches for 5–7 minutes, or until golden brown. • Drain well on paper towels. • Place half the eggplant in a large baking dish. Cover with the meat sauce, followed by the remaining eggplant. Top with the cheese sauce. • Bake for 25–35 minutes, or until the cheese is golden brown. • Serve hot or warm.

Serves 8–10 • Prep: 30 min. + 1 hr to drain the eggplants • Cooking: 143–155 min. • Level: 2

- 3 eggplants/aubergines, each weighing about 12 oz/350 g, cut into ¹/₄-inch/5-mm thick slices
- salt
- ³/₄ cup/180 ml extra-virgin olive oil
- 2 red onions, finely chopped
- 1¹/₂ lb/750 g ground/minced beef
- ¹/₂ cup/125 ml dry red wine
- freshly ground black pepper
- 1 lb/500 g peeled and chopped tomatoes
- 1 tablespoon finely chopped fresh parsley
- ¹/₄ teaspoon freshly grated nutmeg
- ¹/₄ teaspoon ground cinnamon
- water (optional)
- ¹/₄ cup/60 g butter
- ¹/₃ cup/50 g + 1 tablespoon all-purpose/plain flour
- 2 cups/500 ml milk
- ¹/₂ cup/60 g freshly grated Kefalotiri or Parmesan cheese
- 2 large egg yolks, lightly beaten

Vegetables

SWEET POTATOES WITH ONIONS AND CAYENNE PEPPER

Glikopatates

- 3 tablespoons extra-virgin olive oil
- 2 large red onions, finely chopped
- 2 cloves garlic, chopped
- 1 tablespoon sweet paprika
- 1 teaspoon cayenne pepper
- 1 tablespoon tomato paste
- 3 lb/1.5 kg sweet potatoes, peeled and quartered
- 1 1/4 cups/310 ml dry white wine
- 1 cup/250 ml water
- salt and freshly ground black pepper

Heat the oil in a large frying pan over medium heat. • Sauté the onions and garlic for 8–10 minutes, or until lightly browned. • Add the paprika, cayenne pepper, and tomato paste. • Stir in the sweet potatoes and cook for 1 minute. • Pour in 1/2 cup (125 ml) wine and the water and bring to a boil. • Lower the heat, cover, and cook for 12–15 minutes, or until the sauce has thickened. Season with salt and pepper. • Pour in the remaining 3/4 cup (180 ml) wine. Cover and cook for 10–15 minutes, or until the sweet potatoes are tender. • Serve hot.

Serves 4 • Prep: 15 min • Cooking: 30–40 min • Level: 1

BAKED VEGETABLES

Briami

Sprinkle the eggplant with salt in a colander and let drain for 1 hour. • Preheat the oven to 350°F/180°C/gas 4. • Set out a large roasting pan. • Mix the eggplant, potatoes, zucchini, tomatoes, onion, oil, parsley, and basil in the pan. Season with salt and pepper and mix well. • Bake for 55–65 minutes, or until the vegetables are tender. If the vegetables start to burn, cover with aluminum foil. • Serve hot.

Serves 6 • Prep: 15 min + 1 hr to drain the eggplants • Cooking: 55–65 min. • Level: 1

- 2 medium eggplants/ aubergines, peeled and cut into cubes
- salt
- 1 lb/500 g potatoes, peeled and cut into cubes
- 1 lb/500 g zucchini/ courgettes, sliced
- 2 lb/1 kg firm-ripe tomatoes, cut into 1/2-inch/1-cm slices
- 1 large red onion, sliced
- 1 cup/250 ml extra-virgin olive oil
- 2 tablespoons finely chopped fresh parsley
- 2 tablespoons finely chopped fresh basil
- freshly ground black pepper

FAVA BEANS COOKED WITH LEEKS AND POTATOES

Fassolakia me patates kai prasso

- 1/2 cup/125 ml extra-virgin olive oil
- 3 medium leeks, white parts only
- 4 large potatoes, peeled and cut into cubes
- 2 lb/1 kg fresh fava/ broad beans, shelled
- salt and freshly ground black pepper
- 2 cups/500 ml water

Heat the oil in a large frying pan over medium heat. • Sauté the leeks for 8–10 minutes, or until lightly browned. • Add the potatoes and fava beans. Season with salt and pepper. • Pour in the water and bring to a boil. Lower the heat, cover, and cook for 20–25 minutes, or until the fava beans and potatoes are tender. • Season with salt and pepper. Remove from the heat and serve hot.

Serves 4–6 • Prep: 15 min • Cooking: 30–35 min. • Level: 1

Fresh vegetables

Vegetables are an essential aspect of any Greek meal. Whether raw or cooked, vegetables are prepared in simple ways to draw out their fresh flavors. Due to the geography of Greece, what is available on one island may not be available on the mainland, or vice versa. However, you can be sure that whatever vegetables are served, they will be deliciously fresh and prepared with lightness and simplicity.

Desserts

ATHENIAN WALNUT CAKE

Karidopita

- 1¹/₂ cups/225 g all-purpose/plain flour
- ¹/₂ cup/75 g semolina flour
- 2 teaspoons baking powder
- 1 teaspoon baking soda/bicarbonate of soda
- 1 teaspoon ground cinnamon
- ¹/₈ teaspoon ground cloves
- ¹/₈ teaspoon salt
- 4 large eggs, separated
- 1¹/₂ cups/300 g firmly packed dark brown sugar
- 1 cup/250 ml extra-virgin olive oil
- ¹/₂ cup/125 ml milk
- 1¹/₂ cups/150 g walnuts, finely chopped
- 2 tablespoons brandy

Syrup
- 1¹/₂ cups/300 g granulated sugar
- 2 cups/500 ml water
- ¹/₂ cup/125 ml honey

- ¹/₂ cup heavy/double cream
- walnuts, to decorate

Preheat the oven to 350°F/180°C/gas 4. • Butter a 10-inch (25-cm) round cake pan. Line with waxed paper. • Sift both flours, baking powder, baking soda, cinnamon, cloves, and salt into a medium bowl. • Beat the egg yolks and brown sugar in a large bowl with an electric mixer at high speed until pale and creamy. • Use a large rubber spatula to fold in the dry ingredients, followed by the oil, milk, walnuts, and brandy. • In a separate bowl, with mixer at high speed, beat the egg whites until stiff peaks form. • Carefully fold the beaten whites into the batter. • Spoon the batter into the prepared pan. • Bake for 40–45 minutes, or until golden brown and a toothpick inserted into the center comes out clean. • Cool the cake in the pan for 15 minutes. Turn out onto a rack to cool completely. • Syrup: Bring the sugar, water, and honey to a boil in a small saucepan. • Prick holes all over the cake. Drizzle the syrup over the cake, until it has all been absorbed. • With mixer at high speed, beat the cream in a small bowl until stiff. Spoon over the cake in a decorative manner and decorate each dot of cream with walnuts.

Serves 8 • Prep: 25 min • Cooking: 40–45 min • Level: 2

GREEK NUT BAKLAVA

Baklavas me karydia

Preheat the oven to 350°F/180°C/gas 4. • Fit four sheets of phyllo dough into a large baking pan. Brush both sides of the sheets of phyllo with melted butter. • Stir together the walnuts, ¹/₄ cup (50 g) of sugar, cinnamon, and nutmeg in a medium bowl. • Spread one-third of the walnut mixture over the top phyllo sheet. Cover with two more sheets of phyllo and top with another third of the walnut mixture. Top with two more sheets of phyllo. Sprinkle with the remaining walnut mixture and cover with four sheets of phyllo (all brushed with butter). • Use a sharp knife to cut the phyllo sheets into squares. • Bake for 35–40 minutes, or until golden brown. • Remove from the oven and let cool. • Syrup: Boil the water, sugar, honey, lemon zest and juice, and cinnamon in a small saucepan. • Pour over the baklava. • Let stand for 2 hours before serving.

Serves 6 • Prep: 25 min + 2 hr to cool • Cooking: 35–40 min • Level: 1

- 12 sheets frozen phyllo dough, thawed
- 1 cup/250 g butter, melted
- 1 lb/500 g walnuts, coarsely chopped
- ¹/₄ cup/50 g granulated sugar
- 1 teaspoon ground cinnamon
- ¹/₂ teaspoon freshly grated nutmeg

Syrup
- ¹/₂ cup/125 ml water
- 1 cup/200 g granulated sugar
- ³/₄ cup/180 ml honey
- grated zest and juice of 1 lemon
- 1 teaspoon ground cinnamon

Athenian walnut cake

Rice with milk

CINNAMON COOKIES

Krithina

- 7 cups/750 g all-purpose/plain flour
- 1/2 teaspoon salt
- 1 cup/250 ml water
- 1 stick cinnamon
- 5 cloves
- 1 1/2 cups/375 ml extra-virgin olive oil
- 1 1/2 cups/300 g granulated sugar
- 1 cup/250 ml brandy
- 2 teaspoons baking soda/bicarbonate of soda

Sift the flour and salt into a medium bowl. • Bring the water, cinnamon, and cloves to a boil in a small saucepan. Discard the cinnamon and cloves. • Beat the oil and sugar in a large bowl with an electric mixer at high speed until creamy. • Add the brandy, spiced water, and baking soda. • Fold in the dry ingredients. • Turn out onto a lightly floured work surface and knead until a stiff dough has formed. • Shape into a ball, wrap in plastic wrap, and let rest for 30 minutes. • Preheat the oven to 375°F/190°C/gas 5. • Line three large baking sheets with parchment paper. • Discard the plastic wrap, break off pieces of dough, and shape into balls the size of walnuts. Roll out into finger shapes. • Place on the prepared baking sheets. • Bake for 12–15 minutes, or until firm to the touch. • Transfer to racks and let cool completely.

Serves 6 • Prep: 20 min + 30 min • Cooking: 12–15 min • Level: 1

RICE WITH MILK

Rizoghalo

Bring 2 cups (500 ml) of water, salt, cinnamon, and lemon zest to a boil over medium heat in a medium saucepan. • Remove the cinnamon stick and lemon zest. • Add the rice. Lower the heat and cook for 15 minutes over very low heat, stirring often to make sure that the mixture does not stick to the pan. • Bring the milk to a boil and pour into the rice. Cook for 20 minutes. • Stir the cornstarch into the remaining 2 tablespoons water in a small bowl. Stir into the rice. Add the sugar. • Cook for 15 minutes more, stirring often, then remove from the heat. • Pour into individual bowls and let cool completely. • Cover with plastic wrap and refrigerate for at least 2 hours. • Dust with the cinnamon and serve.

Serves 6 • Prep: 15 min + 2 hr to chill • Cooking: 50 min • Level: 1

- 2 cups/500 ml + 2 tablespoons water
- 1/8 teaspoon salt
- 1 stick cinnamon
- zest of 1 lemon, cut in 1 long spiral
- 1 cup/200 g short-grain rice
- 2 cups/500 ml milk
- 1 tablespoon cornstarch/cornflour
- 3/4 cup/150 g granulated sugar
- ground cinnamon, to dust

Desserts

GREEK CINNAMON PUDDING
Ekmek

Syrup
- 1 cup/250 ml water
- 1 cup/200 g granulated sugar
- 1/2 cup/125 ml cognac
- 1/4 cup/60 ml honey

Custard
- 3 cups/750 ml milk
- 3/4 cup/150 g granulated sugar
- 2 egg yolks
- 2 tablespoons all-purpose/plain flour
- 2 tablespoons cornstarch/cornflour

Base
- 1 package (8 oz/200 g) square rusks (dried bread, like melba toast)
- 2 teaspoons ground cinnamon

Topping
- 1 cup/250 ml heavy/double cream
- 2 tablespoons granulated sugar
- 1 teaspoon ground cinnamon
- 1/2 cup/50 g slivered almonds

Syrup: Bring the water, sugar, cognac, and honey to a boil in a medium saucepan over medium-low heat. Simmer for 15 minutes. Set aside to cool. • Custard: Place the milk and sugar in a saucepan and whisk in the egg yolks, flour, and cornstarch. Place over medium-low heat and stir with a wooden spoon until thickened and the mixture registers 160°F (80°C) on an instant-read thermometer. • Remove from heat, let cool a little, then cover with plastic wrap to prevent a skin from forming on the top (or stir often). • Base: Line a glass dish with the rusks. Pour the cooled syrup over the top. The syrup should cover the rusks completely. Dust with the cinnamon. • Spoon the cooled custard over the rusks. Refrigerate for 2 hours. • Topping: Beat the cream and sugar in an electric mixer at high speed until thickened. • Spoon over the pudding just before serving. Dust with the cinnamon and sprinkle with the nuts.

Serves 6 • Prep: 40 min + 2 hr to chill • Cooking: 30 min • Level: 2

HONEY NUT FRITTERS
Dipples

Bring the honey, water, and sugar to a boil in a medium saucepan. Simmer for 15 minutes. Turn heat down to very low until ready to use. • Beat the eggs and vanilla in a large bowl until pale. • With mixer on low speed, gradually add the flour, alternating with the olive oil. • Divide the dough into three or four pieces. Roll each piece out to about 1/4 inch (6 mm) thick. Cut into strips about 2 inches (5 cm) wide. • Twist the pieces of dough around the tines of a fork. • Heat the oil in a deep frying pan to very hot. Fry the dough in batches until pale golden brown. Drain on paper towels. • Dip in the hot syrup, sprinkle with the cinnamon and nuts, and serve.

Serves 6–8 • Prep: 10 min • Cooking: 30 min • Level: 2

- 2 cups/500 ml honey
- 1 cup/250 ml water
- 1/4 cup/50 g granulated sugar
- 6 eggs
- 1 teaspoon vanilla extract
- 3 cups/450 g all-purpose/plain flour
- 1/4 cup/60 ml extra-virgin olive oil
- 2 cups/500 ml oil, for frying
- 1 tablespoon ground cinnamon
- 1 1/2 cups/150 g toasted walnuts or almonds, finely chopped

YOGURT WITH HONEY
Yiaourti me meli

Beat the yogurt in a large bowl with an electric mixer at high speed until stiff. • Use a spatula to fold in the honey until well blended. • Pour the mixture into bowls, cover with plastic wrap, and refrigerate for at least 2 hours. • Sprinkle with the walnuts and serve.

Serves 6 • Prep: 10 min + 2 hr to chill • Level: 1

- 1 1/2 quarts/1.5 liters plain yogurt
- 1/3 cup/80 ml honey
- 1 cup/100 g walnuts, coarsely chopped

MAKING YOGURT AT HOME

1. Pour 1 quart (1 liter) boiling milk into a large bowl.

2. When the milk has cooled to 98°F/37°C, use a wooden spatula to fold in 1 cup (250 ml) plain yogurt until well blended.

3. Cover with a clean cloth and top with a serving plate. Let stand for 24 hours.

BALKANS

To the north of Greece, Albania, Yugoslavia, Croatia, Bosnia and Herzegovina look across the Adriatic Sea toward Italy. Cooking styles in these countries have much in common with Italian, Greek, and Mediterranean cuisines in general. However, there are also some more exotic influences from Eastern Europe and some special flourishes from the great Ottoman and Austro-Hungarian empires of the past.

Cabbage rolls
(see page 230)

Appetizers & Salads

POTATO AND BEAN PUREE

Matevz

- 1 lb/500 g potatoes
- 2¹/₂ cups/250 g cooked cannellini or white kidney beans
- ¹/₄ cup/60 ml extra-virgin olive oil
- 1 medium onion, finely chopped
- 2 cloves garlic, finely chopped
- salt and pepper

Cook the potatoes in their skins in a large pot of salted boiling water for 15–20 minutes, or until tender. Drain, let cool a little, and slip off their skins. • Use a fork to mash the potatoes and beans until smooth. • Heat the oil in a small frying pan over medium heat and sauté the onion and garlic for 8–10 minutes until pale gold. • Stir the onion and garlic into the potato mixture. • Season with salt and pepper and serve hot.

Serves: 4 • Prep: 15 min • Cooking: 25–30 min • Level: 1

DANDELION SALAD

Regratova

- 2 medium potatoes
- 10 oz/300 g dandelion leaves, well-washed
- 2 hard-cooked eggs, quartered
- 1 clove garlic, finely chopped
- 2 tablespoons extra-virgin olive oil
- 1 tablespoon white wine vinegar
- salt and freshly ground black pepper

This salad comes from Slovenia, where it is served in springtime when wild dandelion greens are at their tastiest.

Cook the potatoes in their skins in a medium pot of salted boiling water for 15–20 minutes, or until tender. Drain, let cool a little, and slip off their skins. cut into small cubes. Arrange the dandelion leaves in a large salad bowl. • Place the potatoes on top and add the eggs and garlic. • Mix the oil and vinegar in a small bowl until well blended. Season with salt and pepper. • Pour over the salad and toss carefully.

Serves 4 • Prep: 10 min • Cooking: 15–20 min • Level: 1

CABBAGE ROLLS

Sarmas

These delicious rolls are of Turkish origin, although this recipe comes from Croatia, where they are very popular.

Blanch the cabbage leaves in boiling water for 5–10 minutes, or until the leaves have softened. Drain well. • Preheat the oven to 350°F/180°C/gas 4. • Set out a large baking dish. • Heat the oil in a large saucepan over medium heat. Sauté the onion and bacon for 8–10 minutes, or until lightly browned. • Mix the onion mixture, pork, ham, beef, garlic, and rice in a large bowl. Season with salt and pepper. Add the egg. • Place 3–4 heaping tablespoons of filling in the center of each cabbage leaf. Tuck the ends over the filling and roll up. • Place the cabbage rolls in the pan seam side down. • Pour in the tomato sauce and cover with aluminum foil. • Bake for about 2 hours, or until the meat is cooked.

Serves 8–10 • Prep: 15 min • Cooking: 2 hr 13–20 min • Level: 1

- 8–10 large cabbage leaves, or 16–20 small cabbage leaves
- ¹/₄ cup/60 ml extra-virgin olive oil
- 1 large onion, finely chopped
- 4 oz/125 g bacon, finely chopped
- 1¹/₂ lb/750 g ground/minced pork
- 1 lb/500 g ground/minced ham
- 8 oz/250 g ground/minced beef
- 1 clove garlic, finely chopped
- 1 cup/250 g cooked rice
- salt and freshly ground black pepper
- 1 large egg
- 1 cup/250 ml tomato sauce

SPICY TOMATO AND FETA SALAD

Sopska salata

Place the tomatoes, chiles, and bell pepper in a large bowl. • Mix the oil, vinegar, salt, and garlic in a small bowl. • Pour over the tomato mixture and toss well. • Sprinkle with the Feta and garnish with the parsley.

Serves 4 • Prep: 15 min • Level: 1

- 6 medium tomatoes, cut into cubes
- 3 green chile peppers, finely chopped
- 1 green bell pepper/capsicum, seeded and cut into thin strips
- ²/₃ cup/150 ml extra-virgin olive oil
- ¹/₃ cup/80 ml white wine vinegar
- ¹/₂ teaspoon salt
- 1 clove garlic, finely chopped
- 12 oz/350 g Feta cheese, cut into cubes
- 1 tablespoon finely chopped fresh parsley

Bell pepper and eggplant puree

BELL PEPPER AND EGGPLANT PUREE

Ajvar

- 3 bell peppers/ capsicums, mixed colors
- 3 eggplants/aubergines
- $^1/_2$ cup/125 ml extra-virgin olive oil
- 3 cloves garlic, finely chopped
- salt and freshly ground black pepper
- 2 tablespoons white wine vinegar

This dish can be served as an appetizer or as a side dish with kebabs or grilled meats.

Preheat the oven to 400°F/200°C/gas 6. • Arrange the bell peppers and eggplants in a baking pan. • Roast for 20 minutes, turning often, until the skins have blackened and the insides are tender. • Remove from the oven and let cool completely. • Peel, removing the seeds, and chop coarsely. • Heat the oil in a large frying pan over medium heat. Sauté the garlic for 2–3 minutes, or until pale gold. • Add the garlic and oil to the bell pepper mixture. Season with salt and pepper and drizzle with the vinegar. • Serve hot or at room temperature.

Serves 4 • Prep: 15 min • Cooking: 25 min • Level: 1

CARROT AND YOGURT APPETIZER

Sargarera

Place the yogurt in a medium bowl and stir in the tarragon. • Melt the butter in a large frying pan. Add the carrots, onion, and sugar and cook, stirring frequently, over low heat for 30 minutes, or until the carrots are tender. • Season with salt and pepper. • Add the yogurt mixture and stir over low heat until the yogurt has lost all its extra moisture. • Serve hot as is or spread on slices of warm toast.

Serves 4 • Prep: 10 min • Cooking: 35 min • Level: 1

- 2 cups/500 ml plain yogurt
- 6 tablespoons finely chopped fresh tarragon
- $^1/_4$ cup/60 g butter
- 6 large carrots, thinly sliced
- 1 small white onion, finely chopped
- 2 teaspoons granulated sugar
- salt and freshly ground black pepper

Savory Pies & Vegetables

BEEF AND ONION PIE

Byrek

- 1/3 cup/80 ml extra-virgin olive oil
- 3 medium onions, finely chopped
- 5 oz/150 g lean ground/minced beef
- salt and freshly ground black pepper
- 6 sheets frozen phyllo dough, thawed

Preheat the oven to 400°F/200°C/gas 6. • Butter a 9-inch (23-cm) baking pan. • Heat 2 tablespoons of oil in a large frying pan over medium heat. Sauté the onions for 8–10 minutes, or until lightly browned. • Add the beef and brown for 5–7 minutes. Season with salt and pepper. • Lay out the sheets of dough and cover with a damp cloth. • Place a sheet of dough in the baking pan, trimming to fit the pan. • Cover with a layer of the beef and onion filling. • Cover with another sheet of dough. Brush with oil. • Cover with another layer of filling. Repeat until all the filling is used up, finishing with a sheet of dough. • Bake for 25–30 minutes, or until golden brown. • Serve hot.

Serves 4 • Prep: 15 min • Cooking: 40–45 min • Level: 2

ALBANIAN CHEESE PIE

Gibanica

Preheat the oven to 350°F/180°C/gas 4. • Brush a 9-inch (23-cm) square baking pan with oil. • Mix the eggs, yogurt, Feta, and 1/4 cup (60 ml) oil in a large bowl until well blended. Season with salt. • Lay out the sheets of dough and cover with a damp cloth. • Place four phyllo sheets in the prepared pan, brushing each sheet with oil and allowing the dough to drape over the sides of the pan. • Spoon half the cheese mixture into the pan. • Cover with another four phyllo sheets, each brushed with oil, trimming to fit the pan. • Spoon the remaining cheese mixture into the pan. • Fold the overlapping dough over the top. • Cover with the remaining four phyllo sheets, each brushed with oil. • Prick all over with a fork. • Bake for 25–30 minutes, or until golden brown. • Serve hot or at room temperature.

Serves 6 • Prep: 20 min • Cooking: 25–30 min • Level: 1

- 3 eggs, lightly beaten
- 2 cups/500 ml plain yogurt
- 1 lb/500 g Feta cheese, crumbled
- 2/3 cup/180 ml extra-virgin olive oil
- salt
- 12 sheets frozen phyllo dough, thawed

RED CABBAGE KRAUTI

Prazeno rdece zelje

- 1/4 cup/60 g butter
- 1 small onion, finely chopped
- 2 tablespoons all-purpose/plain flour
- 1 medium red cabbage, shredded
- 1 cup/250 ml boiling water
- 1 tablespoon granulated sugar
- 1 teaspoon caraway seeds
- salt and pepper
- 2 tablespoons red wine vinegar

Melt the butter in a large frying pan over medium heat. Sauté the onion for 5–7 minutes, or until translucent. • Stir in the flour and toast until lightly browned. • Add the cabbage, water, sugar, and caraway seeds. Cover and simmer over very low heat for 1 hour. • Drizzle with the vinegar about 15 minutes before the end of the cooking time. • Serve hot or at room temperature.

Serves 4–6 • Prep: 20 min • Cooking: 65 min • Level: 1

BURNANIJA

Braised green beans

Melt 2 tablespoons of butter in a large frying pan over medium heat. Sauté the onion and garlic for 5–7 minutes, or until translucent. • Add the beans and tomatoes and season with salt and pepper. Cover and cook over low heat for 15 minutes, stirring frequently. • Melt the remaining 2 tablespoons butter in a small saucepan and stir in the flour and paprika. • Add the stock to the sauce and stir until thickened. • Pour the sauce into the beans and cook, stirring often, for 5 more minutes, or until the beans are tender. • Sprinkle with the parsley and mint and serve hot.

Serves 4–6 • Prep: 25 min • Cooking: 30–35 min • Level: 1

- 1/4 cup/60 g butter
- 2 onions, finely chopped
- 2 cloves garlic, finely chopped
- 1 1/2 lb/750 g green beans, cut into 1-inch/2.5 cm lengths
- 2 large tomatoes, peeled and chopped
- salt and freshly ground black pepper
- 1 tablespoon all-purpose/plain flour
- 1 teaspoon paprika
- 1/2 cup/125 ml boiling beef stock or broth
- 1 tablespoon each finely chopped fresh parsley and mint

Soups & Fish

SERBIAN BEAN SOUP

Pasulj

- 1 lb/500 g dried cannellini or white kidney beans, soaked overnight and drained
- 2 tablespoons extra-virgin olive oil
- 2 medium onions, coarsely chopped
- 3 cloves garlic, finely chopped
- 2 bay leaves
- 2 tablespoons finely chopped fresh parsley
- 2 large tomatoes, peeled and chopped
- 2 large carrots, thinly sliced
- 1 teaspoon black peppercorns, coarsely crushed
- 1 quart/1 liter water
- 1 lb/500 g garlic sausages, thickly sliced
- salt

This thick soup is really more of a stew or goulash. If you like spicy dishes, increase the amount of coarsely crushed peppercorns to 1–2 tablespoons.

Heat the oil in a large saucepan and sauté the onions, garlic, bay leaves, and parsley for 8–10 minutes. • Add the tomatoes, carrots, and peppercorns. • Rinse the beans, drain, and add to the pan with the water. Cover and simmer over very low heat for 45 minutes. • Add the sausages and cook for 1 hour, or until the beans are tender. • Season with salt and serve hot.

Serves 4–6 • Prep: 15 min • Cooking: 2 hr • Level: 1

POTATO SOUP

Juha od krumpira

Melt the butter in a large saucepan over medium heat. Sauté the onion and bacon for 8–10 minutes, or until lightly browned. • Add the chile, potatoes, allspice, marjoram, and bay leaf. Season with salt and pepper. • Add the flour, stirring well, followed by the water. • Cook for 15–20 minutes, or until the potatoes are tender. • Transfer the soup to a food processor and process until smooth. • Add the parsley, garlic, and vinegar. • Return the soup to the saucepan and bring to a boil. • Serve hot.

Serves 6 • Prep: 15 min • Cooking: 25–30 min • Level: 1

- ¼ cup/60 g butter
- 1 medium onion, finely chopped
- 2 oz/60 g bacon, coarsely chopped
- 1 fresh red chile pepper, seeded and finely chopped
- 1½ lb/750 g potatoes, peeled and cut into small cubes
- 1 tablespoon ground allspice
- 1 tablespoon finely chopped fresh marjoram
- 1 bay leaf
- salt and freshly ground black pepper
- 1 tablespoon all-purpose/plain flour
- 1 quart/1 liter water
- 1 tablespoon finely chopped fresh parsley
- 2 cloves garlic, finely chopped
- 1 teaspoon white wine vinegar

Potato soup

Adriatic fish in sauce

ADRIATIC FISH IN SAUCE

Brodet

- 2 lb/1 kg fresh fish fillets (red mullet, sea bass, ocean perch)
- salt
- juice of 1 lemon
- $^1/_2$ cup/75 g all-purpose/plain flour
- $^1/_3$ cup/80 ml extra-virgin olive oil
- 2 medium onions, finely chopped
- 2 cups/500 g chopped tomatoes
- $^3/_4$ cup/180 ml dry white wine
- 1 tablespoon finely chopped fresh basil
- 3 bay leaves
- 1 teaspoon finely chopped fresh rosemary
- 1 tablespoon finely chopped fresh parsley
- freshly ground black pepper

Variations on this recipe are served all along the eastern coast of the Adriatic.

Sprinkle the fish with salt and drizzle with the lemon juice. Marinate for at least 30 minutes. • Drain well and dip the fish in the flour, making sure it is well coated. • Heat the oil in a large saucepan over medium heat. Fry the fish for 5–7 minutes, or until golden brown on both sides. Set aside. • Sauté the onions in the same saucepan for 8–10 minutes, or until lightly browned. Stir in the tomatoes. • Lower the heat and pour in the wine. Add the basil, bay leaves, and rosemary. Season with salt and pepper. • Cook for 5–7 minutes, or until the wine has reduced. • Place the fish in the sauce, shaking the pan gently. • Cook over very low heat for 20–25 minutes, or until the sauce has thickened. • Sprinkle with the parsley and serve hot.

Serves 6 • Prep: 20 min + 30 min to marinate • Cooking: 40–50 min • Level: 1

CROATIAN MUSHROOM SOUP WITH BUCKWHEAT

Hubova polievka

Heat the oil in a large saucepan over medium heat. Sauté the onion for 5–7 minutes, or until translucent. • Stir in the mushrooms and garlic. Cook for 3–5 minutes, or until the mushrooms have softened slightly. • Add the buckwheat and bay leaf. Pour in the water. • Bring to a boil, lower the heat, and simmer for 20 minutes. • Season with salt and pepper. Swirl in the sour cream and garnish with the thyme. • Serve hot.

Serves 4 • Prep: 20 min • Cooking: 30 min • Level: 1

- $^1/_4$ cup/60 ml extra-virgin olive oil
- 1 medium onion, finely chopped
- 6 oz/180 g mixed wild mushrooms, thinly sliced
- 2 cloves garlic, finely chopped
- scant $^2/_3$ cup/90 g buckwheat groats, well-washed
- 1 bay leaf
- 1 quart/1 liter water
- salt and freshly ground black pepper
- $^1/_4$ cup/60 ml sour cream, to garnish
- 1 tablespoon finely chopped fresh thyme, to garnish

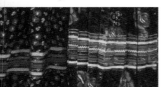

Fish & Seafood

BAKED FISH AND POTATOES
Tavë peshku me patate

- 2 lb/1 kg firm-textured fish, such as sea bass, carp, mullet, trout, or tuna, gutted
- salt and freshly ground white pepper
- 5 cloves garlic, finely chopped
- 3 tablespoons finely chopped fresh parsley
- 3/4 cup/180 ml extra-virgin olive oil
- 2 lb/1 kg potatoes, cut into bite-sized pieces
- 1/4 teaspoon dried oregano
- 3 tablespoons fresh lemon juice
- 1 cup/250 ml dry white wine

Preheat the oven to 325°F/170°C/gas 3. • Set out a large roasting pan. • Season the fish with salt and pepper. • Place the garlic, parsley, and 1/4 cup (60 ml) oil in the pan. • Drizzle the potatoes with 1/4 cup (60 ml) oil and season with salt and pepper. Sprinkle with oregano. • Spoon the potatoes on top of the parsley and garlic. • Bake for 20 minutes. • Mix the lemon juice, wine, and remaining 1/4 cup (60 ml) oil. Arrange the fish on top of the potatoes. • Return the pan to the oven and bake for 15–20 minutes more, or until the fish is well cooked, basting frequently with the lemon juice mixture. • Serve hot.

Serves 4 • Prep: 15 min • Cooking: 35–40 min • Level: 1

STUFFED SQUID
Punjene lignje

- 1 1/2 lb/750 g squid, cleaned
- 1 bunch parsley
- 2 cloves garlic, finely chopped
- 2 cups/200 g cooked rice (about 1/3 cup/70 g dry short-grain rice)
- 1/2 cup/125 ml extra-virgin olive oil
- salt and freshly ground white pepper
- 1/2 cup/125 ml dry white wine

Preheat the oven to 400°F/200°C/gas 6. • Butter a large ovenproof dish. • Chop the squid tentacles and parsley finely with a large knife. • Mix with the garlic and rice in a medium bowl. Add 1/4 cup (60 ml) oil and season with salt and pepper. • Stuff the squids' bodies with the rice mixture using a plastic bag (see step 4). Fasten them shut with a toothpick. • Arrange the stuffed squid in the prepared dish. Season with salt and pepper. • Bake for 20 minutes. • Drizzle with the wine. Return to the oven and bake for 20 minutes more. • Serve hot.

Serves 4 • Prep: 30 min • Cooking: 40 min • Level: 2

CLEANING AND STUFFING SQUID

1. Cleaning: Rinse the squid. Grasp the head with one hand and the body in the other and pull—most of the interiors and translucent quill will come away with it. Scrape out the rest with a blunt knife. Cut off the tentacles at the hard ball, or beak, just behind the eyes. Discard the head. Use your fingers to remove the mottled skin.

2. Finely chop the parsley and tentacles of the squid.

3. Mix the rice, parsley, and squid in a medium bowl until well blended.

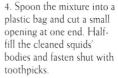

4. Spoon the mixture into a plastic bag and cut a small opening at one end. Half-fill the cleaned squids' bodies and fasten shut with toothpicks.

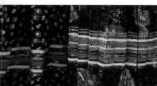

Fish & Seafood

Octopus and potato stew

OCTOPUS AND POTATO STEW

Salata od hobotnice i krumpira

- 1 octopus, weighing about 1¹/₂ lb/750 g, or 1¹/₂ lb/750 g squid, cleaned
- 2¹/₄ quarts/2.25 liters water
- ¹/₂ onion + 1 medium onion, finely sliced
- ¹/₂ carrot
- ¹/₂ stalk celery
- 1 bunch parsley
- ¹/₂ cup/125 ml white wine vinegar
- ¹/₃ cup/80 ml extra-virgin olive oil
- 2 cloves garlic, finely chopped
- ¹/₂ cup/125 ml dry white wine
- 1 lb/500 g potatoes, peeled and cut into large cubes
- 1 tablespoon finely chopped fresh parsley
- salt and black pepper

Place the octopus in a large saucepan and pour in 2 quarts (2 liters) of water. • Add the ¹/₂ onion, carrot, celery, parsley, and vinegar. Bring to a boil and simmer for 40–50 minutes, or until the octopus is tender. • Drain well and cut into chunks. • Heat the oil in a large saucepan over medium heat. Sauté the sliced onion and garlic for 5–7 minutes, or until translucent. • Pour in the wine and cook until it has evaporated. • Add the potatoes and remaining 1 cup (250 ml) of water, and boil for 10 minutes. • Stir in the chopped octopus and parsley. • Simmer for 20–25 minutes, or until the potatoes are tender. • Season with salt and pepper. • Serve hot.

Serves 2–4 • Prep: 40–50 min • Cooking: 80–97 min • Level: 1

TROUT WITH GOLDEN RAISINS

Pastrmka od sugov grozdja

Preheat the oven to 400°F/200°C/gas 6. • Set out a large ovenproof dish. • Mix the bacon and ¹/₄ cup (45 g) of raisins in a medium bowl. Stuff the fish with the raisin mixture. • Use a sharp knife to make a number of small cuts on the backs of the fish. • Arrange the garlic and parsley in the prepared pan. Place the fish in the pan and drizzle with the oil, vinegar, and water. • Bake for 40–45 minutes, or until the fish is very tender. • Transfer to a heated serving dish. • Pour the eggs, remaining ³/₄ cup raisins, and lemon juice into a small saucepan. Cook over medium heat for 2–3 minutes, then pour over the fish. Season with salt and pepper. • Serve hot.

Serves 4 • Prep: 25 min • Cooking: 40–45 min • Level: 1

- 1 cup/125 g finely chopped bacon
- 1 cup/180 g golden raisins/sultanas
- 2 trout, weighing about 1¹/₂ lb/750 g, gutted
- 4 cloves garlic, finely chopped
- 2 tablespoons finely chopped fresh parsley
- ¹/₂ cup/125 ml extra-virgin olive oil
- ¹/₂ cup/125 ml white wine vinegar
- 1 cup/250 ml water
- 2 large eggs, lightly beaten
- juice of 1 lemon
- salt and freshly ground black pepper

BAKED FISH WITH BEANS

Saran na pasulja

- 1 cup/100 g dried cannellini or white kidney beans, soaked overnight and drained
- 1/2 cup/125 ml extra-virgin olive oil
- 1 large onion, thinly sliced
- 2 carp or trout, weighing about 14 oz/400 g each, gutted
- salt and freshly ground black pepper
- 1 fresh red chile pepper, finely chopped

Preheat the oven to 400°F/200°C/gas 6. • Cook the beans in a large pot of salted boiling water for 1–1 1/2 hours, or until the beans are tender. Drain well, reserving 1/4 cup (60 ml) liquid. • Heat the oil in a large Dutch oven or saucepan. Add the onion and sauté for 8–10 minutes, or until lightly browned. • Cover with the cooked beans and the reserved liquid. • Place the carp on top. • Season with salt and pepper and sprinkle with the chile. • Bake for 15–20 minutes, or until the flesh yields easily from the bone. • Serve hot.

Serves 4 • Prep: 20 min • Cooking: 95–140 min • Level: 2

FISH WITH CABBAGE

Riba s kistim zelyem

Cook the cabbage in a large pot of boiling salted water for 10–15 minutes, or until tender. Drain well, reserving the water. • Heat the oil in a large saucepan over medium heat. Stir in the flour to make a smooth paste. Cook until fragrant, 2–3 minutes. • Sprinkle with paprika and season with salt and pepper. Add the bay leaf. • Stir in the cabbage and reserved water. • Bring to a boil, add the fish, and cook for 20 minutes. • Pour in sour cream and bring to a boil. • Serve hot.

Serves 6 • Prep: 15 min • Cooking: 42–48 min • Level 1

- 1 lb/500 g cabbage, shredded
- 1/3 cup/80 ml extra-virgin olive oil
- 2 tablespoons all-purpose/plain flour
- 1/8 teaspoon paprika
- salt and freshly ground black pepper
- 1 bay leaf
- 1 lb/500 g white-fleshed fish, such as bream or snapper, cut into chunks
- 3/4 cup/180 ml sour cream

FRIED TROUT

Pec'ene posrvi

Season the fish with salt and pepper. • Heat the oil in a large frying pan over medium heat and add the fish. Sprinkle with the parsley, garlic, lemon juice, and bay leaves. • Fry over medium heat for 10 minutes, or until the fish is well cooked. • Serve hot.

Serves 6 • Prep: 10 min • Cooking: 10 min • Level: 1

- 2 lb/1 kg trout, cleaned
- salt and freshly ground white pepper
- 1/4 cup/60 ml extra-virgin olive oil
- 1 tablespoon finely chopped fresh parsley
- 3 cloves garlic, finely chopped
- 2 tablespoons fresh lemon juice
- 2 bay leaves

Baked fish with beans

Chicken & Beef

Dalmatian pot roast

CHICKEN AND RICE

Pulë me pilaf

- 1 small chicken, weighing about 1¹/₂ lb/750 g
- 1¹/₂ quarts/1.5 liters boiling water
- ¹/₃ cup/80 g butter
- ¹/₄ cup/30 g all-purpose/plain flour
- ¹/₂ cup/125 ml milk
- 2 large egg yolks, lightly beaten
- salt and freshly ground white pepper
- 2 cups/400 g long-grain rice

Boil the chicken in the water for 15 minutes. • Remove the chicken, reserving the stock. • Cut the chicken into quarters. • Melt 2 tablespoons of butter in a large saucepan over medium heat. Add the chicken. • Cover and cook over low heat for 20–25 minutes, or until the chicken is tender. • Melt 2 tablespoons of butter in a medium saucepan. Stir in the flour to make a smooth paste and cook until fragrant, 2–3 minutes. Pour in the milk and 1 cup (250 ml) of the reserved stock, stirring constantly to prevent lumps. Cook for 5–10 minutes, or until thick. • Remove from the heat and let cool to warm. • Stir in the egg yolks. Season with salt and pepper. • Toast the rice in the remaining 2 tablespoons butter in a medium saucepan over high heat until lightly golden. Add the remaining reserved stock. Season with salt. • Lower the heat and cook for 18–20 minutes, or until the rice is tender. • Spoon the rice onto a heated serving dish, place the chicken on it, and drizzle the sauce over the top.

Serves 4 • Prep: 15 min • Cooking: 50–55 min • Level: 2

DALMATIAN POT ROAST

Pasticada

This hearty dish is traditionally served at Christmas lunch in Croatia.

Use a sharp knife to make slashes in the beef. Press garlic into the slashes and around the meat. • Place the beef in a large roasting pan and pour in the wine. Add the onions, thyme, bay leaf, rosemary, and celery. Season with salt and pepper. • Cover with aluminum foil and refrigerate for 12 hours. • Heat the oil in a large saucepan or Dutch oven over medium heat. Brown the beef and bacon for 5 minutes. • Remove the beef from the pan. Add the liquids from the marinade and cook for 1 minute. • Add the beef, parsley, carrots, tomatoes, and mustard. Simmer, covered, for 2–3 hours, or until the meat is very tender. • Serve hot.

Serves 8 • Prep: 30 min + 12 hr to marinate • Cooking: 2–3 hr • Level: 1

- 4 lb/2 kg top loin of beef
- 4 cloves garlic, finely chopped
- 2 quarts/2 liters dry red wine
- 4 large onions, finely chopped
- 1 tablespoon finely chopped fresh thyme
- 1 bay leaf
- 1 tablespoon finely chopped fresh rosemary
- 3 stalks celery, finely chopped
- salt and freshly ground black pepper
- ¹/₂ cup/125 ml extra-virgin olive oil
- 8 oz/250 g bacon, finely chopped
- 2 tablespoons finely chopped fresh parsley
- 4 large carrots, thinly sliced
- 1 lb/500 g tomatoes, peeled and chopped
- 2 teaspoons Dijon mustard

BAKED CHICKEN WITH VEGETABLES

Pulë e pjekur me perime

- 1 chicken, weighing about 1¹/₂ lb/750 g, quartered
- salt and freshly ground white pepper
- ¹/₂ cup/125 g + 2 tablespoons butter
- 1 medium onion, finely chopped
- 1 cup/250 ml dry white wine
- 2 tablespoons water
- 8 oz/250 g tomatoes, peeled and thinly sliced
- 2 cups/250 g peas
- 8 oz/250 g carrots, peeled and thinly sliced
- 1 lb/500 g potatoes, peeled and thinly sliced
- 2 tablespoons finely chopped fresh parsley

Preheat the oven to 350°F/180°C/gas 4. • Season the chicken with salt and pepper. • Melt ¹/₄ cup (60 g) butter in a large deep Dutch oven or saucepan over medium heat. Sauté the chicken and onion for 8–10 minutes, or until lightly browned. • Pour in the wine, water, and tomatoes. • Bake for 30 minutes. • While the chicken is baking, sauté the peas, carrots, and potatoes in the remaining ¹/₄ cup (60 g) butter in a large frying pan over medium heat for 5 minutes. • Remove the chicken from the oven and add the sautéed vegetables. Sprinkle with the parsley and season with salt and pepper. • Cover with aluminum foil and bake for 60–70 minutes, or until the juices run clear and the vegetables are tender. • Serve hot.

Serves 4 • Prep: 20 min • Cooking: 103–115 min • Level: 2

YUGOSLAVIAN MEATBALLS

Fashir

Preheat the oven to 350°F/180°C/gas 4. • Oil a large baking pan. • Place the beef, ²/₃ cup (100 g) of bread crumbs, parsley, red pepper flakes, salt, pepper, caraway seeds and 1 egg in a large bowl and mix until well blended. • Shape the mixture into balls the size of golf balls. • Lightly beat the remaining egg. Dip the meat balls in the egg, then in the remaining ¹/₃ cup bread crumbs. • Heat the oil to very hot in a large frying pan and fry the meatballs in batches for 5 minutes, turning frequently to brown evenly. • Transfer the meatballs to the baking dish and bake for 1 hour. • Serve hot on a bed of rice.

Serves 4 • Prep: 20 min • Cooking: 1 hr 15 min • Level: 1

- 1¹/₂ lb/750 g ground/ minced beef
- 1 cup/150 g dry bread crumbs
- 1 tablespoon finely chopped fresh parsley
- 1–2 teaspoons red pepper flakes
- salt and freshly ground black pepper
- 1 tablespoon caraway or cumin seeds
- 2 eggs
- 1 cup/250 ml olive oil, for frying
- hot cooked rice, to serve

Baked chicken with vegetables

Lamb & Variety Meats

ALBANIAN CALVES' LIVER

Fërgesë me melçi

- 10 oz/300 g calves' liver, trimmed and thinly sliced
- 3 cloves garlic, finely chopped
- 4 teaspoons red pepper flakes
- 3 tablespoons all-purpose/plain flour
- ¼ cup/60 ml extra-virgin olive oil
- salt
- ¼ cup/60 ml Ricotta cheese
- 2 large red onions, very thinly sliced
- 1 tablespoon finely chopped fresh dill
- 1 tablespoon finely chopped fresh parsley

Sprinkle the liver with the garlic, 2 teaspoons red pepper flakes, and the flour. • Heat 2 tablespoons of oil in a large frying pan over medium heat. Add the liver, a few pieces at a time, and cook for 5 minutes, or until lightly cooked. Season with salt. • Arrange the liver on a heated serving dish. • Heat 1 tablespoon of oil in a separate skillet over medium heat. Sauté the remaining 2 teaspoons red pepper flakes for 1 minute. • Remove from the heat, stir in the remaining 1 tablespoon oil and the Ricotta. • Spoon the Ricotta mixture over the liver. • Season the onions with salt and set aside for 15 minutes. Squeeze the onion gently and pat dry with paper towels. • Stir together the onions, dill, and parsley in a medium bowl. • Arrange the onion mixture over the liver and serve.

Serves 4 • Prep: 15 min + 15 min to drain • Cooking: 15 min • Level: 1

CROATIAN LAMB STEW

Hrvatski lonac

Arrange the lamb, cabbage, potatoes, tomatoes, carrots, onions, and celery in layers in a large saucepan. Season with the salt and pepper. Garnish with the parsley. • Pour in the stock, cover, and cook over medium heat for about 3 hours, or until the lamb is very tender. • Serve hot.

Serves 4 • Prep: 10 min • Cooking: 3 hr • Level: 1

- 1½ lb/750 g boneless lamb, cut into small cubes
- 1½ lb/750 g cabbage, finely shredded
- 10 oz/300 g potatoes, cut into cubes
- 3 firm-ripe tomatoes, thinly sliced
- 2 medium carrots, peeled and thinly sliced
- 2 red onions, finely chopped
- 1 stalk celery, finely chopped
- salt and freshly ground black pepper
- 1 tablespoon finely chopped fresh parsley
- 1 quart/1 liter beef, chicken, or vegetable stock or broth

Albanian calves' liver

MIXED MEAT AND VEGETABLE STEW

Turli tava

- 1 medium eggplant/ aubergine, thinly sliced
- salt
- $^1/_3$ cup/80 ml extra-virgin olive oil
- 1 lb/500 g lean lamb, pork, and veal, cut into small chunks
- 1 medium carrot, sliced
- 2 medium red onions, thinly sliced
- 3 large potatoes, peeled and cut into cubes
- 1 medium red bell pepper/capsicum, cut into thin strips
- 3 oz/100 g green beans
- 8 oz/200 g mushrooms, coarsely chopped
- 3 firm-ripe tomatoes, cut into cubes
- salt and freshly ground black pepper
- 1 cup/100 g cooked borlotti or red kidney beans
- 1 tablespoon paprika
- 1 tablespoon water

Place the eggplant slices in a colander. Sprinkle with salt and let drain for 1 hour. • Heat the oil in a large frying pan over high heat. Brown the meat for 5 minutes. • Add the carrot, eggplant, onions, potatoes, bell pepper, green beans, mushrooms, tomatoes, and 1 tablespoon water. Season with salt and pepper. • Lower the heat, cover, and cook for 30 minutes. • Stir in the borlotti beans and sprinkle with paprika. • Cover and cook over very low heat for 25–30 minutes, or until the meat is tender, adding more water if the stew begins to dry. • Serve hot.

Serves 4 • Prep: 30 min + 1 hr to drain • Cooking: 60–65 min • Level: 1

HAM AND CABBAGE STEW

Jota

Cook the ham and cabbage with the bay leaf in a large pot of salted boiling water for 15–20 minutes, or until the cabbage is tender. • Cook the beans in a large pot of salted boiling water for 25–30 minutes, or until tender. • Cook the potatoes in a large pot of salted boiling water for 15–20 minutes, or until tender. • Add the beans and their liquid to the cabbage mixture. Use a fork to mash the potatoes and add them to the cabbage. • Heat the oil in a large frying pan over medium heat. Sauté the onions for 8–10 minutes, or until lightly browned. • Add the onions to the cabbage. • Stir in the garlic and tomato paste. • Season with salt and pepper. • Serve hot.

Serves 4 • Prep: 15 min • Cooking: 65–80 min • Level: 2

- 1 lb/500 g ham on the bone
- 1 lb/500 g cabbage, shredded
- 1 bay leaf
- $2^1/_2$ cups/250 g fresh or frozen (not dried) cannellini beans or other shell beans
- 12 oz/350 g potatoes, peeled and cut into large chunks
- $^1/_4$ cup/60 ml extra-virgin olive oil
- 2 medium onions, finely chopped
- 1 clove garlic, finely chopped
- 1 tablespoon tomato paste
- salt and freshly ground black pepper

LAMB MEATBALLS

Jagnjeca pljeskavica

- $1^1/_2$ lb/750 g ground/ minced lamb
- 1 large red onion, finely chopped
- salt and freshly ground black pepper
- 1 teaspoon paprika
- 2–4 tablespoons olive oil

Mix the lamb and onion in a large bowl. Season with salt, pepper, and paprika. • Use your hands to knead the mixture. • Shape into twelve balls the size of golf balls, flattening slightly. • Heat 2 tablespoons oil in a large frying pan over high heat. Add a single layer of meatballs and cook for 5 minutes on each side, until cooked through. Remove from the pan and keep warm. Cook the remaining meatballs, adding the additional oil as needed. • Serve hot.

Serves 4 • Prep: 20 min • Cooking: 20 min • Level: 1

Cabbage

Cabbage is used extensively in Balkan cuisines. Economical and adaptable, it is popular as a wrap for rice- or meat-based dishes. It is also the basis for many stews and roasted meals.

Kebabs

YUGOSLAVIAN SAUSAGE

Cevapcici

- 8 oz/300 g ground/ minced chicken
- 8 oz/200 g ground/ minced lamb
- 8 oz/200 g ground/ minced pork
- 1 teaspoon black peppercorns
- 1 small onion, finely chopped
- 4 cloves garlic, finely chopped
- salt
- 12 bay leaves

Mix the chicken, lamb, and pork with the peppercorns, onion, and garlic in a large bowl. Season with salt and shape into sixteen oval meatballs. • Thread onto four metal skewers, alternating the meat with bay leaves. • Cook the skewers under a broiler (grill) or on a barbecue for 15 minutes, turning often. • Serve hot.

Serves 4 • Prep: 10 min • Cooking: 15 min • Level: 1

FRIED PORK SKEWERS

Raznjici

Carefully thread the meat, alternating with the peppers, potatoes, scallions, and bacon onto four metal skewers. • Drizzle with the extra-virgin olive oil and season with salt and pepper. Roll in the cornmeal. • Heat the frying oil in a large frying pan to very hot. Fry the skewers, turning them frequently, for 15–20 minutes, or until the meat is well cooked. • Serve hot.

Serves 4 • Prep: 10 min • Cooking: 15–20 min • Level: 1

- 1¹/₂ lb/750 g lean pork, cut into 16 cubes
- 2 red bell peppers/ capsicums, cut into large chunks
- 10 oz/300 g small new potatoes, parboiled
- 10 oz/300 g scallions/ spring onions
- 5 oz/150 g bacon, in thick strips and cut into squares
- 2–4 tablespoons extra-virgin olive oil
- salt and freshly ground black pepper
- 1 cup/150 g coarsely ground cornmeal
- 2 cups/500 ml olive oil, for frying

Yugoslavian sausage

Desserts

WALNUT COOKIES

Lokumi

- 1¹/₂ cups/225 g all-purpose/plain flour
- ¹/₈ teaspoon salt
- 1 cup/150 g confectioners'/icing sugar
- 2 cups/200 g finely chopped walnuts
- grated zest of 1 lemon
- ¹/₂ teaspoon vanilla extract
- ¹/₃ cup/80 g butter, melted

Preheat the oven to 400°F/200°C/gas 6. • Butter a cookie sheet. • Sift the flour and salt into a medium bowl. Stir in ¹/₂ cup (75 g) of confectioners' sugar, walnuts, lemon zest, and vanilla. • Mix in the butter to form a smooth dough. Let stand for 20 minutes. • Roll the dough out on a lightly floured work surface into a 1-inch (2.5-cm) thick rectangle. Use a sharp knife to cut diagonally into slices about 2 x 1-inch (4 x 1-cm) wide. • Arrange the cookies on the prepared cookie sheet. • Bake for 15–20 minutes, or until lightly browned. • Cool the cookies completely on racks. • Dust with the remaining ¹/₂ cup (75 g) confectioners' sugar.

Serves 8 • Prep: 40 min • Cooking: 15–20 min • Level: 1

COOKIES IN SYRUP

Sheqerpare

<u>Syrup</u>: Bring the sugar, water, vanilla bean, and cloves to a boil in a small saucepan over medium heat. Boil for 3 minutes. • Strain, discarding the cloves and vanilla beans, and set aside at room temperature. • <u>Cookies</u>: Preheat the oven to 325°F/170°C/gas 3. • Line a cookie sheet with parchment paper. • Beat the butter and sugar in a large bowl with an electric mixer at high speed until creamy. • Add the egg yolks, one at a time, until just blended after each addition. • With mixer at low speed, gradually beat in the the flour, baking soda, and salt. • Roll out to ¹/₄ inch (5 mm) thick on parchment paper. Refrigerate for 15 minutes. • Use a pastry cutter to cut out 1-inch (2.5-cm) disks. Lay them on the prepared cookie sheet. • Bake for 15–20 minutes, or until golden brown. • Cool the cookies completely on the sheet. • Serve the cookies in the lukewarm syrup.

Serves 6 • Prep: 45 min • Cooking: 15–20 min • Level: 2

Syrup
- 1 cup/200 g granulated sugar
- 1 tablespoon water
- 1 vanilla bean
- 3 cloves

Cookies
- ³/₄ cup/180 g butter, softened
- 1 cup/200 g granulated sugar
- 2 large egg yolks
- 1¹/₄ cups/180 g all-purpose/plain flour
- ¹/₄ teaspoon baking soda/bicarbonate of soda
- ¹/₈ teaspoon salt

Cookies in syrup

Cherry and yogurt pie

CHERRY AND YOGURT PIE

Tresnja strudle

- 2 cups/300 g all-purpose/plain flour
- 2 teaspoons baking powder
- $^1/_8$ teaspoon salt
- 3 large eggs
- $1^1/_4$ cups/250 g granulated sugar
- 2 cups/500 g plain yogurt
- 2 cups/200 g pitted sour cherries
- 2 medium apples, peeled and cut into small cubes
- 1 tablespoon brandy
- 1 tablespoon dark rum
- $^1/_4$ teaspoon cinnamon
- $^1/_2$ teaspoon vanilla extract
- $^1/_3$ cup/50 g confectioners' sugar

Preheat the oven to 350°F/180°C/gas 4. • Butter a 9-inch (24-cm) round cake pan and line with waxed paper. • Sift the flour, baking powder, and salt into a medium bowl. • Beat the eggs and 1 cup (200 g) of sugar in a large bowl with an electric mixer at high speed until pale and creamy. • With mixer at low speed, gradually beat in 1 cup (250 ml) yogurt, followed by the dry ingredients. • Pour half the batter into the prepared pan. • Bake for 10–15 minutes. • Mix the cherries, apples, brandy, rum,

remaining 2 tablespoons of sugar, and cinnamon in a small saucepan. Cover and cook for 15 minutes over medium heat. Stir in the vanilla. • Pour the fruit mixture over the baked cake. • Spoon the remaining batter over the fruit. • Bake for 10–15 minutes, or until golden brown and a toothpick inserted into the center comes out clean. • Dust with the confectioners' sugar. Serve warm or at room temperature, with the remaining 1 cup (250 ml) yogurt passed on the side.

Serves 6–8 • Prep: 25 min • Cooking: 20–30 min • Level: 2

Desserts

SLOVENIAN DOUGHNUTS
Krofi

- 1¹/₂ oz/45 g fresh yeast or 3 packages (¹/₄-oz/7-g) active dry yeast
- ¹/₄ cup/60 ml lukewarm water
- 1 teaspoon + ¹/₂ cup/100 g granulated sugar
- 1 cup/250 ml milk
- 1 cup/250 ml half-and-half/single cream
- ²/₃ cup/150 g butter
- 6 large eggs
- 1 teaspoon salt
- 1 cup/250 ml sour cream
- 10 cups/1.5 kg all-purpose/ plain flour, or more if needed
- grated zest and juice of 1 lemon
- 1 quart/1 liter oil, for frying
- ¹/₂ cup/75 g confectioners'/icing sugar, to dust

Mix the yeast, water, and 1 teaspoon sugar in a small bowl. Let stand for 5–10 minutes, or until foamy. • Heat the milk, half-and-half, and butter in a small saucepan until the butter melts. Let cool to lukewarm. • Beat the eggs, ¹/₂ cup (100 g) sugar, salt, and sour cream in a large bowl with an electric mixer at high speed until creamy. Use a large rubber spatula to fold the milk mixture into the beaten egg mixture. • Stir in the yeast mixture, lemon zest and juice, and 2 cups (300 g) flour. Add enough of the remaining flour to form a soft dough. • Turn the dough onto a lightly floured work surface and knead for 5–7 minutes, or until smooth and elastic. Place in a well-oiled bowl and cover with a clean cloth. Let rise for 1 hour, or until doubled in bulk. • Turn the dough out onto a lightly floured surface and stretch to ¹/₂ inch (1 cm) thick. Use a cutter to stamp out rounds. Reroll the trimmings. • Place the rounds on a lightly floured cloth. Cover with a clean cloth and let rise for about 30 minutes, or until doubled in bulk. • Heat the oil to very hot in a deep fryer. • Fry the doughnuts in batches for 10–15 minutes, or until golden brown. Drain well on paper towels. • Dust with the confectioners' sugar and serve warm.

Serves 12–14 • Prep: 30 min + 90 min to rise • Cooking: 45 min • Level: 3

RICE CAKE
Torta od rize

Bring the milk and rice to a boil in a saucepan over medium heat. Lower the heat and cook until the rice is tender, about 20 minutes. Remove from the heat and set aside to cool. • Preheat the oven to 350°F /180°C/gas 4. • Butter a 9-inch round cake pan. Line with waxed paper. Butter the paper. • Process the rice mixture in a food processor until smooth. • Transfer to a large bowl and beat in the egg yolks, granulated sugar, and butter. • Stir in the candied fruit and chocolate. • Beat the egg whites in a large bowl with an electric mixer at high speed until stiff peaks form. Use a rubber spatula to fold them into the rice mixture. • Spoon the batter into the prepared pan. • Bake for 35–45 minutes, or until a toothpick inserted into the center comes out clean. • Cool the cake in the pan for 15 minutes. Turn out onto a rack. Carefully remove the paper and let cool completely. • Dust with the confectioners' sugar. Decorate with the candied cherries and angelica.

Makes one 9-inch cake · Prep: 25 min. · Cooking: 35–45 min. Level: 1

- 2 cups/500 ml milk
- ³/₄ cup/150 g short-grain rice
- 4 large eggs, separated
- ³/₄ cup/150 g granulated sugar
- ¹/₂ cup/125 g butter, softened
- ¹/₂ cup/100 g chopped mixed candied fruit
- 2 oz bittersweet chocolate, chopped
- ¹/₃ cup/75 g confectioners' sugar, to dust
- candied cherries and angelica, to decorate

Rice cake

Yugoslavian pastries

YUGOSLAVIAN PASTRIES

Kolacki

- 2 cups/300 g all-purpose/plain flour
- ²/₃ cup/150 g butter, cut up
- 1 package (8 oz/250 g) cream cheese, cut up

Filling
- 1 cup/300 g apricot, peach, or plum preserves
- 1 cup/100 g finely ground walnuts
- 1 large egg, lightly beaten
- ¹/₂ cup/75 g confectioners'/icing sugar, to dust

Preheat the oven to 400°F/200°C/gas 6. • Butter a large baking sheet. • Sift the flour into a large bowl. • Use a pastry blender to cut in the butter and cream cheese. Shape into a ball. • Cover with a clean cloth and refrigerate overnight. • Divide the dough into three pieces. Roll out to ¹/₄ inch (5 mm) thick. • Cut the dough into 2- or 3-inch (5–8-cm) squares. • Filling: Mix the jam, walnuts, and egg in a small bowl until well blended. • Spoon a teaspoonful of the filling in the center of each piece of dough. Fold the dough over the filling to form small triangles, sealing the edges with a fork. • Bake for 12–15 minutes, or until lightly browned. • Dust with the confectioners' sugar.

Serves 6 • Prep: 30 min + overnight to chill • Cooking: 12–15 min • Level: 1

NINE-LAYER PIE

Bregovska pita

- 1 cup/125 g walnuts
- 1¹/₂ cups/150 g poppy seeds
- 1 cup/180 g raisins, plumped in ¹/₄ cup/60 ml dark rum for 1 hour
- 1¹/₂ cups/300 g granulated sugar
- 1 tablespoon ground cinnamon
- 10 sheets frozen phyllo dough, thawed
- ³/₄ cup/180 g butter, melted
- 10 oz/300 g apples, finely grated
- 1²/₃ cups/400 ml sour cream
- 2 large eggs, lightly beaten

Butter a 13 x 9-inch (33 x 23-cm) baking pan. • Preheat the oven to 400°F/200°C/gas 6. • Finely chop the walnuts and poppy seeds. • Mix the walnuts with ¹/₂ cup (100 g) sugar and 1¹/₂ teaspoons cinnamon. Mix the poppy seeds with ¹/₂ cup (100 g) sugar. Mix the raisins, rum, apples, remaining ¹/₂ cup (100 g) sugar, and cinnamon. • Brush two sheets of phyllo with butter and place in the pan, trimming the edges to fit. Spread with half the apple mixture and 3 tablespoons sour cream. • Brush two more sheets of dough with butter and place in the pan. Cover with the walnut mixture and 3 tablespoons sour cream. • Brush two more sheets of dough with butter and place in the pan. Cover with the poppy seed mixture and 3 tablespoons sour cream. • Brush two more sheets of dough with butter and place in the pan. Cover with the remaining apple mixture and 3 tablespoons sour cream. Top with the remaining dough and butter it. • Mix the eggs with the remaining sour cream. Pour over the pastry. Prick well with a fork. • Bake for 50–60 minutes, or until golden brown. • Cool completely in the pan.

Serves 8 • Prep: 25 min + 1 hr to soak raisins • Cooking: 50–60 min • Level: 2

INDEX

Acknowledgments

All photos by Marco Lanza and Walter Mericchi and © McRae Books, except:
p. 7, House on Santorini, © Walter Mericchi, Florence; pp10–11, Greek Islands © Walter Mericchi, Florence; pp. 12–13, Portovenere © Marco Nardi, Florence; pp. 64–65, Lavender fields, Plateau du Valensole, Provence, France © Marka; pp. 100–101, Bench, Parco Guell, Barcelona, Spain © Marka; pp. 130–131, North Africa © The Image Works; pp. 150–151, The archeological site at Byblos, Lebanon © Brenda Turnnidge/Lonely Planet Images; pp. 186–187, Fishing Village Harbor, Kekova, Turkey © Chris Hellier/Corbis; pp. 202–203, House on Santorini, © Walter Mericchi, Florence; pp. 228–229, Dubrovnik © Roman Soumar/Corbis